BALZAC AND THE DRAMA OF PERSPECTIVE
THE NARRATOR IN SELECTED WORKS
OF *LA COMÉDIE HUMAINE*

FRENCH FORUM MONOGRAPHS

60

Editors R.C. LA CHARITÉ and V.A. LA CHARITÉ

For complete listing, see page 173

The cover illustration is a sculpture by Auguste Rodin of Balzac. Reproduced by kind permission of the Musée Rodin, Paris.

Balzac and the Drama of Perspective
The Narrator in Selected Works of *La Comédie humaine*

JOAN DARGAN

FRENCH FORUM, PUBLISHERS
LEXINGTON, KENTUCKY

Copyright © 1985 by French Forum, Publishers, Incorporated,
P.O. Box 5108, Lexington, Kentucky 40505.

All rights reserved, including the right to reproduce this book, or parts thereof, in any form, except for the inclusion of brief quotations in reviews.

Library of Congress Catalog Card Number 85-80419

ISBN 0-917058-61-5

Printed in the United States of America

To my parents

ACKNOWLEDGMENTS

If in each life there are seven ages, in each book there are many more; and in writing this one I have often received kind and generous help. I would like to thank Léon-François Hoffmann of Princeton University for reading this study in all its various forms, for going over my work with me painstakingly and for sharing an enthusiasm for Balzac that has become mine also. I would like to thank Suzanne Nash for her encouragement and her careful reading of those chapters originally part of my dissertation and for calling my attention to pertinent works of critical theory. I thank also Patricia Murphy of the University of New Mexico for her interest in the book and for her corrections and suggestions for improving the final version.

I would like to acknowledge a summer stipend from the University of New Mexico which made it possible for me to revise and expand the original study. I am grateful to St. Lawrence University for its generous support of my research and in particular to the Owen D. Young Library for assistance I received while preparing the final manuscript.

Finally, I would like to thank my aunt M. Margaret Dargan for her loving support in this endeavor, as in many other things.

TABLE OF CONTENTS

ACKNOWLEDGMENTS 7

INTRODUCTION 11

I. *LOUIS LAMBERT* 19

II. *LE COLONEL CHABERT* 45

III. *HISTOIRE DES TREIZE: FERRAGUS* 65

IV. *HISTOIRE DES TREIZE: LA DUCHESSE DE LANGEAIS* 87

V. *HISTOIRE DES TREIZE: LA FILLE AUX YEUX D'OR* 106

VI. *EUGÉNIE GRANDET* 132

CONCLUSION 159

NOTES 161

SELECTED BIBLIOGRAPHY 167

INTRODUCTION

> Le but de profonde moralité caché dans mon livre [*La Peau de chagrin*] échappe à beaucoup de critiques malveillants, qui ne voient que la forme, et j'avoue que je suis vivement touché lorsque quelque critique veut bien dégager mes intentions de leur sauvage enveloppe. Tous nos maîtres ont mis la moelle dans un os, à l'exemple de la nature.
>
> (*Correspondance*, 1831)

In 1831 Balzac had just completed his first major work, *La Peau de chagrin*, and had embarked upon the first and most prolific phase of his mature career. By 1835 he had written close to forty novels and stories, many of which would be subject to revision and expansion with each new edition of *La Comédie humaine*. But in 1831 *La Comédie humaine* as such did not yet exist; it was only with *Le Père Goriot*, in 1834, that the unifying concept of the reappearing character flashed through his mind "comme un rêve ... une chimère," as Balzac would note in the "Avant-Propos" to his collective work.

Balzac's early works are especially interesting because they are "*isolés les uns des autres et présentés comme des œuvres différentes.*"[1] Unknown even to their creator, these novels already possessed the dynamic qualities, the inner consistency of theme and symbol, upon which he could build a comprehensive analysis of society. With the discovery of the reappearing character—a kind of familiar landmark in a vast symbolic territory—Balzac was able to present his work in such a way that its analytical dimension became more accessible to the reader. In the "Avant-Propos," introducing the categories into which the novels are divided—*Etudes philosophiques, Scènes de la vie parisienne, Scènes de la vie privée,* and so on—the author acknowledges his responsibility as teacher or guide and tells us how to approach his work as a whole.

But for all practical purposes, we must still begin with each individual work, each "sauvage enveloppe," and through it discover that "but de profonde moralité" of authorial vision, of Balzac's poetical consciousness. And so we may contemplate Balzac here, at the threshold of his career, already plagued by misapprehension of the fundamental seriousness of his work, already supplying a metaphor—"la moelle dans un os"—affirming the organicity of form and, therefore, his novel's autonomy as work of art. Already he adopts the defensive posture that will become a hallmark of his prefaces; and in referring to the "sauvage enveloppe" of narrative form, he appeals to us as benevolent readers to reconsider the intelligence hidden within its rough appearance. This most maligned of authors was in fact supremely conscious of literary influence ("*Tous nos maîtres* ont mis la moelle dans un os...") and frequently had recourse to melodrama to impress upon the reader symbolic truths implicit in a prose renowned for its meticulous, even relentless, naturalistic detail.

The apparent incongruity between bone and marrow, form and content, between the autonomy of the single work and the unity of the collection, may dismay any number of "critiques malveillants" and disconcert even the most favorably disposed reader. But these same paradoxes reflect a basic tension at the heart of Balzac's fiction, a condition of poetical discourse itself. The relation of the particular and the universal, of mimesis and myth, takes us back to a fundamental principle of Aristotelian poetics, one underlying the tensions inherent in all literary creation:

> La poésie, disait-il [Aristotle], est une imitation des actions humaines; mais cette *mimesis* passe par la création d'une fable, d'une intrigue, qui présente des traits de composition et d'ordre qui manquent aux drames de la vie quotidienne.... si la tragédie n'atteint son effet de *mimesis* que par l'invention du *mythos*, le *mythos* est au service de la *mimesis* et de son caractère foncièrement dénotatif....
>
> Cette jonction entre *mythos* et *mimesis* n'est pas l'œuvre de la seule poésie tragique; elle y est seulement plus aisée à détecter parce que, d'une part, le *mythos* prend la forme d'un "récit" et que la métaphoricité s'attache à l'intrigue de la fable, et parce que, d'autre part, le référent est constitué par l'action humaine qui, par son cours de motivation, présente une affinité certaine avec la structure du récit. La jonction entre *mythos* et *mimesis* est l'œuvre de toute poésie.[2]

If we consider Balzac's fiction as a conjunction of myth and mimesis, of symbolic truth and naturalistic detail, of visionary insight and observation of human appearances and behavior, then it is easy to appreciate his impatience with those who misread *La Peau de chagrin*. At the same time, if we are to accept *La Comédie humaine* as the elaboration of a single authorial vision already present in the early works before the organization of *La Comédie humaine* as such, we must recognize the presence of one more apparent incongruity, one more necessary conjunction: that of perspective in the individual novel or story in its relation to the vision of the author. The perspective afforded by the "sauvage enveloppe" of a single work indirectly reveals the "but de profonde moralité" of authorial vision, just as the latter informs the former as its instrument. Hence, the organicity or autonomy of each narrative necessarily implies a closure with respect to the particular conjunction of myth and mimesis effected within it. But with respect to the single poetic imagination at its source, each narrative is also a means of access and exploration, one of many such openings that invite comparison and that reveal repeated, characteristic preoccupations of the author on the formal and thematic levels.

Although it would be presumptuous, not to say impossible, to determine Balzac's own "intentions," no reader is barred from the symbolic universe each of his novels invites us to enter. Thus, in examining a number of works Balzac originally wrote before 1835 and which he later included in *La Comédie humaine*, I would like to explore the relation of narrative perspective to authorial vision, to study the narrator as a kind of avatar or instrument of a writer whose genius for formal innovation was as remarkable as his insight into language, history and human behavior. In each of these works—*Louis Lambert, Le Colonel Chabert*, the trilogy *Histoire des Treize* and *Eugénie Grandet*—the narrator adopts a distinctive point of view, often openly addressing problems of form and transition while relating his story; and the process of narration itself, therefore, unfolds as a drama in conjunction with the plot or action of the novel. It is this drama of technique that will be the subject of the readings of these individual works, which are addressed in the approximate chronological order of their inception (the first versions of *Louis Lambert* and *Le Colonel Chabert* were written in 1832, those of the novels of the *Histoire des Treize*, between 1833 and 1835; and *Eugénie Grandet* was begun in 1833, but not completed until 1839). This sequence suggests a refinement of technique culminating in the masterpiece *Eugénie Grandet*; in fact, no such rigid, linear technical development can be said to have taken place, since Balzac continually revised these as well as many other novels throughout the course of his career. However, I would like to suggest a possible inner development by means of the sequence that may parallel Balzac's gradual mastery of technique and expansion of its range—from the confused perspective in *Louis Lambert* to the masterfully told chronological narration of *Le Colonel Chabert*, to the experimentation with fragmented perspective and chronology in the *Histoire des Treize*, to the harmonious fusion of social panorama and story in *Eugénie Grandet*.

Louis Lambert is arguably the most autobiographical of Balzac's novels; it is also an essay in philosophical speculation. In the guise of the dead hero's friend and self-appointed biographer, the narrator attempts to reconstruct Lambert's life and thought from surviving evidence—written fragments, letters, the narrator's own reminiscences. As he progresses further into the recesses of memory and the open space of speculation, the narrator finds himself alternately locked within—or out of—the closed world of Lambert's private vision and often impenetrable discourse. In the end he can only acknowledge his failure truly to unify his "histoire intellectuelle," to fuse storytelling with analysis. Thus, we watch the narrator unsuccessfully struggle to integrate the various forms of expression that find their way into the narrative—letters, philosophical tenets and speculation, poetical myth and mimesis. And yet the narrator's problematical identification with his subject is instructive, illuminating some of the fundamental, recurring themes in Balzac's work generally, and enabling us the better to appreciate the detachment of perspective he achieves in other novels.

Whereas in *Louis Lambert* the narration sometimes borders on near-despair of intelligibility—the hero's cryptic speech, the narrator's inability to conjoin poetical and philosophical discourse—the narrator of *Le Colonel Chabert* forcefully asserts the referential capacity of language as a source of power and responsibility both in society, where it is frequently misused, and in poetry, where it participates in the symbolic. Through a perspective that explores the relationship of many different levels of meaning, the novel explores linguistic ground beyond the mere recognition of the denotative relation of sign to referent—a relation dangerously severed by Lambert in his last ravings. We enter the realm of moral and intellectual responsibility: the truthfulness and simplicity of Chabert's claim—"Je suis un homme!"—contrast utterly with the dishonesty and compromise too often tolerated by conventional language. The ambiguous relation of language and, by extension, of social justice to truth that, in this dispassionately told story, leads to willful personal and collective blindness, inspires in the lawyer Derville a kind of metaphysical horror. On the formal level the narrator addresses this ambiguity with respect to the symbolic truth of poetical discourse by deferring certain dramatic incidents in order to impress upon us the distanciation between sign and referent so richly exploited by metaphorical language. In so doing, he distinguishes between the tolerance of ambiguity of meaning essential to poetry and, through Derville's gradual disillusionment, its very different, often unjust application practiced in society.

In the preface to the trilogy *Histoire des Treize* Balzac introduces the persona of a narrator, an anonymous figure in whom the three stories have ostensibly been confided, only to abandon all pretense of a single narrative perspective once embarking on the narration of the first work, *Ferragus*. This and the other novels, *La Duchesse de Langeais* and *La Fille aux yeux d'or*, address the problem of fragmented perspective; they relate stories in which chronology, or the rearrangement of it, requires obvious and concerted shifting of the narrator's point of view. Hence, the way in which the narrator manages transitions within these works is a measure of technical accomplishment and growing mastery. In *Ferragus* the narrator indirectly and successively embodies the perspective of two of the characters, male figures in jealous pursuit of the mysterious Madame Jules; and then he steps back to adopt an "omniscient" pose, revealing her relationship as daughter to the hero, Ferragus, and inscribing the story in the larger context of a global vision of Paris. Thus, the narrator at one point carefully distinguishes between "récit" and "histoire," reminding us that the mere anecdote of the story depends upon the art of narration for its effectiveness and meaning. Although the work is not so compelling in its drama of persecution and loss as is the superior *Le Colonel Chabert*, it is instructive for its attempt to meet the challenge of coordinating several different perspectives within a single narrative, all the while respecting the law of chronology.

In *La Duchesse de Langeais* the narrator openly flouts that law, relating a story in flashback form, its suspense and timing representing Balzac's dramatic sense at its best. Technically, the deliberate rearrangement of chronology structurally imitates the operation of memory, associating past with present and endowing both with a sense of urgency and meaning. On a thematic level, insofar as the narrator would recreate the social and political environment of the Restoration and shows the hero Montriveau in his attempt to kidnap the cloistered Duchess, there also the narration is an act of retrieval. The transitions require that the narrator, who adopts throughout the detached, "omniscient" pose, convey depth and background, as opposed to the sense of linear continuity in *Ferragus*. Because the flagrant disregard of strict chronology makes this a self-conscious work, the narrator makes no explicit distinction between "récit" and "histoire"—only a final, inevitable tribute to the power of poetry to preserve feeling and memory. "Ce n'est plus qu'un poème," says Montriveau of the eponymous heroine; the adventure, once over, is a source of mystery, not disappointment.

Of the works in the *Histoire des Treize*, the third and last, *La Fille aux yeux d'or*, is formally and thematically the most audacious. It opens with the famous panorama of the chapter entitled "Physionomies parisiennes," invoking Classical mythology and Romantic allegory in its vision of industrial society and modern art; then abruptly, with only implicit transition through metaphor, the narrator relates an anecdote of a hero's exotic and grotesque initiation to the passions of greed, homosexuality and incest, all of which is prefigured in the first scene. By virtue of its appendage to the opening vision, the stylized tale acts as a metaphor for Balzac's poetical vision, stressing the fundamental consistency and identity of his imaginary universe, one that fuses myth with mimesis. The story of the hero de Marsay's eventual discovery of his relation to a rival and artist figure, his half-sister, corresponds to the formal effect of the disjointed two-part structure, which delays the reader's recognition of the esthetic unity of the work as a whole.

In an obvious parallel to *La Fille aux yeux d'or*, *Eugénie Grandet* begins with a quiet, classic description of the provincial town Saumur entitled "Physionomies bourgeoises"; but rather than sharply breaking with the description in the service of formal innovation, the narrator of *Eugénie Grandet* develops the themes of history, melancholy and solitude in an unobtrusive continuation of his initial scene. He allows that even he cannot fully interpret, completely understand, the world of symbols he opens before us; like the ancient markings carved into wooden doors, like the grotesque figures embellishing the town's mute, often forbidding architecture, lives and faces are hieroglyphs, full of mystery and unspoken stories. Unlike Louis Lambert and his biographer, this narrator renounces the ambition of omniscience; and although he sounds many of the themes explored in *Le Colonel Chabert*, he chooses an inherently less remarkable and articulate protagonist. Thus, the interest of *Eugénie Grandet* shifts away from the gradual resolution of an open conflict, such as Chabert's personal war against society, towards the drama of discernment, through the narrator's eyes, of hidden conflict, passion and the silent depths of experience. The process of seeing coincides with the progress of the heroine's rite of passage on the thematic plane; more clearly than the other works, *Eugénie Grandet* illustrates the painstaking art, the patient evolution of visionary insight Balzac so memorably described in *Facino Cane*:

Chez moi l'observation était déjà devenue intuitive, elle pénétrait l'âme sans négliger le corps; ou plutôt elle saisissait si bien les détails extérieurs, qu'elle allait sur-le-champ au-delà; elle me donnait la faculté de vivre la vie de l'individu sur laquelle elle s'exerçait, en me permettant de me substituer à lui comme le derviche des *Mille et Une Nuits* prenait le corps et l'âme des personnes sur lesquelles il prononçait certaines paroles.

It is, after all, this process of "observation"—its exploitation on the level of perspective, its constant deepening on the level of authorial vision—that initiates the reader into the special poetical consciousness of any author. The "sauvage enveloppe" Balzac so staunchly defended in his letter requires no apology for its superficial lack of refinement; distortions of theme or rearrangements of chronological order may serve to stress profound symbolic insights. A serious writer will cultivate first of all his vision, his "but de profonde moralité"; all the rest will follow. For all its technical faults, *Louis Lambert* is the work of such a writer, a work flawed by the absence of a controlling perspective sufficiently removed to coordinate insights from many sources—philosophy, religion, autobiography, invention. Told by a narrator who is not torn by so many conflicting impulses, *Le Colonel Chabert* elevates the poignant social criticism it contains far above the level of mere didacticism; it brings us to the crossroads where conventional language meets its obligation to truth, and explores the uses of compromise and ambiguity with respect to law, ordinary speech and symbolic expression. In the *Histoire des Treize* we see in three reprises the experimental uses of perspective in the relation of stories in which desire becomes a metaphor for the search for absolute, eternal meaning, one in which the identity and difference between the sexes can be reconciled and transcended. The inevitable failure of this endeavor leads, in these novels, to endings affirming the limitations and the possibilities of poetical discourse. Finally, in *Eugénie Grandet*, in less flamboyant and more measured style, the narrator departs from the solemn historicity of his opening vision to relate an adventure of the heart that does not entirely decipher the physical and moral façades of ordinary provincial life, but only deepens their mystery. Indeed, it is an attitude of wonder, of exploration, of scrutiny, that the drama of perspective would communicate to us in all these works. The revelation that one cannot change or control the world by divining its essence (*Louis Lambert*), by proclaiming one's personal truth (*Le Colonel Chabert*), by possessing one's beloved (*Histoire des Treize*), in *Eugénie Grandet* takes the form of a drama of relation: Eugénie meets her destiny, and herself, by accepting her paternal inheritance—the inescapable material and spiritual fruit of her father's avarice and of her own provincial roots. This ending, however bleak, is an esthetically compelling one, stating in its way the ultimate subordination of the life of the individual to the forces of history, and of the novel as work of art to the era from which it springs. It is as if Balzac would bequeath his work to us with a benevolent detachment prefigured by his narrator; as Martin Kanes observes:

Eventually we come full circle, for by recognizing the aesthetic status of the text, we make of the novel an object in its own right: not a copy of something else, but an autonomous object whose structures of perception and consciousness are those of the age that produced it. Inevitably, then, it will return us to history, not by what it refers to, but by what it is, thus fulfilling Balzac's fondest dream.[3]

Thus, the close readings of the novels that follow will take as their premise that an examination of narrative perspective will enable us to glimpse the "but de profonde moralité" implicit within a profusion of detail, in melodrama, in formal innovation, in the adventure of poetic feeling given permanence in words. Each work is a means of access to the single authorial vision in which it originates; but each work establishes its own unique symbolic world also. The relation of each narrative to the underlying poetical vision remains ambiguous, revealing as much as it conceals; we cannot explain away or categorize the qualities of such a vision; we can only respond as readers to the works before us. The accumulation of painstaking descriptive detail in Balzac's fiction reminds us, even as we question its linguistic and metaphysical underpinnings, that worlds become possible through language and that language cannot preclude the representation of humble detail expressed in accessible form. It is Louis Lambert's tragedy to have sacrificed the particular in the sounding of the universal—a helplessness, or temptation, firmly rejected by his creator. Colonel Chabert, Ferragus—these haunting, moving figures of wounded intelligence—convey an author's urgent sense of the fragility and limitations of the human mind —and of the intrinsic seriousness and value of its creative works and knowledge. This commitment to poetic vision, implicit in the drama of perspective in its many and enduring forms, illuminates the "sauvage enveloppe" of Balzac's art by fusing bone with marrow and marrow with bone.[4]

Chapter I

LOUIS LAMBERT

Part of *Le Livre mystique*, a subdivision of the *Etudes philosophiques*, *Louis Lambert*[1] is, according to the author's preface, "le mysticisme pris sur le fait" (507; 608). But authors' prefaces often can deceive, as Balzac's apparent ambivalence towards his chosen theme suggests: at the same time that he proclaims his interest in the writings of the mystics, he wistfully takes leave of the subject:

> ... de bonne heure, il [the author] avait pressenti là comme une nouvelle Divine Comédie. Hélas! le rythme voulait toute une vie, et sa vie a exigé d'autres travaux; le sceptre du rythme lui a donc échappé. La poésie sans la mesure est peut-être une impuissance? peut-être n'a-t-il fait qu'indiquer le sujet à quelque grand poète, humble prosateur qu'il est! Peut-être le Mysticisme y gagnera-t-il en se trouvant dans la langue si positive de notre pays, obligé de courir droit, comme un wagon sur le rail de son chemin de fer. (506;607)

In his intuition of a new rhythm, of a new *Divine Comedy*—all the while professing loyalty to its human counterpart—Balzac qualifies his vision as one subject to the laws of narrative perspective; his language, as one bound by referentiality, the discipline of orderly progression in thought, and rhythms reflecting the poetical nature of discourse in fiction. Yet it is clear that in Balzac's fictional mythology Louis Lambert was to have been that poet whose divine inspiration the author would invoke. It is Louis's mission, even as a child, to penetrate the natural and supernatural worlds with his extraordinary vision: "Louis embrassait les faits, il les expliquait après en avoir recherché tout à la fois le principe et la fin avec une perspicacité de sauvage" (591; 287). Pride, society and a too tenuous grasp upon the world outside his mind all contribute to Lambert's downfall. The story, in many ways a cautionary tale, probes into the origins of literary creativity and, indirectly, into Balzac's own coming of age as an artist.

The son of a provincial tanner, Louis Lambert attracts the attention of Madame de Staël, who sees in him *"un vrai voyant"* (595; 288) and sponsors his education at the Collège de Vendôme. There Louis meets a fellow traveler along the paths of philosophical speculation; he and his friend, the future narrator, are together known as "Le Poète-et-Pythagore" (606; 293), partly in honor of the youthful narrator's predilection for rhyming. During this period Lambert's intellectual development leads him from uncritical acceptance of Swedenborg's mystical doctrines to a fervent advocacy of materialism. At the age of fifteen he formulates his thought in a brilliant *Traité de la volonté*, seized and destroyed by an over-zealous schoolmaster. Leaving the *collège*, Louis and adolescence behind, the narrator learns only much later of his friend's student days in Paris, a career marked primarily by intellectual and romantic frustrations. His self-destructive impulses already visible, Louis returns to Mer, near Blois, to stay with his uncle, a parish priest. Upon meeting there a young woman, Pauline de Villenoix, he divines in her an *"ange-femme"* (670; 316), vindicating his earlier beliefs in mysticism and promising him sexual fulfillment through marriage; but on the eve of his wedding, unable to reconcile the conflicting demands of his physical and spiritual natures, Lambert lapses into a coma. After meeting by chance Louis's distraught uncle, the narrator resolves to write the intellectual history of his former companion, now crippled by catalepsy, his mind forever lost to science and to art. At the end of the novel we learn that Lambert, 28 years old, dies in his fiancée Pauline's arms; presumably a suicide, he is buried on her estate beneath an unmarked cross of stone.

Thematically and formally a precarious undertaking, the fictional biography of Louis Lambert suffers from weaknesses symptomatic of the preoccupation with the difficulties of writing shared by the hero, the narrator and, we may infer, the author. On the thematic level the fragmentary condition of Lambert's works reflects the ambiguity at the heart of his poetical-mystical vision: the truth known by mystics does not have the radical dependence on words characteristic of the symbolic truths expressed by poets.[2] When Lambert is said to encounter the inexpressible, we cannot distinguish his incoherence from madness; and the narrator's distance from his subject, a cue to interpretation, shifts inconsistently throughout the novel. On the formal level the narrator has assigned himself the unenviable task of describing a form of awareness—Lambert's illumination—supposedly independent of or incompatible with verbal expression:

The narrator is attempting to reduce to communicable language a doctrine largely composed of nonverbal perceptions, which nevertheless depends on verbal expression to exist at all outside Lambert's mind. In a sense, all texts fall short of their ideal of referentiality; but what makes the narrator's attempt even remotely reasonable is the possibility that even if he cannot set forth his hero's doctrine explicitly, he can hope to convey its sense by the contextual arrangement of his words. While there is no verification or proof of correspondence, the reader in the real world may find some sense of Lambert's doctrines in the reality of the text.[3]

The narrative, then, must accommodate as its subject a vision whose relation to language is quite different from that of the author's own poetical vision. Even with the narrator as a sort of obliging midwife, helping to give birth in words to a consciousness alien to them, *Louis Lambert* may have been doomed to failure; Balzac himself called it "le plus triste de tous les avortons"[4]—a stillborn poem.

A further complication on the level of discourse, one that becomes conspicuous towards the end of the book, involves Lambert's frequent ventures into philosophical speculation. Although related insofar as they are modes of intellectual inquiry, speculation in philosophy and speculation in poetry approach experience and metaphor in very different ways.[5] The narrator, who often reproduces Lambert's thoughts verbatim, makes no attempt to integrate them into the flow of the narrative, stating only his determination not to lend a false coherence to his work:

Peut-être aurais-je pu transformer en un livre complet ces débris de pensées. . . . La vie de cet immense cerveau, qui sans doute a craqué de toutes parts comme un empire trop vaste, y eût été développée dans le récit des visions de cet être, incomplet par trop de force ou par faiblesse; mais j'ai mieux aimé rendre compte de mes impressions que de faire une œuvre plus ou moins poétique. (692; 123)

The narrator's reluctance to shape a unified whole or dramatic unit from his "impressions" reveals the tension inherent in his bringing together the modes of poetical and philosophical discourse. It is as if storytelling and analysis, presumably the two impulses behind what was originally called the "*Histoire intellectuelle* de Louis Lambert" (my emphasis), refuse the yoke of a single unifying perspective.[6]

These preoccupations with language affecting character and the process of narration have in this novel conspicuous psychological import as well. Lambert's conflicting attractions to spirituality and sensuality condemn him to the physical, intellectual and spiritual isolation of catalepsy, unproductivity and madness. It is entirely possible, as Marthe Robert asserts, that Balzac's own experience and intuition gave him authoritative insight into Lambert's pathology:

Nous ne savons pas comment Balzac a triomphé intérieurement des tendances pathologiques graves—tendance au meurtre, au suicide, à l'automutilation—dont il donne dans son histoire intellectuelle un tableau clinique si exact (on s'est toujours extasié sur cette exactitude clinique sans toutefois oser se demander d'où l'auteur tirait ses connaissances). Mais nous pouvons l'inférer de la place tout à la fois centrale et excentrique que tient l'autobiographie [*Louis Lambert*] dans *la Comédie Humaine*, l'œuvre gigantesque qu'il a durement gagnée, jour après jour, mot après mot, sur le fond angoissant de sa propre sauvagerie.[7]

Thus, without insisting on whatever personal demons Balzac may have exorcised in writing the novel, we can read *Louis Lambert* as a novel of vocation, the demands of which are successfully met not by the nominal hero, but by the narrator, who never openly declares his superiority. It is, therefore, with a certain false modesty that the narrator finally declines to cross over the boundary separating fact or document ("ces débris de pensées") from literary creation ("une œuvre plus ou moins poétique"). With this exaggerated austerity as a shield, he need not pronounce the verdict against Lambert—writer of mere fragments—implied by the existence of the present, completed biography. As Otto Rank writes:

The artist, too, has [a] feeling of *Weltschmerz* in common with the handicapped neurotic; but here the paths diverge, since the artist can use this introverted world not only as a protection but as a material; he is thus never wholly oppressed by it—though often enough profoundly depressed—but can penetrate it by and with his own personality and then again thrust it from him and re-create it from himself. This extrusion is a process both of begetting and of bearing, not at the level of sexual differentiation of male and female, but at a deeper and more fundamental level: the liberation of the individual from the burden of generation by repulsion of part of the ego, which is felt as a relief and not as a loss.[8]

The relation between the narrator and Louis Lambert may be said to dramatize this process. The narrator abandons the attempt to write a "poetical" work in favor of a more studied form of introspection, that is, the present narrative; he has presumably overcome the neurotic tendencies to which his friend and double eventually succumbs. It is significant that the separation of the two figures is occasioned by the narrator's own lapse into a coma and subsequent withdrawal from school—a turn of events prefiguring Lambert's demise, which itself fully accentuates the narrator's implicit recovery and ultimate ascendency. The narrator's is not the voice in the authorial preface, hurrying on to other self-appointed labors ("le rythme voulait toute une vie, et sa vie a exigé d'autres travaux"); the narrator's pause for reflection towards the end of the novel ("Peut-être aurais-je pu transformer en un livre complet ces débris de pensées") attests to his difficult, protracted rupture with an earlier, soon-to-be-discarded self. No longer basing his authority on the fusion of identity between "Le Poète-et-Pythagore," the narrator contemplates his friend's decline as he establishes, albeit awkwardly, his own distinctive perspective, one no longer associated with adolescence. In graduating from the status of disciple to that of biographer,[9] the narrator achieves an identity as writer won at the cost of acknowledging Lambert's pathetic failure as such. His ambivalence towards his former companion—outwardly praising him, implicitly condemning him—may be said, according to Rank's analysis, to stem from a certain guilt feeling accompanying the process of creative growth:

As the artist, during the process of liberation from the ideology [of an earlier state], has to include in what he surrenders the person or persons who were concerned with it, he has to justify this action, which is usually done by magnification. That is, he will either really create something greater, in order to justify his action, or in the effort to create this greater [work] he will be impeded by a still more enhanced feeling of guilt. In the first case he will use the guilt-feeling directly for creation; in the second even his previous creative power will be impeded.[10]

If we read *Louis Lambert* in light of this possible symbolic meaning—the author's dramatization of the shedding of an earlier self impeding his artistic development—then the novel may be said to represent the second of the possibilities cited by Rank, an inferior work in this case flawed by lack of dramatic unity, the interference of different modes of discourse and a certain amount of self-indulgence. But in turn we must then recognize *La Comédie humaine* as a whole as representing the first of the possibilities: the greater work, the creation of which proves the author's triumph over the conflicts and problems with language afflicting his less resourceful characters (the narrator and Lambert), insofar as they are autobiographical.

It is necessary to emphasize that *Louis Lambert* is not literally the technical breakthrough that made Balzac's mature career possible; *Les Chouans* or *La Peau de chagrin* most likely had that function. *Louis Lambert* is, however, as Martin Kanes has noted,[11] one of the few works in which Balzac openly analyzes the origins of poetic creation. The narrator's difficulty in establishing his distance from the hero is not merely a problem of first-person narration, but a reflection of the inquiry itself: the contemplation of literary creation as a product of the will and intellect ("Peut-être aurais-je *pu* transformer ces débris de *pensées*"), and as a meaningful communication with others (the destruction of Lambert's treatise and his insanity as cautionary symbols).

It is with this exploration of the possibilities and limitations of poetical discourse that the drama of perspective begins: *Louis Lambert* is like a threshold predicated by the immense achievement of *La Comédie humaine*. The authorial consciousness embodied by Derville in *Le Colonel Chabert*, the visible experimentation with form in the *Histoire des Treize*, the almost impersonal voice narrating the classic *Eugénie Grandet*—these technical accomplishments presuppose an acceptance of the restrictions of genre, the control of language and of perspective. In the self-definition of the narrator in *Louis Lambert* Balzac allows us to glimpse, even as he explores them, the preconditions of literary creation. *Louis Lambert* is the first step of a journey making other journeys possible.

In the first pages of *Louis Lambert* the narrator, as yet unidentified, introduces the hero as a child of remarkable intellectual and, it is suggested, spiritual gifts. The first lines are marked by the solemn tone characteristic of saint's life or fairy tale, and promise a story full of mystical and poetic feeling:

> Louis Lambert naquit, en 1797 à Montoire, petite ville du Vendômois, où son père exploitait une tannerie de médiocre importance et comptait faire de lui son successeur; mais les dispositions qu'il manifesta prématurément pour l'étude modifièrent cet arrêt paternel.... L'Ancien et le Nouveau Testament étaient tombés entre les mains de Louis à l'âge de cinq ans; et ce livre, où sont contenus tant de livres, avait décidé de sa destinée. Cette enfantine imagination comprit-elle déjà la mystérieuse profondeur des Ecritures, pouvait-elle déjà suivre l'Esprit-Saint dans son vol à travers les mondes, s'éprit-elle seulement des romanesques attraits qui abondent en ces poèmes orientaux; ou, dans sa première innocence, cette âme sympathisa-t-elle avec le sublime religieux que des mains divines ont épanché dans ce livre? Pour quelques lecteurs, notre récit résoudra ces questions. Un fait résulta de cette première lecture de la Bible: Louis allait par tout Montoire, y quêtant des livres qu'il obtenait à la faveur de ces séductions dont le secret n'appartient qu'aux enfants, et auxquelles personne ne sait résister.... Le peu de fortune des pauvres tanneurs ne leur permettant d'acheter un homme à leur fils, ils trouvèrent dans l'état ecclésiastique le seul moyen que leur laissât la loi de le sauver de la conscription, et ils l'envoyèrent, en 1807, chez son oncle maternel, curé de Mer, autre petite ville située sur la Loire, près de Blois. (589-90; 286)

The future religious or mythical hero, if indeed he fulfills his implied destiny, is already a child of great promise, distinguished from his humble background by extraordinary virtue, in this case of an intellectual nature. The sacrifices of his parents, his persecution by society (in the form of military conscription), the flights to religious sanctuary—these childhood events call to mind the fate of the child Moses (to whom Lambert will be compared) and the Flight into Egypt (Lambert will call Jesus a fellow *Spécialiste*, or seer). Indeed, Lambert amazes his parents, and later his patroness, Madame de Staël, with his intelligence and wisdom; we witness what appears to be a modern child Jesus instructing the elders in the temple of Romantic allegory. Appropriately, it is the written word—sacred scriptures—that both awakens Lambert's imagination and, as implied by the use of the passive voice ("étaient tombées"), seals his fate. Thus, the narrator establishes Lambert as an intellectual hero and attributes to the boy's giftedness the power to modify conventional destiny—the "arrêt paternel," military service. Lambert's becomes a privileged existence, his genius a kind of talisman. Nothing stands in his way—not even locks upon libraries, mysteries of Scripture.

In the opening lines the forces of myth and mimesis enter into an intriguing dialectic that promises much to the reader. On the one hand, the narrator supplies abundant naturalistic detail: allusions to time, geography, age, historical conditions, distinct and specific characters. On the other, in the echoes of the Bible and folklore, and in his own speculation, the narrator invites the undercurrents of myth to tug at the still slender reed of descriptive reference, as if preparing to transform it. But upon closer inspection we find that this creative tension has already been released and driven to the surface. The narrator does not use irony to exploit or subvert his sweeping claims; instead, in the fourth sentence ("Cette enfantine imagination . . .") he establishes an unqualified opposition of poetry and religion—"romanesques attraits" and "sublime religieux"—that puts both on equal symbolic footing. The Old and New Testaments do not help form Lambert's moral character; they excite his imagination as "poèmes orientaux" whose "sublime religieux" and "mystérieuse profondeur"—that is, their power of evocation—leave a lasting impression. For Lambert, it is implied, the Bible is primarily literary in value, an interpretation confirmed by the resulting "fact": his almost epic quest for books. Is Lambert's first reading the foundation for a search for truth, or is it the beginning of a lifelong passion for reading? Do these reflect the same impulses? The narrator in his musings seems to shroud in deliberate ambiguity this hint of ambivalence towards the truth of religious symbol. By withholding irony or criticism, he suggests that Lambert's future mysticism may have its origins in an excessively stimulated imagination and not in spiritual illumination. Already the myth of the hero or saint has encountered the obstacle of doubt, defying the creative impulse to transform this beginning into a drama of mythological proportions. The narrator's indecisiveness—he volunteers possible meanings only to retreat from them—is like an early frost killing the symbolic bloom just flowering here.

The narrator need not have sacrificed an attitude of ironic, though sympathetic detachment, one that might have led him and Lambert both to deeper understanding of their young, heroic dreams. In *Le Grand Meaulnes*, for example, the narrator François, also the adolescent friend of the hero, re-experiences the admiration, wonder and sense of adventure he knew in the company of his friend and reenacts his gradual initiation into the prosaic territory of adulthood. Alain-Fournier develops François's inner transformation as a counterpoint to Meaulnes's more dramatic adventures; but Balzac gives the reader of *Louis Lambert* no such inner compass by which to gauge the dimensions of Lambert's tragedy. We are to consider Lambert's story much in the same way he approached the Bible: inspired by its poetry and at an ambiguous remove from its doctrines.

The narrator continues to insist on the hero's exceptional character. In 1811, at age fourteen, Lambert enrolls in the Collège des Oratoriens in Vendôme under the sponsorship of Madame de Staël:

Lambert dut la protection de cette femme célèbre au hasard ou sans doute à la Providence qui sait toujours aplanir les voies au génie délaissé. Mais pour nous, de qui les regards s'arrêtent à la superficie des choses humaines, ces vicissitudes, dont tant d'exemples nous sont offerts dans la vie des grands hommes, ne semblent être que le résultat d'un phénomène tout physique; et, pour la plupart des biographes, la tête d'un homme de génie tranche sur les masses comme une belle plante qui par son éclat attire dans les champs les yeux du botaniste. (590; 286)

In presenting Lambert's benefactress as a sort of fairy godmother or guardian angel, the narrator again sounds a note of ambiguity with respect to religious belief—the "sans doute" appearing as an afterthought—and again proceeds to the superficial level at which effect, and not source or substance, is registered. He invites us to stop with the disinterested curiosity of scientists to examine a marvelous anomaly somehow persisting in nature; but it is not Lambert's physiognomy that should detain us. We have no physical portrait of him yet; it is the narrator's skill—"*l'aventure* de Louis Lambert")—that should hold our interest:

Cette comparaison pourrait s'appliquer à l'aventure de Louis Lambert . . . il emportait dès le matin du pain et des livres; puis il allait lire et méditer au fond des bois pour se dérober aux remonstrances de sa mère, à laquelle de si constantes études paraissaient dangereuses. Admirable instinct de mère! (590; 287)

We can now gratefully welcome the narrator's assumption of the guise of mere humanity in our behalf ("pour nous de qui les regards s'arrêtent à la superficie des choses humaines"). We look forward, like the young Lambert, to the dangerous pleasures lying in store for us as his fellow travelers, that is to say, inveterate readers. Like an able politician, the narrator has elicited our sympathy by superficially identifying himself with us; and in finally presenting himself, he resorts to another ingratiating tactic, referring to himself modestly with an indirect object pronoun:

—Souvent, me dit-il, en parlant de ses lectures, j'ai accompli de délicieux voyages, embarqué sur un mot dans les abîmes du passé, comme l'insecte qui posé sur quelque brin d'herbe flotte au gré du fleuve. Parti de la Grèce, j'arrivais à Rome et traversais l'étendue des âges modernes. . . . Qui nous expliquera philosophiquement la transition de la sensation à la pensée, de la pensée au verbe, du verbe à son expression hiéroglyphique, des hiéroglyphes à l'alphabet, de l'alphabet à l'éloquence écrite, dont la beauté réside dans une suite d'images classées par les rhéteurs, et qui sont comme les hiéroglyphes de la pensée? (591; 287)

Now that the reassuring collective "nous" has been transformed into the unobtrusive singular "me" ("me dit-il"), we readers have been drawn, implicated, absorbed into the narrator's point of view. Significantly, the first words Lambert pronounces in the course of the narrative concern the development of written language; this mutual preoccupation brings the narrator and hero intellectually and syntactically together. Equally significantly, no dialogue occurs: Lambert speaks and the narrator, his disciple, listens and remembers. The latter's reticence invites us, upon rereading the novel, to interpret Louis's words as a caution or parable illustrated by the work as a whole: however delightful the voyage launched by words, fragile vessels of collective memory, the mind that travels in isolation may dangerously skirt an abyss of self-absorption, of incommunicability. Already haunted by the lost ideal of perfect referentiality, Lambert has recourse to metaphor, describing ideas as ultimately inaccessible, glimpsed only through "les hiéroglyphes de la pensée." He does not imagine his consciousness to have roots in a particular time and place, nourished by the life-giving river of language; he compares himself instead to a lower form of life at the mercy of the river's arbitrary currents: "un insecte qui posé sur quelque brin d'herbe flotte au gré du fleuve."

The narrator qualifies Lambert's penchant for reflection of this sort to "un de ces jeux effrayants auxquels se plaît parfois la Nature, et qui prouvait l'anomalie de son [Lambert's] existence" (591; 287). Insisting on the hero's precocity, the narrator makes no evaluation of the ideas themselves. It is with another, and similar, passage that he voices concern over the misguided direction of Lambert's inner voyages. In the repetition of the grammatical structure casting him as Louis's passive audience ("me dit-il," "me disait-il"), we can detect the narrator's ambivalence towards his subject. In the first instance of this structure he introduces Lambert's preoccupation with the collective and, we may infer, individual mastery of the skills of writing; and now in the second instance the narrator introduces his own misgivings about Lambert's speculation—a kind of thought that threatens to dispense with language altogether:

Un grand penchant l'entraînait vers les ouvrages mystiques. "*Abyssus abyssum,*" me disait-il. Notre esprit est un abîme qui se plaît dans les abîmes. . . . Cette prédilection lui fut fatale, s'il est permis toutefois de juger sa vie selon les lois ordinaires. . . . Ce goût pour les choses du ciel . . . était dû peut-être à l'influence exercée sur son esprit par les premiers livres qu'il lut chez son oncle. Sainte Thérèse et Mme Guyon lui continuèrent la Bible . . . . (594; 288)

The narrator's hesitation and use of the word *juger* announce his wariness, as if Lambert himself were an abyss ready to engulf the narrator's identity and perspective. At present, however, the narrator seems unwilling to make any judgment as to relative value; the profound and the superficial converge upon the same plane of thought, a process that occurs also in the sweeping vision of Paris introducing *La Fille aux yeux d'or*. But in the latter work it is precisely the horror of the urban landscape that the narrator would have us contemplate; the narrator of *Louis Lambert* would impress upon us instead the vastness of a genius whose vision is said to penetrate material and spiritual reality. The ambivalence with which he approaches his subject casts doubt on his ultimate seriousness and on the immensity of Lambert's intelligence—a fiction we might otherwise readily accept. The deference of the narrator, the determining influence of Lambert's reading, the exhilaration of a mind absorbed in thought—these motifs again accompany the association of purely literary pleasure with religious or mystical texts. This disconcerting juxtaposition is even repeated internally by the association of Madame de Guyon and Saint Teresa, the one a minor figure and the other unquestionably a religious genius.

Avoiding judgments as to relative value, the narrator leads us, too, towards an abyss in which genius is valued merely for its brilliance and rarity—"la superficie des choses"—and not for its intellectual and moral qualities and works. The narrator's attitude towards mysticism is more quietistic than Christian in inspiration, again exempting Lambert from the "ordinary laws" of human existence. But we are willing to forgive his unqualified praise when he promises to bring the character dramatically alive:

> Etonnée, Mme de Staël prit le livre [*Du ciel et de l'enfer* by Swedenborg, which she surprises Lambert reading] avec cette brusquerie qu'elle affectait de mettre dans ses interrogations ... puis, lançant un coup d'œil à Lambert: "Est-ce que tu comprends cela?" lui dit-elle. —Priez-vous Dieu? demanda l'enfant. —Mais ... oui. —Et le comprenez-vous?
>
> La baronne resta muette pendant un moment; puis elle s'assit auprès de Lambert et se mit à causer avec lui. Malheureusement ma mémoire, quoique fort étendue, est loin d'être aussi fidèle que l'était celle de mon camarade, et j'ai tout oublié de cette conversation, hormis les premiers mots. (595; 288)

Like the first paragraph, this moment, too, is rich in tensions: the meeting of a historical personage and fictional character, of an author and an imaginary creature, of naturalistic description and an exchange reminiscent of Buddhist or New Testament parables, of striking dialogue and meditative silence. But nothing further happens; it is as if the narrator compulsively sabotages the potential drama of his own work by intruding upon it, reducing effective imagery to mere, and inadequate, feats of memory. In this instance the intertwining of history and fiction is particularly ineffective; we learn that Madame de Staël enrolls "son petit Moïse" (596; 289) in the school where the narrator meets him, and that sometime later, in 1817, Lambert "vint à pied de Blois à Paris dans l'intention de la voir, et arriva malheureusement le jour où la baronne mourut" (596; 289). The narrator would have us share his astonishment before "le merveilleux de cette histoire" (596; 289), but the weakness of his claims lies precisely in their implausibility. In the work bearing his name, Colonel Chabert's bond to Napoleon is supported by every detail in the story, whereas the narrator of *Louis Lambert* must rely on extraordinary, not to mention incomplete, evidence to reinforce a tenuous conjunction of mimesis and myth.

Now that the narrator prepares to enter the story as a character, as Lambert's adolescent friend, he abruptly rids his story of the trappings of myth and hagiography. He embarks upon a description of the history, campus and curriculum of the Collège des Oratoriens. So detailed and convincing are these "quelques renseignements" (596; 289) that the narrator's earlier apology for his faulty memory seems suspect. Now, as he describes his childhood, the narrator's "nous" refers explicitly to himself and his fellow students; the reader, no longer his tacit accomplice, is addressed as a free, and separate, agent: "Quiconque voudra se représenter l'isolement de ce grand collège avec ses bâtiments monastiques, au milieu d'une petite ville ... aura certes une idée de l'intérêt que devait nous offrir l'arrivée d'un *nouveau*, véritable passager survenu dans un navire" (600; 290). The peaceful, prosaic rhythms of scholarly life are about to be magically disrupted by the appearance of Lambert: "L'arrivée de Louis Lambert fut le texte d'un conte digne des *Mille et Une Nuits*" (600; 290). Again referring to an "Oriental poem," the narrator resumes his temporarily suspended efforts at myth-making. His remarks, as before, intensify our awareness of the literary nature of the narrative, identifying Lambert's arrival as a "texte" and even introducing the figure of a storyteller:

> Tous les Petits arrivèrent en silence pour écouter l'aventure de ce Louis Lambert, trouvé, comme un aérolithe, par Mme de Staël au coin d'un bois. M. Hagoult dut nous expliquer Mme de Staël: pendant cette soirée, elle me parut avoir dix pieds; depuis j'ai vu le tableau de Corinne, où Gérard l'a représentée et si grande et si belle; hélas! la femme idéale rêvée par mon imagination la surpassait tellement, que la véritable Mme de Staël a constamment perdu dans mon esprit, même après la lecture du livre tout viril intitulé *De l'Allemagne*. (600-01; 290)

It is as if Lambert himself were the germ of creative consciousness; the very evocation of his name and story brings with it a host of literary, artistic and mythological allusions. The narrator now refers to Lambert, formerly Mme de Staël's "petit Moïse," as an "aérolithe"—again trivializing the religious theme in what may be an Old Testament anticipation of Apollinaire's Christ as aviator ("Zone"). The exaggerated dimensions the narrator attributes to Mme de Staël inspire deception associated with artistic representation; but rather than dismiss the illusory "femme idéale" from his mind, he only cultivates the image: "la véritable Mme de Staël a *constamment perdu dans mon esprit*." Of course, he is joking; but even this anecdote conforms to the process implicit from the beginning of the novel: a persistent idealization of the subject, Lambert, and everything associated with him, accompanied by expressions of doubt and disillusionment with respect to the imagination's own powers. Religious imagery and poetry once again fuse: the priest narrates not the Gospels, but a magical adventure; and its subject, Louis Lambert, is a poet formerly destined by his family to the clergy.

Even though the narrator looks back upon this episode with bemusement and nostalgia, he does not hesitate to exploit it as a pretext for speculation:

> L'impression que les discours du père Hagoult firent sur moi pendant cette soirée est une des plus vives de mon enfance, et je ne puis la comparer qu'à la lecture de *Robinson Crusoé*. Je dus même plus tard au souvenir de ces sensations prodigieuses une remarque peut-être neuve sur les différents effets que produisent les mots dans chaque entendement . . . mais l'étude de ce phénomène exige de larges développements, hors de propos ici. (602; 291)

This passage is reminiscent of the beginning of *Ferragus*, in which the narrator establishes the susceptibility of his imagination to even the slightest visual stimulus. Here the narrator shows his sensitivity to the effect of words, spoken or printed, in storytelling; and he goes on to tell of his "intempestive passion" (603; 291) for reading and for writing poetry, a practice that earned him the derisive nickname "le Poète" and made him particularly receptive to Lambert's friendship and ideas: "Cette digression autobiographique doit faire comprendre la nature des réflexions par lesquelles je fus assailli à l'arrivée de Lambert" (603; 292). As in *Ferragus*, the narrator's own subjectivity is presented as interesting in its own right before he gives us detailed portraits of the characters. Accordingly, the description of Lambert that follows must be read in light of the attitude implicit in the narrator's earlier use of imagery:

> Louis était un enfant maigre et fluet, haut de quatre pieds et demi; sa figure hâlée, ses mains brunies par le soleil paraissaient accuser une vigueur musculaire que néanmoins il n'avait pas à l'état normal. Aussi, deux mois après son entrée au collège, quand le séjour de la classe lui avait fait perdre sa coloration presque végétale, le vîmes-nous devenir pâle et blanc comme une femme. Sa tête était d'une grosseur remarquable . . . . Son œil ressemblait alors à une vitre d'où le soleil se serait retiré soudain après l'avoir illuminée . . . . Sa voix se faisait douce comme une voix de femme qui laisse tomber un aveu; puis elle était, parfois, pénible, incorrecte, raboteuse, s'il est permis d'employer ces mots pour peindre des effets nouveaux. (605; 292)

For the first time we are invited to visualize this extraordinary creature, whose literary sensitivity seems to have been translated into physical delicacy, according to Romantic prescription. The massiveness of his head, the penetration of his gaze, the musicality of his voice—these attributes meet our expectations. But the narrator implies that their exceptional character borders on the monstrous or degenerate: "à l'état normal"—the last a conspicuous word in this context—Lambert lacks vigor; his deceptively healthy coloring, called "végétale"—sub-human—fades to a feminine pallor;

his gaze calls to mind a sun that has vanished, not one that radiates; his voice alternately sings and loses its pleasing quality. Typically conscious of the supposed novelty of his observations, the narrator reminds us of our dependency on his skill with language. Like the subject of his portrait, the verbs he uses are weak—forms of *être, paraître, devenir* abound; it is a static description, one in keeping with the continual frustration of the dramatic impulses in this novel.

Having diminished the hero's stature, the narrator merges with him—and in so doing, he subtly elevates his own. Now he ascribes to Lambert godlike qualities absent from the physical portrait and, with customary false modesty, basks in their reflected glory:

> Je fus donc seul admis à pénétrer dans cette âme sublime, et pourquoi ne dirais-je pas divine? qu'y a-t-il de plus près de Dieu que le génie dans un cœur d'enfant? ... Notre fraternité devint si grande que nos camarades accolèrent nos deux noms; l'un ne se prononçait pas sans l'autre; et, pour appeler l'un de nous, ils criaient: *Le Poète-et-Pythagore!* ... ma vie se trouva, pendant cette époque, assez intimement unie à la sienne pour qu'il me soit possible aujourd'hui d'écrire son histoire intellectuelle. (606; 292-93)

It is this "conjugalité" (618; 297) that authorizes the narrator's biography, that is his pretext for writing. When we reconsider the mythological overtones of the first lines of the novel in light of the phenomenon of identification occurring here, the narrator's moments of hesitation and defensiveness are more understandable: he comes uncomfortably close to mythicizing an aspect of himself, part of a life "intimement unie" to his own. In symbolically "marrying" Lambert, the narrator contemplates his identity with and difference from the subject of his words, and becomes so supremely self-conscious that he again justifies his actions:

> Il a fallu que j'arrivasse à trente ans ... pour que je comprisse la portée des phénomènes desquels je fus alors l'inhabile témoin ... mais aujourd'hui ma mémoire les a coordonnés, et je me suis initié aux secrets de cette tête féconde en me reportant aux jours délicieux de notre jeune amitié. (606-07; 293)

Although the narrator ostensibly asserts that the passage of time has given him an informed perspective as witness to Lambert's genius, he also states that this understanding originates within himself, in the practice of introspection. An unwitting disciple, his initiation takes place only in the absence of the master, only in the journey into memory; Lambert is seen, as during Père Hagoult's narration, most interesting when he is a stimulus for thought, a virtual myth, a fantasy descending, like the aerolith, into the sphere of reality. Like Colonel Chabert, Ferragus and Paquita in *La Fille aux yeux d'or*—all of whom are called "fantaisies"—Louis Lambert exists primarily as an intriguing, symbolic figure; but rather than dramatically state "la grandeur" and "le mécanisme" (606; 293) of his genius, the narrator falls back upon himself, upon the condition of his own intellectual development. His role as witness and initiate obliquely calls to mind Lambert's remark that "le plus bel ouvrage à faire aujourd'hui était l'Histoire de l'Eglise primitive" (640; 305); just as only after the death of Jesus were the Gospels written and doctrines formulated, so only after Lambert's death can the narrator at last evaluate his life and thought. Perhaps this evangelical approach to his subject—for the New Testament is present from the very first paragraph of the novel—explains in part the narrator's failure to sustain a single dramatic action throughout the work. Lambert, despite a period of doubt, believes in the doctrines of Swedenborg; the narrator, who must distance himself, does not; and although he collects Lambert's sayings and recollections of him, he cannot suffuse them with either mystical feeling or a sense of poetical freedom, of creative adventure.

Indeed, the narrator's use of metaphor in recounting his life with Lambert shows how little faith he has in the progress of spiritual evolution. He and Lambert, as yet undifferentiated, resemble subhuman and despised forms of life, the monstrous exception: "Le Poète-et-Pythagore furent donc une exception, une vie en dehors de la vie commune.... Nous vivions donc exactement comme deux rats tapis dans le coin de la salle où étaient nos pupitres... nous demeurions là tranquilles, heureux à demi, semblables à deux végétations..." (613; 295). As if to dramatize further their status as pariahs, they share the cental role in a play put on at school, *Le Lépreux de la vallée d'Aoste* (614; 295). The memory of this occasion inspires in the narrator a hyperbolic regret that intimates his own literary ambitions: "Les soupirs de Lambert m'ont appris des hymnes de tristesse bien plus pénétrants que ne le sont les plus belles pages de *Werther*" (614; 295). He does not refer instead to a mystical text or scriptures.

The situation of the narrator's perspective in memories of the "conjugalité" of adolescent friendship makes it difficult to assess the value the narrator would place on the mysticism said to preoccupy the hero. In this domain the narrator is strictly Lambert's pupil, as always susceptible to the storyteller's magic: "J'écoutais avidement ses récits empreints de ce merveilleux qui fait dévorer avec tant de délices, aux enfants comme aux hommes, les contes où le vrai affecte les formes les plus absurdes" (616; 296). It is not a search for religious truth that consumes the narrator—he will only later turn to Swedenborg "par curiosité" (616; 296); it is instead a love of language and poetry that illuminates his memories. Even after briefly stating the Swedish mystic's doctrines, the narrator abruptly turns from the subject of mystical theology to begin a discussion of literary effects:

Cette doctrine ... m'était présentée par Lambert avec toutes les séductions du mystère, enveloppée dans les langes de la phraséologie particulière aux mystographes: diction obscure, pleine d'abstractions, et si active sur le cerveau, qu'il est certains livres de Jacob Boehm, de Swedenborg ou de Mme Guyon dont la lecture pénétrante fait surgir des fantaisies aussi multiformes que peuvent l'être les rêves produits par l'opium. ... J'aimais néanmoins à me plonger dans ce monde mystérieux, invisible aux sens, où chacun se plaît à vivre, soit qu'il se le représente sous la forme indéfinie de l'Avenir, soit qu'il le revête des puissantes formes de la Fable. (617-18; 297)

It is not direct experience of mystical union that leads the narrator into speculation; "phraséologie," "diction" and "la lecture" inspire his "fantaisies." The reference to an opium-induced trance reduces Lambert's spiritual journeys to one of a variety of sensations provoked artificially by drugs —or by reading—in an excessively stimulated imagination. Of all the effects the narrator describes, only the "puissantes formes de la Fable" have any force or shape. Thus, he subtly distances himself from the "mysterious world" he praises: "*J'aimais* néanmoins à me plonger ...."

Consigning his mystical reverie to the past, the narrator implies that he no longer finds meaning or solace in formless thought or contemplation. With the more mature perspective his thirty years have earned him, he watches his former dreams—Lambert's "travaux spirituels" (616; 296)—dissolve into a sea at the edge of consciousness, into which the two principals dive "comme deux poissons qui nagent dans les mêmes eaux" (616; 296). What for Swedenborg represents an evolution of the spirit, for the narrator, using an animal metaphor, implies a traveling backward to a more primitive state. He also associates advancement in the spheres of spiritual awareness with paralysis of speech, inhibition of expression:

Dans le monde invisible, comme dans le monde réel, si quelque habitant des régions inférieures arrive, sans en être digne, à un cercle supérieur, non seulement il n'en comprend ni les habitudes ni les discours, mais encore sa présence y paralyse et les voix et les cœurs. Dans sa *Divine Comédie*, Dante a peut-être eu quelque légère intuition de ces sphères .... (617; 297)

The angels speak only to those who have already won certain insights; but for the narrator, whose ascendancy is poetical—whose seeing depends on unimpeded access to words—vision is a process in conjunction with language and not a status determined by past experience. Having metaphorically allied spiritualism with a kind of biological regression, the narrator would be like that unworthy, displaced intruder, inspiring in the angels— and implicitly in his subject, Lambert—an awkward silence he ambiguously associates with delusion. Only his double, Lambert—the failed poet and genius—can afford to seek "la clef des cieux" (617; 297); the narrator prefers to analyze Dante. Lambert will see the angels, but the narrator will write his story. That Balzac privileges the narrator over Lambert in this way insinuates an oppressive ambiguity at the center of his spiritual universe, the will to write not at one with an attraction to mysticism.

As if to crystallize the insight implicit here, the narrator shows Lambert brought to the same rejection of Swedenborg's teachings in the next stage of his intellectual development. Reflecting upon a prophetic dream in which he vividly pictured a site he was to visit the next morning, Lambert concludes that this experience must predicate a human consciousness intrinsically bound to sensory perception—an interdependence of matter and spirit that renders the concept of dualism, stating their incompatibility, unnecessary and false:

> Peut-être sommes-nous tout simplement doués de qualités intimes et perfectibles dont l'exercice, dont les développements produisent en nous des phénomènes d'activité, de pénétration, de vision encore inobservés. Dans notre amour du merveilleux, passion engendrée par notre orgueil, nous aurons transformé ces effets en créations poétiques, parce que nous ne les comprenions pas. Il est si commode de déifier l'incompréhensible! Ah! j'avoue que je pleurerai la perte de mes illusions. (622; 298-99)

Again, implicitly equating "créations poétiques" and "déification," poetry and religion, Lambert repeats the imaginative association established in the first lines of the novel. Now that the then potentially mythic hero has come to question the very foundation of his myth, he, like the narrator, must outgrow his childhood dreams—"des langes qu'il lui faudrait bientôt quitter" (622; 299)—and, again like the narrator, affirm his intellectual independence by writing: "Il commença le lendemain même un ouvrage qu'il intitula *Traité de la Volonté*" (623; 299). It is as if, in anticipation of Lambert's eventual disbelief, the narrator failed to allow the creative tension between poetry and mysticism to generate an allegory. He now presents Lambert after his own image: thinker, skeptic, writer. Confirming the ascendancy of poetical discourse over Lambert's penchant for mysticism and now philosophy, the former teller of Lambert's legend, Père Hagoult, confiscates the treatise (624; 299): the storyteller triumphs over the would-be philosopher. The circle of metaphorical influence widens further to include another work (*La Peau de chagrin*) and, apparently, the author: "Ce fut en mémoire de la catastrophe arrivée au livre de Louis que, dans l'ouvrage par lequel commencent ces Etudes, je me suis servi pour une œuvre fictive du titre réellement inventé par Lambert" (624; 299). The hero's intellectual autonomy eclipsed at last, the narrator reproduces fragments of Lambert's thoughts "à la couleur des miennes" (625; 300).

This insinuation of the narrator's presence into a presumably inaccessible domain, Lambert's mind, is one of the identifying traits of the Balzacian narrator, who penetrates into minds, households, laboratories and boudoirs with the passkey of "omniscience." Here he commits an invasion of intellectual privacy, describing in his own words Lambert's system based on the principles of *Volonté, Pensée* and *Idée*. Just as he had previously tested the distinction between poetry and mysticism, so now the narrator would accommodate poetry and philosophical speculation in the context of what is specifically a work of prose fiction. This new complication on the level of discourse actually represents a coming to terms with language itself; for in his flirtation with mysticism the narrator contemplated the possibility of a way of seeing that would have eclipsed his art, rendered language expendable. Now he brings together two kinds of discourse based on speculation of different natures, the poetical and the philosophical, working within the sphere of language itself.

When he goes to resume his story, the narrator evokes images of psychological and intellectual paralysis, his own and Lambert's. It is as if these were the outcome of the interference of poetical and philosophical modes of discourse, only one of which can govern a narration:

Six mois après la confiscation du *Traité sur la Volonté*, je quittai le collège.... Ma mère, allarmée d'une fièvre qui depuis quelque temps ne me quittait pas, et à laquelle mon inaction corporelle me donnait les symptômes du *coma*, m'enleva du collège....
(637; 304)

Arrêté dans sa course, et trop faible encore pour contempler les sphères supérieures, il se contempla intérieurement. Il m'offrit alors le combat de la pensée réagissant sur elle-même et cherchant à surprendre les secrets de sa nature, comme un médecin qui étudierait les progrès de sa propre maladie.... Lambert est l'être qui m'a donné l'idée la plus poétique et la plus vraie de la créature que nous appelons *un ange*, en exceptant toutefois une femme de qui je voudrais dérober au monde le nom, la personne et la vie, afin d'avoir été seul dans le secret de son existence et pouvoir l'ensevelir au fond de mon cœur. (644; 306-07)

In his last reference to Lambert's adolescence the narrator evokes two images of pathology: the disease of genius and the delusion of angels. Recalling the previous reference to *La Peau de chagrin*, the apparent allusion to Madame de Berny (1566; 307; identified by Michel Lichtlé and Citron) has the effect of trivializing Lambert's theories or of mocking the reader. Even though the narrator and Lambert have at this point come to reject Swedenborg's theocracy, why is there the uncalled-for pun on the word "angel"? And if we have carefully followed the exposition of Lambert's thought, why are we now so artlessly reminded of the artificial nature of the narrative by this conspicuous intrusion? It is as if the author, this time, would ingratiate himself with one reader only, passing implicit judgment on the weight of Lambert's philosophy. In withdrawing from the narrative as an active character, the schoolboy, the narrator-author assumes the same attitude with which he begins the novel: a false sense of wonder in contemplating his subject.

Thus, as the narrator relates the final phase of Lambert's story, he conveys through imagery the negative verdict he has indirectly rendered against him:

> ... peut-être voulait-il résoudre l'œuvre de sa destinée par l'extase, et rester *sous une forme presque végétale* .... (646; 307; my emphasis)
>
> En lisant ces pages [Lambert's letter to his uncle] écrites au hasard, prises et reprises suivant les caprices de la vie parisienne, ne semble-t-il pas voir *un chêne pendant un temps où son accroissement intérieur fait crever sa jolie peau verte, le couvre de rugosités, de fissures* ... ? (646; 307; my emphasis)
>
> Il faut un angle facial déterminé, une certaine quantité de plis cérébraux pour obtenir Colomb, Raphaël, Napoléon, Laplace ou Beethoven: *la vallée sans soleil donne le crétin*; tirez vos conclusions. (654-55; 307; my emphasis)

These observations continue the narrator's constant association of the movement towards a luminous source of consciousness and the abdication of the intelligence, of ecstasy and vegetation, of interior growth and superficial degeneration, of genius and abnormality. Lambert, sharing the narrator's preoccupation with the unequal distribution of intellectual ability ("la tête d'un homme de génie tranche sur les masses comme une belle plante qui ... attire ... les yeux du botaniste" [590; 206]), condemns himself by using an image signifying an extreme, dangerous, exclusive cultivation of the intellect. Genius, like idiocy, is the abnormal extreme, a monstrous deviation, insofar as this character is concerned. Lambert is the metaphorical brother of Colonel Chabert, whose head is (unforgivably) compared to a mushroom when he first emerges from the mass grave on the battlefield. Both characters, failing to receive the recognition they seek, finally lapse into madness, with occasional moments of lucidity—a result, perhaps, of the cruel botanical curse against anomaly and intelligence.

And again like Chabert, Lambert suffers from the inaccessibility of the woman he would possess, a deprivation reinforcing his status as pariah. The narrator recounts an incident to which he attributes as great a significance as that accorded the earlier prophetic dream. Leaving the theater of his private meditations for the Théâtre-Français, Lambert glimpses a young woman in the company of her lover and conceives a jealous rage. Rather than interpret the meaning of this event, the narrator presents a letter, written by Lambert to his uncle, "dans laquelle se peint l'état de son âme" (645; 307). The letter of the young student's reflection on his reading and ambitions contains no overt allusion to the evening at the theater. At the end of the letter, however, comes this unexpected announcement:

> Je suis revenu à Swedenborg.... Il a lavé Dieu du reproche que lui font les âmes tendres sur la pérennité des vengeances par lesquelles il punit les fautes d'un instant, système sans justice ni bonté. Chaque homme peut savoir s'il lui est réservé d'entrer dans une autre vie, et si ce monde a un sens. Cette expérience, je vais la tenter. Cette tentative peut sauver le monde, aussi bien que la croix de Jérusalem et le sabre de la Mecque. (654-56; 311)

The letter receives no gloss, and it is for us to interpret its suicidal and Messianic overtones. Lambert willingly returns to his early beliefs, presumably a regression in response to profound sexual frustration. In implying this sequence of events, the narrator vitiates the theme of mysticism even more than he had previously, reducing it to the level of psychology and not respecting its traditional meaning of spiritual illumination. Having indirectly restated the theme of pathological genius, the narrator suggests that we have been prepared to understand this dénouement:

> Ceux auxquels ce livre ne sera pas encore tombé des mains comprendront, je l'espère, les événements qui me restent à raconter, et qui forment en quelque sorte une seconde existence à cette créature; pourquoi ne dirais-je pas à cette création en qui tout devait être extraordinaire, même sa fin? (657; 311)

Again distinguishing Lambert from ordinary "creatures," removing him this time to the category of "creation," the narrator prepares the hero's downfall. Lambert returns to Blois and falls in love with a woman who incarnates all his bookish fantasies and dreams of angels:

> Une innocence biblique éclatait sur son front.... Aussitôt que Lambert aperçut Mademoiselle de Villenoix, il devina l'ange sous cette forme.... Cette passion fut un abîme où le malheureux jeta tout, abîme où la pensée s'effraie de descendre, puisque la sienne, si flexible et si forte, s'y perdit. (659; 312)

A recapitulation of the themes and imagery of the first lines, this description announces the imminent dénouement. Pauline de Villenoix is like an "Oriental poem," a Swedenborgian seraph—an image of the Scriptures and mystical writings that have dominated Lambert's imagination. His passion for reading has been succeeded by an equally dangerous one, another lure of the abyss; and the role of his first protectress, Madame de Staël, now devolves on Pauline. Lambert finds poetry, passion and protection in his ardent pursuit first of mystical ecstasy and now of Pauline's love. But the narrator has already implicitly condemned the confusion of religious and sexual feeling in Lambert's letter to his uncle, he has branded Lambert with the stigma of extraordinary consciousness, and he has compared Lambert's passion to an abyss absorbing all intelligence. We are clearly about to receive the moral of this Fable.

Once again, rather than let symbolic events naturally run their course, the narrator intervenes with most unwelcome self-congratulation:

> ... il a fallu toute l'ardeur de mon culte pour sa mémoire, et l'espèce de fanatisme que donne une entreprise de ce genre, pour deviner et rétablir le sens des cinq lettres ... que je conserve avec une sorte de piété .... Mlle de Villenoix a sans doute détruit les véritables lettres qui lui furent adressées. (660; 312)

It is as if the narrator sinks to even lower depths than those of the abyss calling out to Lambert; his pious cult and "fanatisme" notwithstanding, he again violates the privacy of his subject and asks that we admire him for doing so. His action seems to have didactic intent; the five letters illustrate, as the narrator later notes, Lambert's "transition de l'idéalisme pur dans lequel il vivait au sensualisme le plus aigu" (677; 318). Like the earlier letter to his uncle, these contain internal evidence in the form of familiar metaphors dictating our reading of them. The plant imagery reappears with its association with nothingness, darkness, premature destruction:

Aussi faut-il s'élancer de toutes ses forces vers le bonheur, être attiré vers la vie de l'amour comme l'est une plante vers la lumière . . . . (661; 313)

Les feuillages immobiles ne tremblaient même pas dans ces admirables couleurs du couchant qui sont tout à la fois ombre et lumière. (672; 317)

Ce démon impitoyable [his "génie raisonneur"] fauche toutes les fleurs, ricane des sentiments les plus doux, en me disant: "Eh bien, après?" (666-67; 315)

The couple are to plunge into the same dark waters of illusory bliss earlier visited by "Le Poète-et-Pythagore": "je me sens dans l'âme un bonheur qui me fait concevoir le véritable amour comme un océan de sensations éternelles et toujours neuves, où l'on se plonge avec de croissantes délices" (672-73; 317). And on the eve of the announcement of their engagement Lambert confesses to Pauline, in an allusion to the theater incident, an emotion we recognize to be self-destructive: "je puis t'avouer que le jour où j'ai refusé la main que tu me tendais . . . j'étais dans un de ces moments de folie où l'on médite un meurtre pour posséder une femme" (675; 318).

Were this not Balzac, one might be tempted to dismiss the novel as a self-indulgent study in pathology. But in his struggle against the abyss of false mysticism and with the difficulty of adult sexuality, Lambert experiences as conflict those forces which for many other of Balzac's characters are as a single impulse: sexual desire and desire for the infinite. The narrator himself will be moved to say: "Enfin, peut-être a-t-il vu dans les plaisirs de son mariage un obstacle à la perfection de ses sens intérieurs et à son vol à travers les Mondes Spirituels" (680; 319). In Balzac's fiction and perhaps most explicitly in *Louis Lambert* there exists an association of sexuality and the possibility of transcendence—the latter eventually thwarted by human limitation, social institutions, disillusionment, possessiveness or accident. In Yeats' words:

Louis Lambert's withdrawal into a state of dumb helpless wisdom on the day before what should have been his happy marriage, or into that madness which was an escape from the conflict between his desire for eternity and his sexual desire, suggests certain experiments of Balzac's day. As the mesmeric trance deepened the subject attained, not merely that vision of distant scenes described in *Ursula Mirouët*, but wisdom.[12]

But in *Louis Lambert* it is a wisdom forbidding human expression, profoundly at odds with the requirements of poetry. Whatever the symbolic territory explored by Balzac's novels, the dénouements in general emphasize death, sexuality, blood relationship and recognition—a vision anchored deeply in the visible, physical world. Lambert, who vacillates between spiritualism and sensualism, inhabits the Romantic hero's prison of the self in isolation—a space the unfolding drama of the novel ultimately defines as forbidden territory. A "humble prosateur" cannot afford the luxury of characters with private, mystical visions; in "le récit des visions de cet être" (692; 323) the theme of mysticism is inexorably compromised by the necessity of language. Lambert's sad fate and at times unconvincing portrait may simply be due to the constraints imposed upon him as character by the genre. Designated a mystic, he is, so to speak, congenitally incapable of developing freely as a symbolic figure.

In the final pages of the novel the narrator returns as character, accidentally meeting Lambert's uncle on the coach traveling from Mer to Blois. Informed of Lambert's insanity, the narrator already foresees its literary possibilities as theme:

... nous parlâmes alors de mon pauvre camarade, en faisant de longues digressions par lesquelles je m'instruisis des particularités que j'ai déjà rapportées pour présenter les faits dans un ordre qui les rendît intéressants. . . . Tout en écoutant le vieillard, je critiquais intérieurement son récit. (676-77; 318)

Appropriately, he recalls an incident where, inversely, literature inspired his interest in catalepsy: "nous attrapâmes le grand Martyrologe où sont contenus les faits les plus curieux sur l'abolition complète de la vie corporelle . . . . Nous nous passionnâmes pour la catalepsie . . ." (678; 319). But Lambert's horrible illness is not so easily subsumed into literature: as his uncle tells the narrator, "Je me mis à le surveiller . . . et le surpris heureusement au moment où il allait pratiquer sur lui-même l'opération à laquelle Origène crut devoir son talent" (679; 319)—euphemistically relating Lambert's attempt to castrate himself. As if cursed by the epithet "création" (657; 311), Lambert cannot accept his creatureliness, his distance from the spheres of angels. His self-hatred may repeat on the thematic level the rejection of his being, as seer, predicated by the genre. Perhaps for the same reason also, the narrative requires the disentanglement of the narrator's perspective from Lambert's own, begun with their separation at the Collège des Oratoriens and completed in the relation of their final encounter.

Guided by his "sentiments presque religieux" (680; 320), the narrator travels to the Château de Villenoix to visit his former companion. Upon his arrival, he hands a letter of introduction to the old woman who greets him at the door and then becomes his guide:

Bientôt la même femme revint me chercher, et m'introduisit dans une salle basse, dallée en marbre blanc et noir, dont les persiennes étaient fermées, et au fond de

laquelle je vis indistinctement Louis Lambert.... L'obscurité était si forte que, dans le premier moment, Mlle de Villenoix et Louis me firent l'effet de deux masses noires qui tranchaient sur le fond de cette atmosphère ténébreuse. Je m'assis, en proie à ce sentiment qui nous saisit presque malgré nous sous les sombres arcades d'une église.
(681; 320)

His pilgrimage at last ended, the narrator first sees two formless masses looming in the background, as if to personify the indecisive perspective of the earliest part of the novel. There, in the first pages, religion and poetry, myth and mimesis, symbol and irony all rose to a reductive surface; here human form and abstraction, color and shadow, obscurity and depth meet, disturbingly, on equal terms, undifferentiated by light or judgment. The narrator speaks of a "nuit factice" (682; 320), not of a dark night of the soul; and his journey leads him, like the narrator of Conrad's *Heart of Darkness*, to a false idol ravaged by the disease of spiritual isolation:

Il se tenait debout, les deux coudes appuyés sur la saillie formée par la boiserie.... Ses cheveux, aussi longs que ceux d'une femme, tombaient sur ses épaules, et entouraient sa figure de manière à lui donner de la ressemblance avec les bustes qui représentent les grands hommes du siècle de Louis XIV.... Il frottait habituellement une de ses jambes sur l'autre par un mouvement machinal que rien ne pouvait réprimer. ... Auprès de lui se trouvait un sommier de mousse posé sur une planche. (687; 320)

In the "dreamless sleep," or sleepless dream, of his rigid contemplations Lambert has entered a sphere none can penetrate—not even, as he himself is eager to emphasize, the narrator. Lambert's metaphorical assimilation into a work of art—a sculpture detaching head and shoulders from an absent lower torso—symbolically completes the operation he had unsuccessfully attempted earlier. Lambert has surrendered his reason, his wholeness, his distinct and limited being, only to become a creation of the intellect rather than its master. He retains that androgynous appearance characterizing him as early as his arrival at the Collège des Oratoriens—neither wholly masculine nor wholly feminine, yet not an angel either. Excluded from these categories, Lambert literally takes on the identity of vegetable with which metaphor had previously cloaked him. In order to discern his friend's features, the narrator lets light in through the blinds:

Louis se tenait debout comme je le voyais, jour et nuit, les yeux fixes, sans jamais baisser et relever les paupières comme nous en avons l'habitude.... Hélas! déjà ridé, déjà blanchi, enfin déjà plus de lumière dans ses yeux devenus vitreux comme ceux d'un aveugle. Tous ses traits semblaient tirés par une convulsion vers le haut de sa tête.... J'étais là depuis une heure environ, plongé dans une indéfinissable rêverie, en proie à mille idées affligeantes. J'écoutais Mlle de Villenoix qui me racontait dans tous ses détails cette vie d'enfant au berceau. Tout à coup Louis cessa de frotter ses jambes l'une contre l'autre, et dit d'une voix lente: *Les anges sont blancs!* (682; 320)

In this final scene the audience of "nous" resumes its original identity in relationship with the narrator in the society of ordinary mortals. Rather than approach Lambert with the awe and reverence he had formerly accorded the anomaly of genius, the narrator keeps a welcome distance. The repetition of the word *déjà* in the description of Lambert's physiognomy translates both the narrator's insistence on his detachment and the advanced progress of the hero's decline. The association of the horrible distortion of his features with inexpressible thought—with "une indéfinissable rêverie" and the speechless infant in the crib—suggests the power of attraction and repellence the prospect of mystical ecstasy still exerts over the narrator. Having outgrown the symbiotic relationship of "Le Poète-et-Pythagore," he returns to the story as spectator, not disciple; the role of apologist devolves on Pauline, the narrator having discreetly relinquished it.

Upon hearing Lambert's exclamation, the narrator automatically reflects that perhaps the angels do indeed exist and his friend has evolved to a higher sphere. But it is not Lambert's words that penetrate the narrator's soul; it is, typically, the sound of his voice that moves him: "les accents attendus," "les harmonies," "les irrésistibles pouvoirs" conquer the narrator like the "séductions" (590; 286) Lambert once employed in the service of his passion for reading:

> Je ne puis expliquer l'effet produit sur moi par cette parole, par le son de cette voix tant aimée, dont les accents attendus péniblement me paraissaient à jamais perdus pour moi ... les harmonies de sa voix, qui semblaient accuser un bonheur divin, communiquèrent à ces mots d'irrésistibles pouvoirs. Incomplète révélation d'un monde inconnu, sa phrase retentit dans nos âmes comme quelque magnifique sonnerie d'église au milieu d'une nuit profonde .... Cette femme, cet ange restait toujours là, assise devant un métier de tapisserie, et chaque fois qu'elle tirait son aiguille elle regardait Lambert en exprimant un sentiment triste et doux. (682-83; 321)

The narrator likens Lambert's fragmentary revelations to a bell tolling in a church steeple, a summons not to prayer, but to poetic reverie, luring its hearers towards the abyss of formless thought, "un monde inconnu." Although Lambert may have momentarily ceased his grotesque, irrepressible movement, the theme of mindless, mechanical activity is repeated twice, in the tolling of the bell and in the image of Pauline weaving her tapestry, looking up at Lambert each time she pulls the needle. Like the childless queens of fairy tales, she sits in sorrowful resignation before her loom, punctuating with her needle the fabric of a failed, outmoded myth. Less conspicuously than the narrator, who does not let us forget the difficulty of his labors, she, too, is engaged in creative activity associated with the contemplation of Lambert; and like the narrator, she thus implicates the hero into the category of artistic creation. Comparing his sensations to an opium-induced trance (692; 323), the narrator implies that he could not live by vision alone and remain a poet—or, as suggested by his portrait of Lambert, a human being.

As he draws the intellectual history to a close, the narrator reproduces a last group of Lambert's thoughts, presented as fragments in a manner reminiscent of Pascal's *Pensées*—no doubt an intentional resemblance, given an earlier allusion to the philosopher (603; 291). With these texts the narrator at last substantiates his claims of Lambert's genius; he visits his hero with a terrible fate, and yet rather than respond to the dénouement with pity or terror, we are required to infer the tragedy from the evidence—an operation similar to our reading of Lambert's letters. The catastrophe is more didactic than dramatic in nature. Sketching a theory of the evolution of matter to the spirit and union with God (calling to mind the later philosophy of Teilhard de Chardin), Lambert defines the faculty of *Spécialité*, or visionary insight, and announces its approaching apotheosis:

> XXI. Aussi, peut-être un jour le sens inverse de l'*Et Verbum caro factum est* sera-t-il le résumé d'un nouvel évangile qui dira: *Et la chair se fera le Verbe, elle deviendra la Parole de Dieu.*
> XXII. La résurrection se fait par le vent du ciel qui balaie les mondes. L'ange porté par le vent ne dit pas: "Morts, levez-vous!" Il dit: "Que les vivants se lèvent!" (689; 323)

In the first lines of the novel we had been told that Lambert's reading of the Bible "avait décidé de sa destinée" (589; 286), and it is now clear that Lambert did not receive its teachings entirely in the spirit they are given. Rejecting the principle of an absolute distinction between God and man, Lambert articulates a philosophy more in accord with Eastern thought. With these precepts he subverts New Testament theology, proposing a "nouvel évangile" that would usurp the Word of God, that would release humanity from the condition of physical and spiritual limitation by an effort of the will. Whatever the interest of these speculations, the reader of *Louis Lambert* cannot ignore the "affreux spectacle" (683; 321) that accompanies their presentation; the transmutation of the flesh proposed by Lambert's doctrines has only his own horrible decline for dramatic illustration. The themes of poetry and mysticism meet again in mutual contradiction, prompting the narrator's confession: "Peut-être aurais-je pu transformer en un livre complet ces débris de pensées... mais j'ai mieux aimé rendre compte de mes impressions que de faire une œuvre plus ou moins poétique" (692; 323).

As if to confirm that the writing of "poetic" biography in conjunction with mystical theology cancels the visionary character out, prohibits his autonomous evolution on the symbolic plane, *Louis Lambert* ends with images of absence:

> Lambert mourut à l'âge de vingt-huit ans, le 25 septembre 1824, entre les bras de son amie.... Son tombeau consiste en une simple croix de pierre, sans nom, sans date. Fleur née au bord d'un gouffre, elle devait y tomber inconnue avec ses couleurs et ses parfums inconnus.... Cependant Mlle de Villenoix aurait bien eu le droit d'inscrire sur cette croix les noms de Lambert, en y indiquant les siens... Villenoix tombe en ruines. La femme de Lambert ne l'habite plus, sans doute pour mieux s'y voir comme elle fut jadis. Ne lui a-t-on pas entendu dire naguère: "J'ai eu son cœur, à Dieu son génie!" (692; 323-24)

In this muted ending what might have been a poignant symbol—the simple unmarked cross of stone—conveys none of the starkness, the absoluteness of death, none of the urgency of a confrontation with life's meaning. The cross holds no promise of redemption or resurrection; as if assimilated into Lambert's philosophy, "Jésus-Christ était pour lui le plus beau type de son système" (639; 305). Genius is reduced to mere matter, metaphorically a dead plant: the physical anomaly to be preserved and classified by the botanist. The absence of an inscription on the cross severs Lambert forever from the written word; and even were some inscription to be made, the narrator would commemorate Pauline instead. Her devotion to Lambert's memory, like the narrator's cult, infuses this scene with no redeeming, intrinsic substance; in fact, her devotion is not directed to Lambert at all. She physically withdraws from Villenoix only to preserve an image of herself-"pour mieux s'y voir"—a deceptive form of introspection similar to the narrator's own perspective.

When one compares this bleak ending to the beginning of *Eugénie Grandet*, one can glimpse the negative way in which *Louis Lambert* anticipates Balzac's later, more open affirmation of the intrinsic power and value of inscription—of the written word or symbol—as inspiration of drama and historical witness. Death reduces Lambert to the ultimate personal and collective deprivation: the absence of memory, the loss of earned knowledge and experience. Although, within the context of the novel, Lambert's mysticism and philosophy lack the proof of dramatic illustration, the implied ambivalence towards them on the narrator's part may originate as much in technical limitations as in any skepticism on the author's part. Parts of *Louis Lambert* set forth in expository form the thought that informs the drama of more successful novels: the quest for the absolute through the physical, the possible existence of a wisdom accessible to mystics, the participation of the intellect in the process of artistic creation, the conjunction of Romantic myth and mimesis in the study of a specific historical era. The novel gives us access to the field of speculation, philosophically speaking, that is implicit in Balzac's poetic vision. Yeats defined the novel's interest as follows:

> A modern painter, who thinks, like Whistler, that a picture must be perfect from the

sketch, growing in richness of detail but not in unity, knows that a work of art must remain fluid to the finish, that an alteration in some minor character or in some detail of colour compels alteration elsewhere. ... The specialist may add fact to fact, postponing synthesis till greater knowledge, but the man cannot, for, lacking it, he can neither understand nor see correctly. Jane Austen, Scott, Fielding, inherited that other [artistic] sketch in its clearest and simplest form, but Balzac had to find it in his own mind. His sketch is *Louis Lambert*, the demonstration of its truth is that it made possible the *Comédie Humaine*.[13]

Perhaps the narrator of *Louis Lambert* was for Balzac an instrument of artistic self-definition, a means of consolidating his vast knowledge and of articulating the direction of his future work. If so, the narrator's ambiguous attachment to the character Lambert, his unlikely and questionable cult, performs the service of approaching the springs of the author's literary creativity with explicit reference to its philosophical, even mystical, foundations. That the novel leaves much to be desired as a dramatic unit requires no exaggerated commentary, its usefulness as a "fluid" sketch being its own justification. In leaving the intellectual abyss behind him, the author of *La Comédie humaine* sets his work on the rails of poetical discourse, "obligé de courir droit, comme un wagon sur le rail de son chemin de fer" (505; 607).

Chapter II

LE COLONEL CHABERT

Like *Louis Lambert, Le Colonel Chabert*[1] is a "drame... se jouant dans l'âme de l'homme" (315; 311), but in this narrator's economy there is no room for apology or confession. Instead we watch him build a world earned detail by detail with the slow deliberation of a Chabert invisibly working his way up the stairs to the lawyer Derville's study, step by step, and with the freshness and energy of the diabolical clerk Simonnin, perched on the windowsill, armed with missiles of bread and criticism to be aimed at the hapless passer-by. The narrator places his hero in a world—Restoration Paris—where the power of linguistic reference is more than merely acknowledged; it is manipulated, given primacy over justice, willfully abused and ignored. Through Chabert's story the narrator shows that documented fact, such as a man's alleged identity or death, need compel only that interpretation most useful to its hearers. Truth dependent on the strength of words —after *Louis Lambert*, perhaps the only kind, in Balzac's eyes—has limited power in a society that sees in Chabert a disruptive and useless entity who absurdly proclaims his intrinsic value: in this a man is like a work of art. Both Chabert and his creator state their cases eloquently in this novel.

Recorded a casualty at the Battle of Eylau, Colonel Chabert commits the additional error of returning to Paris some time after his wife's remarriage and inheritance of his estate. The lawyer Derville—also representing the former Madame Chabert—mutes the Colonel's childlike plea for justice with the pragmatic counsel of compromise: Chabert should seek only partial restitution of his fortune. In the course of negotiations the Colonel pointedly reminds the present Countess Ferraud of her humble origins, as if to condemn her to a former self; she withholds recognition, provoking him to renounce identity and possessions. In the end it is Derville who is compromised, and by his own profession, for he neither saves Chabert from ruin nor regains the Countess' trust. The implicit indictment of Derville's own hidden complicity casts the tale in the ambiguous light of human sympathy shown in its problematic relation to social justice.

Le Colonel Chabert ends with the embittered lawyer's renunciation of Parisian life, leaving us with an image of utter and unredeemed corruption. This dénouement acts as a catharsis, for we have been made to feel, along with Derville, a kind of contempt for the impotence of social institutions in addressing falsehood and injustice. But we feel with him also a kind of pity for the destitute, mentally deranged Chabert. Melodramatic and often excruciating in its detail, *Le Colonel Chabert* is governed by a perspective that excludes from within its scope neither naturalistic description nor the dimension of moral conflict and ambiguity. Its first pages insist on a sophisticated awareness of the different levels of meaning, of varieties of discourse in language, and yet the author never sacrifices the possibilities of dramatic action. Precisely because of the inherent complexity of language and perspective illuminated by this novel, *Le Colonel Chabert* is compelling testimony to the power of poetical discourse.

The narrator of *Le Colonel Chabert* does not need to go to his subject. Instead it comes to him:

"Allons!" encore notre vieux carrick!"
Cette exclamation échappait à un clerc appartenant au genre de ceux qu'on appelle dans les études des *saute-ruisseaux*, et qui mordait en ce moment de fort bon appétit dans un morceau de pain; il en arracha un peu de mie pour faire une boulette et le lança railleusement par le vasistas d'une fenêtre sur laquelle il s'appuyait. Bien dirigée, la boulette rebondit presque à la hauteur de la croisée, après avoir frappé le chapeau d'un inconnu qui traversait la cour d'une maison située rue Vivienne, où demeurait Me Derville, avoué. (311; 310)

Unconsciously rehearsing a role for which society may have destined him, the clerk Simmonin plays a harmless soldier, in unintentional symbolic resemblance to the slowly arriving Colonel. Unbeknownst to the glib messenger boy, a colleague of sorts has come calling: Death's own messenger, in the person of "le colonel mort à Eylau" (317; 312). Apparently, in Maître Derville's office words are a familiar form of ammunition: the epithet "notre vieux carrick" springs to Simonnin's lips with the same reflexive ease with which he fires pellets of bread over the transom. Perhaps this is the only manna cruel society can entertain: one that falls upon a hat and not upon a man. Even the master clerk is moved to leave his numbers: "'Allons, Simonnin, ne faites donc pas de sottises aux gens, ou je vous mets à la porte. Quelque pauvre que soit un client, c'est toujours un homme, que diable!' dit le Maître clerc en interrompant l'addition d'un mémoire de frais" (311; 310).

Simonnin is quick to reply, with the irrefutable logic of children (even malicious ones): "'Si c'est un homme, pourquoi l'appelez-vous *vieux carrick*?' dit Simonnin de l'air de l'écolier qui prend son maître en faute"

(311-12; 310). In a reflexive movement this time at the level of discourse Simonnin questions the metonymic image with which the novel begins. Chabert's innate identity has been removed to the coat, the outer shell. The clerk's words contain a moral, but they contain a riddle also: why indeed call a man a coat? Why do we speak in figures? Why interrupt the prosaic rhythms of ordinary language to launch, familiarly, a poetic flight of words? How do we determine when such linguistic release is liberating or reductive? Knowing that moralists and inveterate readers are too wise or preoccupied to stop to field such questions, the narrator quickly moves on. Still stationed in the lawyer's study, he regales us with a monstrous and, therefore, unimpeachable specimen of legal prose, complete with gloss:

Mais, dans sa noble et bienveillante sagesse Sa Majesté Louis Dix-Huit (mettez en toutes lettres, hé! Desroches le savant qui faites la Grosse!), *au moment où Elle reprit les rênes de son royaume, comprit...* (qu'est-ce qu'elle comprit, ce gros farceur-là?) *la haute mission à laquelle Elle était appelée par la divine Providence!...* (point admiratif et six points: on est assez religieux pour nous le passer), *et sa première pensée fut, ainsi que le prouve la date de l'ordonnance ci-dessous désignée, de réparer les infortunes causées par les affreux et tristes désastres de nos temps révolutionnaires, en restituant à ses fidèles et nombreux serviteurs* (nombreux est une flatterie qui doit plaire au Tribunal) *tous leurs biens non vendus... car nous sommes et nous nous prétendons habiles à soutenir que tel est l'esprit et le sens de la fameuse et si loyale ordonnance rendue en...*

"Attendez, dit Godeschal aux trois clercs, cette scélérate de phrase a rempli la fin de ma page... *Rendue en...* Hein? papa Boucard, quelle est la date de l'ordonnance? il faut mettre les points sur les i, saquerlotte. (312-13; 310)

The improviser of this sentence, the clerk Godeschal, receives no answer to his question, like Simonnin before him. Transposing the problem of reference into another register—the correspondence of legal terminology to fact —the narrator, assisted by Godeschal's running commentary, dashes any allusion that truth is well served in this domain also. Or rather, as before, he would intimate that meaning in language has many levels: literal and figurative, conventional and symbolic, implicit and explicit. In his linguistic performance Godeschal eschews any direct statement of simple fact; having all the resources of legal jargon at his disposal, he creatively embarks on a sentence, knowing his words to be immediately intelligible to the specialist. Godeschal may not yet be an artist, but he is assuredly a master craftsman. What exactly has he wrought?

The "scélérate de phrase" is built upon two main clauses coordinated by the conjunction *et*: "... Louis ... comprit la haute mission ... et sa première pensée fut ... de réparer les infortunes ..."—a basic structure enriched by a number of participial and prepositional phrases, epithets and nouns in apposition, and subordinate clauses, all acting variously as verb and noun complements. Finally, there is what appears to be a conjunctive subordinate clause introduced by the word *car,* modifying all that precedes it. Whatever the flourishes satirized by its author, the core of the sentence grammatically illustrates the property of coordination, and it semantically endorses the specific coordination of understanding ("Louis . . . comprit") and thought ("sa première pensée fut"). Godeschal comically underscores this very idea when, a moment later, he rebukes one of the clerks for an error: "Allons, ne faites plus de ces bêtises-là, monsieur Huré! Un Normand ne doit pas écrire insouciamment une requête" (313; 311). But what proves that understanding precedes thought, and, in particular, thought lending itself to verbal expression? This is the very question provoked by the indecipherable gaze of Louis Lambert. In this instance fact will do so: "la date de l'ordonnance ci-dessous signée." The date testifies to the almost automatic mental reflex of the king, who, upon grasping the divine will, immediately thought to render justice to his loyal subjects.

Because this unfinished sentence anticipates the dénouement of the novel—it refers to the act legitimizing the redistribution of Chabert's property—it merits further consideration. On both the grammatical and the semantic levels it illustrates also an endless deferral of authority, in a Derridean sense. On the one hand, the king acts on authority derived not from his own "wisdom," but rather from "la divine Providence"—a source that cannot possibly be sounded, delimited, exhausted by an interpreter. If we look even more closely at the phrasing, even this ultimate authority is held at a distance; it is not even there. Not only has God been reduced to mere circumstantial agent in a clause literally governed by "Elle"—His Majesty—but the words also affirm that the king acts upon his *interpretation* of that design which divine Providence has reserved for him. What he understood is in fact what he himself envisioned; it is not a mandate. Even grammar has its hypocrisy. Just as God has been denied an active, decisive presence—rendered immaterial in more ways than one—so the ostensible benevolent act of restitution has no real substance: "sa première pensée fut . . . ." The verb does not translate an action; it merely presents a "thought" governing only a copula equating intention ("pensée") with accomplishment ("réparer les infortunes"). In this labyrinthine prose we never really leave the realm of Louis's subjectivity.

But there is a way out—at the end of the sentence, as promised by these words of encouragement: "ainsi que le prouve . . . ." And so we make our way to the last clause: "car nous sommes et nous nous prétendons habiles à soutenir que tel est l'esprit et le sens de la fameuse et si loyale ordonnance rendue en . . . ." Even before we look for the date we discover a clerkly *lèse-majesté*: for just as the king had interpreted God's will and in so doing had usurped Him, so Godeschal, using the editorial "nous," now interprets the will of Louis XVIII—and in so doing usurps the royal "pensée," fixes it in words. Godeschal masks this subversive gesture, appropriate in these "temps révolutionnaires," by grammatical subordination. The interpreter, not Providence, reigns supreme, whether in the person of the king or in that of his servant. The ellipsis, however, only suspends this authority, deferring proof that the king's benevolent action is indeed prompted by his perception of his role. The distinction between being ("nous sommes") and affirmation ("nous nous prétendons"), between "esprit" and "sens," repeats the earlier distinction, in similar sequence, between the king's understanding ("Louis comprit") and thought ("sa pensée fut"). The foundation of the authority of this "nous" composed of essence and pretense is indefinitely postponed ("rendue en . . ."). What is the original fact, meaning or order justifying these words, calling for interpretation?

Godeschal's mischievous commentary forbids solemnity, but his sentence conforms to a pattern of internal, reflexive criticism on the level of discourse. Simonnin's figural epithet—"notre vieux carrick"—and the legal jargon of the clerk call into question their own accuracy, their own application; and in both cases the introduction of the fact to which they presumably refer—the arriving Charbert, the date of the ordinance—has been deferred. By frustrating our expectations of drama or data, the narrator heightens our awareness of the way in which language deviates from the ideal of direct reference. And this recourse to metonymy and circumlocution—to rhetoric—is seen as automatic: Simonnin, when he catches sight of the Colonel, involuntarily exclaims ("Cette exclamation échappait à un clerc . . ."); the king, when he perceives what he takes to be his mission, thinks; Godeschal, when he needs to produce a document, improvises. Rhetoric mediates between the speaker and the referent: Simonnin uses a figure of speech, the king summons lawyers who in turn speak in jargon. The narrative seems predicated upon an awareness of the varieties of forms of discourse and of the influence of context on the meaning of words. Even the humor and irony of the opening scene spring from the recognition of linguistic convention as such: Simonnin's sarcastic question, Godeschal's irreverent gloss, and finally this:

    —*Saquerlotte!* répéta l'un des copistes . . . .
    —Comment, vous avez écrit saquerlotte! s'écria Godeschal en regardant l'un des nouveaux venus d'un air à la fois sévère et goguenard.
    —Mais oui, dit Desroches le quatrième clerc en se penchant sur la copie de son voisin, il a écrit: *Il faut mettre les points sur les i*, et *sakerlotte* avec un k. (313; 311)

The clerk Huré's failure to distinguish between formal legal terminology and colloquial speech perhaps should not too quickly amuse us. Wading through or skimming over Godeschal's interminable sentence, we may very well overlook its importance: alluding to the legitimacy, socially speaking, of the act despoiling Chabert of his property. The dimwitted clerk is like an uncomplimentary figure of the reader, apprentice to the intricacies of Balzacian prose under the bemused gaze of a patient, long-suffering tutor. The narrator uses the very conventional device of foreshadowing, here predicting Chabert's demise, in highly conspicuous italicized prose. How can we fail to notice? Fortunately, there is no Desroches peering over our shoulder.

All of this has been accomplished before Chabert arrives at the office door after climbing what must be the only staircase measurable in grammatical units. Chabert, the incidental fact precipitating the initial rhetorical figure, appears as if to confirm belatedly the prior ascendancy of poetical discourse. His arrival is announced as nothing more—or less—than an interruption of Godeschal's grandiloquent phrase: "Un coup frappé à la porte de l'Etude interrompit la phrase de la prolixe requête" (313; 311). As if to humiliate the unfortunate character even further, and further try the reader's patience in the process, the narrator declines to describe Chabert's physical appearance and turns his attention to the office instead:

L'Etude était une grande pièce ornée du poêle classique qui garnit tous les antres de la chicane. Les tuyaux traversaient diagonalement la chambre et rejoignaient une cheminée condamnée sur le marbre de laquelle se voyaient divers morceaux de pain, des triangles de fromage de Brie, des côtelettes de porc frais, des verres, et la tasse de chocolat du Maître clerc.... Les rangs inférieurs du casier étaient pleins de cartons jaunis par l'usage, bordés de papier bleu, et sur lesquels se lisaient les noms des gros clients dont les affaires juteuses se cuisinaient en ce moment. (313-14; 311)

Despite appearances, the narrator will implicate the reader, as before, in a seemingly insignificant digressive passage. The room described here is a stereotype, he tells us, remarkable only for its conformity to expectation. The predictable stove, like all symbols of popular taste, suffers from continual overuse, "chauffé sans mesure" (313; 311), and the riotous collection of morsels of food and glasses of wine announces indifference to criticism: even the appearances of order and cleanliness have been forgone in the crude, undisguised working of the law. The narrator exposes a legal system undistinguished by eloquence or dedication to truth and justice or even by its industry. He transforms the unsavory business into a metaphor of unending consumption ("les affaires juteuses se cuisinaient") and then all too graphically depicts the outcome as wastes:

Certes, si les sacristies humides où les prières se pèsent et se payent comme des épices, si les magasins des revendeuses où flottent des guenilles qui flétrissent toutes les illusions de la vie en nous montrant où aboutissent nos fêtes, si ces deux cloaques de la poésie n'existaient pas, une étude d'avoué serait de toutes les boutiques sociales la plus horrible. . . . Peut-être dans ces endroits le drame, en se jouant dans l'âme de l'homme, lui rend-il les accessoires indifférents . . . . (314-15; 311)

In this society faith, beauty and justice have all been reduced to the lowest common denominator, that of negotiable goods and services: ideals do not merely harm, they defile. These public chambers corrupt the private ones, the soul; the drama occurs within, and the setting is incidental. Only the character, however, can afford this indifference to surroundings: for the narrator no detail is insignificant. We cannot help but notice the physical oppressiveness suggested by the description: the stale, dusty smell of yellowing paper, the odor of discarded food, the defrauded elegance of second-hand clothing, the barter of spiritual favors for gold. The narrator has arranged the scene in such a way that when he at last acknowledges Chabert's presence, we grasp another level upon which the gastronomical imagery operates: "Il se mit à regarder modestement autour de lui, comme un chien qui, en se glissant dans une cuisine étrangère, craint d'y recevoir des coups" (315; 312). Alerted by the simile, we can imagine the impoverished man's pride, and hunger, ignored in this den of iniquity, humiliation and half-eaten food. Chabert is merely one of many "gens processifs" (316; 312), who elicit no sympathy. The narrator seems to have embraced the same indifference to his presence, still deferring the anticipated physical portrait of the character. But after Chabert leaves, we discover that he has indeed been keenly observed:

> Ne voilà-t-il pas un fameux *crâne*? dit Simonnin sans attendre que le vieillard eût fermé la porte. . . .
> —Je parie qu'il a été portier, répliqua Godeschal. Les portiers sont seuls doués par la nature de carricks usés, huileux et déchiquetés par le bas comme l'est celui de ce vieux bonhomme. Vous n'avez donc vu ni ses bottes éculées qui prennent l'eau, ni sa cravate qui lui sert de chemise? Il a couché sous les ponts. . . . Ah! je parie un spectacle pour tout le monde qu'il n'a pas été soldat . . . . (316-17; 312)

The narrator has shifted the burden of description to the characters, who indulge in playful speculation at Chabert's expense. Simonnin again situates Chabert's identity in a trope, the synecdoche "*crâne*"; and Godeschal, the most eloquent and observant of the group, misplaces his bet in our favor, promising a spectacle: "une chose à voir à différents prix, suivant les différentes places où l'on veut se mettre" (318; 313). Books are not excluded from this definition, and we look forward to the entertainment. But it is first the drama of Godeschal's sentence that resumes:

> —*Rendue en juin mil huit cent quatorze* (en toutes lettres), dit Godeschal, y êtes-vous?
> . . . *Et nous espérons que Messieurs composant le tribunal*, dit l'improvisateur. Halte! il faut que je relise ma phrase, je ne me comprends plus moi-même. (319; 313)

The date of the ordinance finally committed to paper, the scene ends with a tribute to historical reference—and to the virtues of rereading. But the new coordinate clause is doomed never to be completed: "—Comment! s'écria le Maître clerc, vous vous avisez de faire des requêtes dans l'affaire vicomtesse de Grandlieu contre Légion d'honneur, une affaire pour compte d'étude, entreprise à forfait? . . . Voulez-vous bien me mettre de côté vos copies . . ." (319-20; 313).

In this last example of narrative discontinuity we discover that Godeschal himself never had the authority with which to dictate his literally interminable sentence. The character has no right to upstage the author, usurp his privilege, and Boucard orders the clerks to lay down their pens But much has been explored in this opening scene; as the master clerk says, "Les clercs plaisantent et disent vrai tout ensemble" (320; 313). We have witnessed what appears to be a series of false starts: the hero not arriving, the sentence never finished, Chabert's audience with Derville ever deferred. But we have no doubt of the nature of the spectacle begun from the very first line: "Allons! encore notre vieux carrick!" It is poetical discourse that proclaims its power, that draws attention to itself; there is none of the internal debate between the respective influences of poetry and mysticism, or of poetry and philosophy, that undermines the narrator's authority in *Louis Lambert*. The narrator of *Le Colonel Chabert* raises the level of linguistic speculation to the sphere of effective use: Simonnin questions his own epithet for Chabert, Godeschal ruminates on the definition of the word *spectacle*, he critically rereads his own sentence, Boucard condemns the whole enterprise of unauthorized production. A heightened consciousness of language and its uses animates all these characters, unites them in a single drama firmly anchored in those "accessories" of detail to which no author can be indifferent. By postponing his detailed portrait of the hero Chabert, the narrator dramatically illustrates the properties of multiple levels of meaning and of distance from the referent that distinguish words used metaphorically in poetic discourse.

Indeed, subtly emphasizing the purposeful detachment with which he shapes the unfolding story, the narrator allows us to see Chabert as if through Derville's eyes. Continuing the procedure of presenting the central figure through others' perception of him (as in the clerks' earlier conversation), the narrator privileges the role of witness, as if to furnish necessary collaboration before recounting a highly improbable tale. This technique of describing the character from the outside—from a distinctly removed viewpoint—contrasts utterly with the technique favored by the narrator of *Louis Lambert*, who often fused with his subject and drew on his own personal reminiscences. But it is appropriate that the long-awaited portrait of Chabert should recall the final description of Louis Lambert, when the narrator has by then dissociated himself from the hero.

The figure the narrator describes, as contemplated by Derville, can only provoke incredulity. Waiting in the lawyer's office for his promised appointment, Chabert looms in the darkness like an uneasy offspring of chance and art:

> Le colonel Chabert était aussi parfaitement immobile que peut l'être une figure en cire.... L'ombre cachait si bien le corps à partir de la ligne brune que décrivait ce haillon [his tie], qu'un homme d'imagination aurait pu prendre cette vieille tête pour quelque silhouette due au hasard, ou pour un portrait de Rembrandt sans cadre. (321; 314)

Like Lambert, who reminded his friend of a sculpture bust, Chabert is both less and more than human—a wax figure and "spectacle surnaturel" (321; 314); he is monstrous, compatible with his species only by virtue of some misbegotten resemblance. Grotesquely obsolete, possessing a "physionomie cadavéreuse" (321; 314), the Colonel has outlived the vital functioning of the intelligence: he wears "une certaine expression de démence triste, avec les dégradants symptômes par lesquels se caractérise l'idiotisme" (321; 314). The narrator suggests that such horrible affliction is not always redeemed by grace or wisdom—and certainly not by association with art:

> Un médecin, un auteur, un magistrat eussent pressenti tout un drame à l'aspect de cette sublime horreur dont le moindre mérite était de ressembler à ces fantaisies que les peintres s'amusent à dessiner au bas de leurs pierres lithographiques en causant avec leurs amis. (322; 314)

Chabert is like a mindless "fantaisie" produced by art—an accident of the imagination, somehow given birth into nature. The sight of Derville jars him out of the realm of poetry as well; the Colonel experiences a convulsive movement "semblable à celui qui échappe aux poètes quand un bruit inattendu vient les détourner d'une féconde rêverie" (322; 314). As if to give prominence to the picture he would have us visualize, the narrator relegates reference to art to the category of metaphor, all the while achieving a convincing portrait. Indeed, he is about to shock the reader as if in succession to Derville and Chabert before him: "Le vieillard se découvrit ... et laissa voir à nu son crâne horriblement mutilé par une cicatrice transversale qui prenait à l'occiput et venait mourir à l'œil droit, en formant partout une grosse couture saillante" (322; 314). Had the previous pages not prepared us by literally imposing a distance between our expectations and the description of Chabert, this image and the equally horrible events Chabert is about to describe might have been examples of gratuitous violence against the reader's imagination. Instead, the power of this description stems in part from its deferral—not only because of the suspense thereby created, but also because of the preceding reassurance that a literal interpretation of imagery is only one of many possibilities.

Chabert begins his long and vivid account of his adventures: "—Monsieur, dit le défunt, peut-être savez-vous que je commandais un régiment de cavalerie à Eylau. . . . Malheureusement pour moi, ma mort est un fait historique consigné dans les *Victoires et conquêtes,* où elle est rapportée en détail" (323; 314). The unqualified irony of the word *défunt* incites speculation: either Chabert is insane and an impostor, or he is a figure of mythic proportions, returned from the dead like Orpheus or Christ, a poet-savior in the tradition of Louis Lambert. But as if to refute both hypotheses, Chabert's lucidity and meticulous recall dispel any suspicion of his madness and anchor the narrative in naturalistic detail and not allegory. His remark on the enshrinement of his death in journalistic prose reopens the debate on the truthfulness of language begun with Simonnin's question as to the meaning of "vieux carrick": how is the account in *Victoires et conquêtes* to be interpreted? What is its authority? To the extent that Chabert would correct historical error, his is a disinterested narration; his cautious deposition resembles the work of a scholar or historian in its detachment, circumspection and careful distinction between fact and hypothesis. The comic and pathetic figure who speaks with such gravity and command wholly astonishes Derville—and the reader:

—Savez-vous, monsieur, lui dit-il en l'interrompant, que je suis l'avoué de la comtesse Ferraud, veuve du colonel Chabert?
—Ma femme! Oui, monsieur . . . . Je vous parlerai de mes malheurs plus tard. Laissez-moi d'abord vous établir les faits, vous expliquer plutôt comme ils ont dû se passer, que comme ils sont arrivés. Certaines circonstances, qui ne doivent être connues que du Père éternel, m'obligent à en présenter plusieurs comme des hypothèses. Donc, monsieur, les blessures que j'ai reçues auront probablement produit un tétanos, ou m'auront mis dans une crise analogue à une maladie nommée, je crois, catalepsie. (324; 315)

Like a professor unwilling to disturb the sacred order of his lecture notes, Chabert firmly, though patiently, reprimands Derville for his interruption. Proceeding with a sort of judicious confidence, Chabert asserts (indirectly, of course) that his authority is inferior only to that of one other, the "Père éternel," the elusive divine Providence of Godeschal's sentence. Chabert's words again confirm the kinship of *Le Colonel Chabert* and *Louis Lambert*: both are stories reconstructed from partial evidence, and both heroes pass through an intermediate stage of, or resembling, catalepsy before receiving their very different revelations. In both cases Balzac coldly observes this paralysis of the intelligence, leaving Lambert's horrible deterioration intact before our eyes or allowing Chabert to recount his past matter-of-factly with no sign of emotion. Perhaps only a man purged of feeling could bring himself to articulate the remarkable words that follow:

> Lorsque je revins à moi, monsieur, j'étais dans une position et dans une atmosphère dont je ne vous donnerais pas une idée en vous entretenant jusqu'à demain. Le peu d'air que je respirais était méphitique. . . . deux morts s'étaient croisés au-dessus de moi de manière à décrire un angle semblable à celui de deux cartes mises l'une contre l'autre par un enfant qui pose les fondements d'un château. . . . je rencontrai fort heureusement un bras qui ne tenait à rien. . . . Mais je ne sais pas aujourd'hui comment j'ai pu parvenir à percer la couverture de chair qui mettait une barrière entre la vie et moi. Vous me direz que j'avais trois bras! Ce levier, dont je me servais avec habileté, me procurait toujours de l'air qui se trouvait entre les cadavres que je déplaçais, et je ménageais mes aspirations. (324-25; 315)

As Chabert describes his traumatic ordeal with unflinching precision, a profound, almost surreptitious gathering of metaphorical meaning gives unexpected resonance to his words. The corpses in the grave above him resemble playing cards, products of paper; an arm wielded like a lever enables the critically wounded soldier to escape the mephitic air. *Louis Lambert* is summarized entire in Chabert's aspiration: "percer la couverture de chair qui mettait une barrière entre la vie et moi." The mystic's desire for illumination and the soldier's will to survive meet on equal terms; in the recesses of the earth, in the recesses of the mind, this desire to breathe, this yearning for life dominates all other thought. To contemplate death, one must fully adopt an almost monstrous courage: we see a man with three arms, consumed by a single thought, and yet gifted with perfect lucidity. Chabert descends to that subterranean level of the consciousness that resists its own extinction and that, perhaps, led Balzac to do so with his pen, a kind of lever allowing him to break into the open space of literary creativity. Thus, in one way Chabert's earlier allusion to *Victoires et conquêtes* stands open to positive interpretation: the written word will ultimately triumph—a victory for the writer, a conquest of his subject.

At last Chabert reaches the term of his grim labors:

> Enfin je vis le jour, mais à travers la neige, monsieur! En ce moment, je m'aperçus que j'avais la tête ouverte. . . . je me trouvai, quand je repris connaissance, au centre d'une petite ouverture par laquelle je criai aussi longtemps que je le pus. . . . Bref, monsieur, après avoir eu la douleur, si le mot peut rendre ma rage, de voir pendant longtemps, ah! oui, longtemps, ces sacrés Allemands se sauvant en entendant une voix là où ils n'apercevaient point d'homme, je fus enfin dégagé par une femme assez hardie ou assez curieuse pour s'approcher de ma tête qui semblait avoir poussé hors de terre comme un champignon. . . . j'étais sorti du ventre de la terre aussi nu que de celui de ma mère; en sorte que, six mois après, quand, un beau matin, je me souvins d'avoir été le colonel Chabert, et qu'en recouvrant ma raison je voulus obtenir de ma garde [at a hospital in Heilsberg] plus de respect qu'elle n'en accordait à un pauvre diable, tous mes camarades de chambre se mirent à rire. (325-26; 315-16)

For readers today this gruesome scene takes on special significance—not that the carnage of war was any less horrible before our century—but because we, unlike readers in Balzac's time, are fully acquainted with photographic evidence of such occurrences, especially with respect to the Holocaust. Perhaps *Le Colonel Chabert* could have been written only in the 19th century; the history of our wars resists the force of symbol to transform—and by virtue of the fact inadvertently to trivialize it. The weight of history has largely suppressed the impulse to create images of what, without the witness of photographs, would have been unimaginable, even mythic-seeming suffering. Balzac's evocation of Chabert's grotesque awakening and rescue in no way demeans real tragedies; it did not compete with memory in the contemporary public imagination. And with the fall of Napoleon, Chabert's surrogate father, his cruel ejection from his mother earth and the remarriage of his wife, Chabert stands for all that *can* be taken away from a man, as opposed to the reality of dispossession and death for those who remain frozen in the silent gaze of the camera's eye. Even Balzac's constant admiring praise of the scientist's disinterested research marks the distance between the dawn of the industrial era and a later one in which technology has demonstrated its ability to destroy as well as to liberate.

Chabert's almost clinical detachment from his own predicament adds to the horror in the retelling, and we understand why neither Derville nor the narrator interrupts this long recitation. Chabert's Herculean labors elevate him to the realm of the supernatural—"une voix là où il n'y avait point d'homme"—the Prussian soldiers' cursory glance proving Chabert's territory not one to be trespassed upon. In piercing that "couverture de chair," Chabert has symbolically freed his voice, one that now presents itself like a comic visitation out of a fairy tale or a tragic dislocation of identity as in a Beckett play. The outrageous simile likening Chabert's head to a mushroom qualifies his intelligence as a natural, if superfluous, growth upon the earth's surface; and the implicit biological transformism from plant to man puts Chabert at some intermediate stage in the evolutionary transition. Again like Louis Lambert, Chabert is a biological anomaly of fragile intellect dependent on circumstantial evidence for proof of past existence. Both characters skirt a nothingness in the way that many of Balzac's characters do, but Chabert is pulled back from its brink by the sudden recovery of his memory. Chabert is like an infant given a fully formed intellect and identity, but who needs to learn all over again that human dignity is not automatically respected in the ordinary man—"un pauvre diable"—let alone in a brave and distinguished colonel. The evolution of the intelligence, so glorified by Lambert, does not necessarily entail a corresponding one in the moral sphere. Chabert goes on to say: "Je voudrais n'être pas moi. Le sentiment de mes droits me tue. Si ma maladie m'avait ôté tout souvenir de mon existence passée, j'aurais été heureux!" (327-28; 316).

The reference to his rights alerts us to the nature of the struggle that will eventually overcome Chabert. He would reclaim the privileges of social status from the hospital guard and from his former wife, whereas this kind of restitution has everything to do with accident (name, rank, nationality, profession) and nothing to do with the simple recognition due a downtrodden "pauvre diable." In turning to Derville for help, he mistakenly equates social justice based on law with justice in its absolute, radical sense. The system represented by the lawyer tolerates ambiguity and error; it is not a search for truth: "—Il faudra peut-être transiger, dit l'avoué. —Transiger, répéta le colonel Chabert. Suis-je mort ou suis-je vivant?" (333; 318). Accordingly, in agreeing to take on the Colonel's case, Derville lends his client money for living expenses, a gesture as calculated as it is compassionate:

> "Boucard, dit Derville à son Maître clerc, je viens d'entendre une histoire qui me coûtera peut-être vingt-cinq louis. Si je suis volé, je ne regretterai pas mon argent, j'aurai vu le plus habile comédien de notre époque."
> Quand le colonel se trouva dans la rue et devant un réverbère, il retira de la lettre les deux pièces de vingt francs que l'avoué lui avait données, et les regarda pendant un moment à la lumière.... "Je vais donc pouvoir fumer des cigares," se dit-il. (334; 318)

Thus the first part of *Le Colonel Chabert* ends, with the hero bathed in artificial light, transfixed by the sight of gold—and anticipating an ephemeral pleasure like that he affords Derville. This is the image of social justice, its principles of gold and pleasure preserved intact, already contaminating the Colonel by symbolic association. Death having erased his identifying traits, he is at the threshold of civilization, a man and a voice fully reunited; but society will exact its toll, threaten this hard-won integrity. In first positing the distinction between language and referent ("vieux carrick"), between law and justice, the narrator prepares the distinction between social identity (Colonel Chabert) and the person ("un pauvre diable"), the latter valued as a universal and the former as a particular. Chabert, "un spectacle surnaturel," may have crossed over into the symbolic dimension; but the humble image of a poor man warmed by the prospect of simple pleasure returns him to the sphere of naturalistic description, myth and mimesis reconciled. Having established Chabert as a potential Everyman within the context of this novel, the narrator allows drama to bring him swiftly to catastrophe. *Le Colonel Chabert* becomes a Kafkaesque drama in which none of the familiar props of identity support the character, in which the narrator refuses to relieve his torment with the simple assurance that madness is but a dream, injustice but a nightmare.

In the second chapter, "La Transaction," Derville, its engineer, is made to repeat symbolically Chabert's earlier, frustrating journey to the office; unlike the "omniscient" narrator now reclaiming his rightful place as storyteller, the lawyer must travel to the Colonel. The consistency of imagery allies Chabert and Derville in their different attempts to reconcile the demands of social propriety with those of justice. Having received from abroad documents verifying Chabert's identity, Derville goes to the town just outside Paris where his client lives in poverty:

Arrivé là, Derville fut forcé d'aller à pied à la recherche de son client ... l'avoué finit par trouver ... entre deux murs bâtis avec des ossements et de la terre, deux mauvais pilastres en moellons, que le passage des voitures avaient ébréchés.... Ces pilastres soutenaient une poutre couverte d'un chaperon en tuiles, sur laquelle ces mots étaient écrits en rouge: *Vergniaud, Nouriceure*. A droite de ce nom, se voyaient des œufs, et à gauche une vache, le tout peint en blanc.... Au fond d'une cour assez spacieuse, s'élevait, en face de la porte, une maison, si toutefois ce nom convient à l'une de ces masures bâties dans les faubourgs de Paris, et qui ne sont comparables à rien, pas même aux plus chétives habitations de la campagne, dont elles ont la misère sans en avoir la poésie. (336-37; 319)

In order to meet the Colonel on his chosen ground—a symbolic Eylau—Derville, like Chabert before him, must walk alone, unaided by man or beast, and he must pass through an entryway whose walls are made, grotesquely, of "des ossements et de la terre"—suggesting not only the image of a charnel house, but also that "fumier humain" (325; 315) under which Chabert had been buried. The misspelled sign recalls the clerk Huré's *sakerlotte*, indirectly a reminder of the legal labyrinth through which Chabert must pass, and Derville after him; this sign and the presumably crude drawings next to it remind us of the way in which human symbols only approximate the ideal—Chabert's "douleur inexprimable" (325; 315), the legal system in relation to justice. Ultimately, the narrator questions the linguistic justice of his description, finding the word *maison* inadequate for his purposes and his imagination deficient in metaphor ("masures... comparables à rien"). Chabert, too, will come to question the value of his given name, representing a former self to which he no longer bears resemblance. At last the narrator concentrates on the immediate squalor before his eyes, "la misère," predicting Chabert's future sordid existence; it is as if this passage contains in miniature the symbolic matrix of the story.

Now Derville finds himself in a territory not far removed from his office:

Comme presque tous les endroits où se cuisinent les éléments du grand repas que Paris dévore chaque jour, la cour dans laquelle Derville mit le pied offrait les traces d'une précipitation voulue par la nécessité d'arriver à heure fixe. . . . La maison était restée sous la protection de trois gamins. L'un . . . jetait des pierres dans un tuyau de cheminée de la maison voisine, espérant qu'elles y tomberaient dans la marmite. . . . Quand Derville leur demanda si c'était bien là que demeurait M. Chabert, aucun ne répondit . . . . (337-38; 320)

In the opening scene, in Derville's office, "les affaires juteuses se cuisinaient"; the food imagery is continued here, indeed made literal, by the lawyer's visit to a dairy. Derville, like "notre vieux carrick," faces a gang of malicious, uncooperative children, one of whom resembles Simonnin, aiming ammunition at food instead of using food as ammunition. As Chabert now crosses "une mare pleine de fumier" (337; 320) in order to rescue his benefactor, we recognize that this is another "cloaque de la poésie" (314; 311). There is, nonetheless, a certain safety in the written word: "'Pourquoi ne m'avez-vous pas écrit,' dit-il à Derville" (338; 320).

Although Godeschal is not present to provide a model of legal prose, the men's brief walk to Chabert's room leads them to other documents, "les Bulletins de la Grande Armée" (339; 320) open on the table. The "fameux carrick" (339; 320), now hung on the wall at a distance, proves metonymy relegated to its proper place; and the asceticism of the surroundings marks Chabert a Balzacian hero like Grandet and Montriveau. As Derville confronts his client with the particulars of his case, we find that nothing has changed in their respective attitudes towards the law: "—Colonel, votre affaire est excessivement compliquée, lui dit Derville. . . . —Elle me paraît, dit le soldat, parfaitement simple. L'on m'a cru mort, me voilà!" (340; 321). The lawyer eventually persuades his client discreetly to request only a stipend, asking rhetorically: "vous m'abandonnez à moi comme un homme qui marche à la mort?" (344; 322). The unintended irony only shows how little progress Chabert has made since the battle at Eylau.

Derville, now the arbiter of justice, goes to visit the Countess Ferraud, whose own upward mobility in society establishes a parallel to her former husband's more spectacular story. Reflecting on her history, the lawyer intuits her motive for not recognizing Chabert: "si son mariage était cassé, ne pourrait-il [the Count] faire passer sur sa tête, à la grande satisfaction du roi, la pairie d'un de ces vieux sénateurs qui n'ont que des filles?" (350; 324). The vertical movement of Chabert's escape from the common grave; the biological transformism suggested by the plant metaphor, the mushroom, describing his wounded head; the Ferrauds' obsession with social climbing—repeatedly, the theme of ascendancy is associated with a tenuous transition from one state to another. Derville tells us that Madame Ferraud's assimilation into the aristocracy is only apparent, and the narrator tells us even more about her evolutionary status: "elle déjeunait en jouant avec un singe attaché par une chaîne à une espèce de petit poteau garni de batons de fer" (350; 324). Representing Chabert's cause to her, Derville seems to glory in his privileged perspective: " 'Nous y sommes! se dit en lui-même Derville. Bien, je te tiens, l'affaire du pauvre colonel est gagnée' " (354; 326). But he fails to attach significance to one detail the narrator reserves for his own observant eye:

>   —M'aime-t-il encore? dit-elle.
>   —Mais je ne crois pas qu'il puisse en être autrement.
>   A ce mot la comtesse dressa la tête. Un éclair d'espérance brilla dans ses yeux . . . .
> (354; 326)

Despite appearances, Derville is not truly "omniscient" in imitation of the Balzacian narrator; his transaction is doomed to failure.

A week later Derville invites both clients, eager to negotiate, back to his office. Even Simonnin would congratulate his employer on his extraordinary professional skill: " —Ha! s'écria le petit clerc, qui veut parier un spectacle que le colonel Chabert est général, et cordon rouge? —Le patron est un fameux sorcier! dit Godeschal" (355; 326). Indeed, Derville has made elaborate preparations to bring off a legal, and theatrical, coup. He begins by reading a proposed agreement to Madame Ferraud while Chabert waits in an adjoining room. Just as Derville had once interrupted the soldier's narration, so Madame Ferraud, impatient with the lengthy preamble, asks Derville to move on: "Passez, dit-elle . . . arrivons aux conditions" (356; 327). More matter, with less art, says *Hamlet*'s Queen; but the Countess Ferraud, unfortunately, has missed the point: " 'Madame, dit l'avoué, le préambule explique succinctement la position dans laquelle vous vous trouvez l'un l'autre' " (356; 327). In law the matter *is* the art; birth, death, marriage, property all hinge on the fateful turn of a law clerk's phrase. Unlike Derville, Godeschal, Chabert and, presumably, the reader, she remains in ignorance of the written word's mighty power—until it comes to figures: "Mais c'est beaucoup trop cher" (357; 327), says the Countess when Derville suggests the amount of a yearly stipend. At this point Chabert storms in, in all his righteous fury:

>   —Trop cher! reprit le vieux soldat. Je vous ai donné près d'un million, et vous marchandez mon malheur. . . .
>   —Mais monsieur n'est pas le colonel Chabert, s'écria la comtesse en feignant la surprise.
>   —Ah! dit le vieillard d'un ton de voix profondément ironique, voulez-vous des preuves? Je vous ai prise au Palais-Royal . . .
>   La comtesse pâlit. (357; 327)

Indifferent to Derville's careful orchestration of a compromise, Chabert breaks the fundamental law of illusion-making by his intrusion. He confronts the Countess with the fact of her disreputable past as, we infer, a prostitute; and she confronts the disfigured Colonel with the fact of his unrecognizable physiognomy. Under the circumstances, only she, and not Chabert, is capable of dissimulation; Derville cannot control the characters in his play as if he were an author. Even they reject his work—the written transaction; and like a dutiful parent in a fairy tale, he sends Chabert off into a world where the forces of myth may conspire against him: "Prenez garde à vous, elle serait capable de vous faire tomber dans quelque piège et de vous enfermer à Charenton" (358; 327).

No sooner does the Colonel leave than Madame Ferraud draws him into her carriage and spirits him away to the countryside: "Les chevaux partirent et traversèrent tout Paris" (359; 327). Protected by her "masque de tranquillité" (362; 329), the Countess would convince Chabert that his return is disruptive; at one point her children appear as if on cue: "Les mains étaient étendues vers la mère, et les deux voix enfantines se mêlaient. Ce fut un tableau soudain et délicieux!" (364; 329). The literally vicious circle closes; Chabert overhears Madame Ferraud and her secretary plot his detention at the asylum at Charenton, and he resolves to disappear: "Je ne réclamerai jamais le nom que j'ai peut-être illustré. Je ne suis plus qu'un pauvre diable nommé Hyacinthe. . . . Ne me touchez pas" (367; 331). It is the resurrected Chabert's *Noli me tangere* addressed to an unpardonable Magdalene; we are not told whether this renunciation launches him on an inner spiritual pilgrimage, or if it simply signifies his defeat at the hands of an enemy more cruel than the Prussian army at Eylau. Perhaps there is nothing more to be said; men can be as trapped in their identities as in their boxcoats, and the title "Colonel Chabert" cannot redeem "un pauvre diable."

The appropriately brief ending, "L'Hospice de la vieillesse," actually has two different settings: the antechamber of the Correctional Police office in Paris and the public home for the aged at Bicêtre. At the first location, some time after the aborted transaction, Derville, making his rounds, overhears the sentencing of one "nommé Hyacinthe" (368; 331) for vagrancy. This "laboratoire de la chicane" (369; 331), like his own office, has its hapless clientele: "Tous ceux qui tombent sur le pavé de Paris rebondissent contre les murailles jaunâtres" (369; 331). Derville greets Chabert as if to reassert his authority: "Me reconnaissez-vous? dit Derville au vieux soldat en se plaçant devant lui" (370; 332). But Chabert has no more need for his services: "il vaut mieux avoir du luxe dans ses sentiments que sur ses habits. Je ne crains, moi, le mépris de personne" (371; 332). Chabert has renounced all, even his "vieux carrick." The narrative has exhausted the tension generated by the initial discrepancy between sign and referent questioned in the first scene by Simonnin, and so the narrator presents a final image, recapitulating the novel's major themes.

In 1840 Derville and Godeschal, now a lawyer, catch sight of a man reminiscent of "ces grotesques qui nous viennent d'Allemagne" (371; 332), a resident of the Hospice de la Vieillesse in Bicêtre. Derville recognizes in him his former client: "Ce vieux-là, mon cher, est tout un poème" (371; 332). Derville then retells Chabert's story, "l'histoire qui précède" (372; 332), but implied by this phrasing is the supremacy of the narrator, who alone has fashioned the present "récit," who alone rises above the level of mere story or anecdote. And indeed he has made *Le Colonel Chabert* a complete narrative poem.

The two friends stop to visit the Colonel:

> ... les deux amis trouvèrent assis sur la souche d'un arbre abattu le vieillard qui tenait à la main un baton et s'amusait à tracer des raies sur la sable. En le regardant attentivement, ils s'aperçurent qu'il venait de déjeuner autre part qu'à l'établissement.
> —Bonjour, colonel Chabert, lui dit Derville.
> —Pas Chabert! pas Chabert! je me nomme Hyacinthe, répondit le vieillard. Je ne suis plus un homme, je suis le numéro 164, septième salle, ajouta-t-il en regardant Derville avec une anxiété peureuse, avec une crainte de vieillard et d'enfant. (372; 332)

No longer a man, Hyacinthe has become a number, not even the figure of speech he once was, "vieux carrick," when even that degrading metonymy at least contained within it the promise of contiguous relation—of belonging. We remember Chabert's rage to pierce "la couverture de chair qui mettait une barrière entre la vie et moi" (325; 315), but the covering of flesh, the covering of cloth, serve to preserve human form; and now, it is implied, language recognizes that form in a way numbers cannot. We can reiterate Simonnin's early question: "Si c'est un homme, pourquoi l'appelez-vous vieux carrick?" (311-12; 310)—or rather "le numéro 164"? The precise, or imprecise, use of language has direct social implications; condemned to death in *Victoires et conquêtes* and denied his rightful name, Chabert has learned a cruel fact from which neither childlikeness nor wisdom nor drunkenness can protect him. But Chabert is only an image allowing us to contemplate this condition, this relation of word to action; as he designs with his cane "une arabesque imaginaire" (372; 332), Colonel Chabert participates in that incessant activity of figure-making that brought the novel into being.

As he learns of the Colonel's fate on these two inauspicious occasions, Derville implicitly undergoes an inner transformation, absorbs a difficult knowledge. In recognizing Chabert, he sees injustice for what it is, his vision unshielded by the ethical ambiguities of his profession. But at Bicêtre Chabert does not recognize Derville in turn, implicating the lawyer in the system that drove him to madness, regression and alcohol—all flights from the lessons of experience and reason. Experience and reason do not prevail where injustice is made legitimate:

Savez-vous, mon cher, reprit Derville après une pause, qu'il existe dans notre société trois hommes, le Prêtre, le Médecin et l'Homme de justice, qui ne peuvent pas estimer le monde? Ils ont des robes noires, peut-être parce qu'ils portent le deuil de toutes les vertus, de toutes les illusions. . . . Combien de choses n'ai-je pas apprises en exerçant ma charge! J'ai vu mourir un père dans un grenier, sans sou ni maille, abandonné par deux filles auxquelles il avait donné quarante mille livres de rente! J'ai vu brûler des testaments; j'ai vu des mères dépouillant leurs enfants, des maris volant leurs femmes. . . . Enfin, toutes les horreurs que les romanciers croient inventer sont toujours au-dessous de la vérité. Vous allez connaître ces jolies choses-là, vous; moi, je vais vivre à la campagne avec ma femme, Paris me fait horreur.
—J'en ai déjà bien vu chez Desroches, répondit Godeschal. (375; 333)

In a world where even children unthinkingly, as in play, join in the process of persecution these words have the weight of accumulated experience: not of Derville's career only, but of the narration of Chabert's story, beginning with Simonnin's verbal assault. Forcefully alluding to a number of Balzac's works—*Le Père Goriot, Gobseck, L'Interdiction*—Derville sounds the death knell for "toutes les vertus" and "toutes les illusions" as the scales fall from his eyes. It is not merely that, an honest man, he is sickened by the cupidity and viciousness he has seen, but that he has become part of that sordid world simply by exercising his practice and residing in Paris. The litany of accusations is directed as much against himself as against the society that has destroyed Colonel Chabert; he, Derville, is its witness and accomplice. It is he who would have compromised Chabert's dignity in serving the interests of Madame Ferraud; it is he whom the defeated Colonel finally does not recognize, does not really see. The uncomprehending gaze of the madman pierces Derville, but not merely on account of the soldier's appalling decline. In his sudden outpouring of bitterness and grief the lawyer implicitly indicts himself: what virtue is there in the possession of superior vision ("J'ai *vu*")—the precious gift now denied Chabert—if it changes nothing, watches social evil and indifference run their damaging course, unchallenged?

The catalogue of Balzac's novels does not advertise them so much as it does Balzac's own closeness to his character Derville, who has seen what his creator has imagined, who has rejected what his creator has made. Whatever may have been his attire, Balzac belongs to the confraternity of black-robed professionals cited by Derville: the fourth, unnamed member of this group is, by implication, the writer. Like the doctor, priest and lawyer—all students of human behavior and masters of a highly specialized form of discourse—the writer has seen the ravages of disease, sin and injustice. Poetical vision, like theirs, encompasses the aspirations and failures, the strengths and the corruption of societies and individuals; and the poet, like his peers, knows that affliction in body, soul or collective spirit shatters the ideals of perfection and justice. Again like his colleagues, the poet retires to his office or study and summons his society before him—an imaginary one in the case of the novelist; he observes the mechanisms associated with human needs and passions, the raw material of his art; and, also a specialist, he skillfully exploits language in the service of his knowledge and authority, and in keeping with the demands and traditions of his craft.

Because of the identification of Derville with Balzac, it is significant that the character reminds us of the limited power of the imagination: "Enfin, toutes les horreurs que les romanciers croient inventer sont toujours au-dessous de la vérité." Balzac would perhaps remind us that, however deep a writer's insight or compassionate his instincts, the limitations of art as a civilizing influence are as painfully apparent to the student of history as Derville's limitations are to him in this moment of reflection. As the lawyer's remark implies, it is within the province of the novel to contemplate the possibilities and limitations of narrative art as well as the ambiguities and conflicts within the self and society. In announcing his intention to leave Paris, Derville proposes to abstract himself from the difficulties inherent in the novel's thematic sphere of reference. The author's corresponding gesture, one operating on the formal and linguistic levels, would be to choose simply not to write. Through Derville's condemnation of himself and society Balzac suggests that the exercise of certain professions, or rather the cultivation of realistic vision, involves struggle, disillusionment and the temptation of despair.

It is this "drame . . . se jouant dans l'âme de l'homme"—character and author—that most clearly establishes the parallel between *Le Colonel Chabert* and *Louis Lambert*. Unable to bear the burden of his imperfection, Lambert aspires to the condition of the angels; appalled by the moral squalor in which his practice implicates him, Derville similarly resolves to reject the self he has become. The price of lucidity is for these characters a form of isolation: a geographical one for Derville, who plans to leave Paris for the provinces, and for Lambert—and Colonel Chabert as well—the intellectual and spiritual exile of the self in madness. We may surmise that Balzac, a Parisian by choice, understood both reactions, but found a different course: it is as striking as it is appropriate that the minor figure Godeschal, the erstwhile composer of sentences, should pronounce the final words of the narrative. Derville, because he wears his black robe, has come to see his resemblance—and his responsibility—to the man once ridiculed for his ragged coat. The Colonel and the lawyer have both seen society in all its horror; and perhaps there is no solution but in madness or renunciation—or, as the author subtly implies through Godeschal's returning presence, in the inquiry made possible by poetical discourse. This, after all and despite all, is Balzac's answer to Simonnin's impertinent, and searching, question: "Si c'est un homme, pourquoi l'appelez-vous *vieux carrick*?"

Chapter III

HISTOIRE DES TREIZE: FERRAGUS

Much of the drama in *Louis Lambert* and *Le Colonel Chabert* occurs at the level of perspective, in the narrator's response to the possible modes of discourse open before him. The narrator of *Louis Lambert,* drawn to mysticism and philosophical speculation, struggles to order his insights from different sources, to discipline the course of his narration. The narrator of *Le Colonel Chabert* confidently inscribes his story in the sphere of poetical discourse, approaching his subject freely, without apology or constraint. In the one, moments of discontinuity prompt the narattor's confession of inadequacy; in the other, with the concerted delay of the hero's arrival, the author's technique, his purposeful art, is made visible. If *Louis Lambert* was to have been a narrative structure crystallizing a character's genius, *Le Colonel Chabert* is such a structure illuminating the author's sense of drama, his love of language, his visionary art. The control of perspective fully achieved, experimentation is made possible.

In the trilogy *Histoire des Treize*[1] Balzac openly abandons all pretense of cultivating a fixed perspective in the three works; he introduces in the Preface a narrator who is clearly a pretext for what follows. Each narrative is structured differently, and each addresses the problem of fragmented perspective: how in the single work can a narrator accommodate several points of view, arrange chronology to dramatic advantage? In *Ferragus* the narrator coordinates three different points of view with the requirements of chronology and calls to our attention the distinction between narration ("récit") and story ("histoire") which this approach requires him to make, and sustain, throughout the work. *La Duchesse de Langeais,* told as a flashback, resembles *Le Colonel Chabert* in its thematic and formal insistence on the influence of historical reference, and, like *Ferragus,* requires the narrator to connect moments involving marked shifts of perspective. In the last of the three works, *La Fille aux yeux d'or,* the narrator presents an allegorized portrait of Paris immediately followed by a chronologically ordered tale, inviting the reader to discover the inherent unity of the two temporally segregated parts. The problem of achieving transitions is especially interesting in the *Histoire des Treize*, making the trilogy an excellent subject for an examination of narrative perspective.

The Preface, clearly not an author's foreword, explains, in the manner of an 18th-century epistolary or confessional novel, the way in which the narrator came into possession of the material he is about to present. Actually, he has not merely transcribed the stories confided in him by a member of the secret political society of the Treize; he will retell them in his own words, in the interest of our entertainment. Thus, the narrator in the Preface to the *Histoire des Treize* is not a point of reference; he is a point of departure. He identifies himself only as the recipient of "la permission assez étrange de raconter à sa guise quelques-unes des aventures arrivées à ces hommes [the Treize], tout en respectant certaines convenances" (788; 10); and indeed, he has no other reason for being. He is like a master of ceremonies who will discreetly retire once the entertainment is underway.

Had it entailed the development of an identifiable character, the fiction of a single narrator of the adventures would have proved obtrusive, distracting. It would be technically impossible for such a narrator to report, in *Ferragus*, the contents of letters that were destroyed or to know Madame de Langeais's private reflections or words Paquita spoke too softly for de Marsay to hear. As if he had wished to underplay the necessary fiction of the narrator, Balzac eliminated afterwords to the novels when preparing the Furne edition of his collected works. The narrator is a transparent gesture to the reader, not a formal principle. Balzac commonly flouts the very conventions he resorts to, a practice that prompted Ortega y Gasset to complain that in reading Balzac "we are on every page thrown out of the dream world of the novel because we have bumped into the novelistic scaffolding."[2]

Clearly Balzac's own creation, the narrator is alternately pedantic and humorous: he is not a character whose identity lends coherence to the novels, but a voice that sets the tone. He demystifies the subject: "Voici donc le prestige romanesque attaché au nom de Ferragus et à celui des Dévorants complètement dissipé" (790; 11); he assumes the role of teacher: "Maintenant, que sont les Dévorants? Dévorants est le nom d'une des tribus de Compagnons..." (788; 11); he proclaims faith in the reader's intelligence: "Si quelque lecteur n'était pas rassasié des horreurs froidement servies au public depuis quelque temps, il [the narrator] pourrait lui révéler de calmes atrocités, de surprenantes tragédies de famille" (788; 10); and he has no illusions about the business of storytelling, his obligation to entertain us: "L'auteur connaît trop les lois de la narration pour ignorer les engagements que cette courte préface lui fait contracter" (788; 10). The anxiety of influence afflicts him no more than it does the member of the Treize who engages his literary services: "Ecrire l'*Itinéraire de Paris à Jérusalem,* c'est prendre sa part dans la gloire humaine d'un siècle; mais doter son pays d'un Homère, n'est-ce pas usurper sur Dieu?" (788; 10). By virtue of his choice of subject, the Parisian Treize, the narrator casually reverses the literary pilgrimage undertaken by Chateaubriand: "Dévorants [among the forerunners of the Treize] est le nom d'une des tribus de Compagnons ressortissant jadis de la grande association mystique formée entre les ouvriers de la chrétienté pour rebâtir le temple de Jérusalem" (789; 11). In imitation of the medieval Scholastics, he sits upon the shoulders of literary giants, Homer and Chateaubriand, only to gaze into the underworld (if such is the location, in the literary cosmos, of the Gothic novel), for he will tell "cette vie secrète, curieuse, autant que peut l'être le plus noir des romans de Mme Radcliffe" (787-88; 10).

The narrator also calls our attention to the common themes of the stories: their setting (Paris), their subject (romance), their heroes (the Treize). But these are not unifying structures; they are interesting themes:

Mais il [the narrator] a choisi de préférence les aventures les plus douces, celles où des scènes pures succèdent à l'orage des passions, où la femme est radieuse de vertus et de beauté. (788-89; 10)

Maintenant, il lui est permis de commencer le récit des épisodes qui, dans cette histoire, l'ont plus particulièrement séduit par la senteur parisienne des détails, et par la bizarrerie des contrastes. (792; 12)

In the Preface the Treize are "dans Paris," not "à Paris," as if the city were not a locus, but a context, a stage with several backdrops: "Il s'est rencontré, sous l'Empire et *dans Paris,* treize hommes..." (787; 10); "Il y eut donc *dans Paris* treize frères..." (792; 12) (my emphasis). Only Balzac's vision of Paris can be said to unify the novels, especially insofar as they are novels of manners: Paris, for the characters, is the site of a passage from innocence to experience, of the reconciliation of self-knowledge with conventional wisdom.

Likewise, the theme of romance is hardly restricting in a genre whose traditional subject is the lives of men and women in society. One might say, however, that Balzac's treatment of the theme of the sexes demonstrates the logic of the theme of convention, the pattern of a cultural and linguistic prejudice. As he wrote in the "Avant-Propos," "Ainsi l'œuvre à faire devait avoir une triple forme: les hommes, les femmes, et les choses, c'est-à-dire, les personnes et la représentation matérielle qu'ils donnent de leur pensée; enfin l'homme et la vie." In the novels of the Treize the heroines —Madame Jules, the Duchesse de Langeais, Paquita, la Marquise de San-Réal—are sentenced to death or to exile in a convent by plots that dictate the momentary enlightenment of the heroes—Jules, Montriveau, de Marsay.

But even this almost predictable pattern creates only analogies, or correspondences, among the novels; it is not a framework.

And this is true also of the treatment of the third and central theme, the subject of the trilogy: the Treize. They are above all an exercise in rhetoric. In describing them, the narrator, who has already committed literary heresy in styling himself successor to Chateaubriand and Homer, discreetly parodies the Gospel of Saint John: "Ce monde à part dans le monde, hostile au monde, n'admettant aucune des idées du monde, n'en reconnaissant aucune loi . . ." (791; 11) recalls "Il était dans le monde, et le monde fut par lui, et le monde ne l'a pas connu" (John 1: 10). The Treize, like the Word made Flesh, incarnate a sublime paradox witnessed by a chosen disciple and scribe: "Ce fut horrible et sublime. Puis le pacte eut lieu; puis il dura, précisément parce qu'il paraissait impossible" (792; 12).

But if the narrator's vision is mediated, screened by his observance of "certaines convenances" (788; 10), the author's own is truly direct and creative, given form and substance through his language:

> Il s'est rencontré, sous l'Empire et dans Paris, treize hommes également frappés du même sentiment, tous doués d'une assez grande énergie pour être fidèles à la même pensée, assez probes entre eux pour ne point se trahir, alors même que leurs intérêts se trouvaient opposés, assez profondément politiques pour dissimuler les liens sacrés qui les unissaient, assez forts pour se mettre au-dessus de toutes les lois, assez hardis pour tout entreprendre, et assez heureux pour avoir presque toujours réussi dans leurs desseins; ayant couru les plus grands dangers, mais taisant leurs défaites; inaccessibles à la peur, et n'ayant tremblé ni devant le prince, ni devant le bourreau, ni devant l'innocence; s'étant acceptés tous, tels qu'ils étaient, sans tenir compte des préjugés sociaux; criminels sans doutes, mais certainement remarquables par quelques-unes des qualités qui font les grands hommes, et ne se recrutant que parmi les hommes d'élite.
> (787; 10)

In this, the first sentence of the *Histoire des Treize*, the Treize are neither defined nor identified: they are set into motion. Their existence is only secondarily an accident of certain undisclosed circumstances. It is primarily the effect of the fortuitous balance of phrases in the sentence, its rhythm stressed by the repetition of the adverb *assez* before the first semicolon and after it by the alternation of adjectives ("inaccessibles," "remarquables") and participles ("ayant couru," "s'étant acceptés," "ne se recrutant"). The theme conjured up by this rhythmic pattern, or rather in conjunction with it, would seem to precipitate the creation of the narratives. For the narrator the "Histoire des Treize" is a legend, a rich and irresistible theme:

> Il [the narrator] connaît assez l'*Histoire des Treize* pour être certain de ne jamais se trouver au-dessous de l'intérêt que doit inspirer ce programme [the agreement to tell the adventures]. (188; 10)

Mais il a choisi de préférence les aventures les plus douces, celles où des scènes succèdent à l'orage des passions, où la femme est radieuse de vertus et de beauté. Pour l'honneur des Treize, il s'en rencontre de telles *dans leur histoire*. (788-89; 10; my emphasis)

Maintenant, il lui est permis de commencer le récit des trois épisodes qui, *dans cette histoire*, l'ont plus particulièrement séduit par la senteur parisienne des détails, et par la bizarrerie des contrastes. (792; 12; my emphasis)

It is, therefore, only thematically that the *Histoire des Treize* alludes to a single history. Its narratives maintain the appearances of a trilogy, with preface and narrator, in the same way that the Parisian society they criticize, in the full sense of the word, adheres to insincere conventions of its own. The social contract, for Balzac, defines the human condition; the literary one, the requisites of form, including, in the *Treize*, the traditional gesture to the reader in the form of a preface. In a way, the Preface to the *Histoire des Treize* is a meditation on the possibilities of fiction, for Balzac contemplates through his narrator the tension between the creative play of the imagination and formal discipline so intensely felt by the artist. The three novels that follow the Preface both preserve and resolve that tension, reminding us of the double nature of literary form itself: that which leads us through words into the wilderness of memory and the imagination, but will never abandon us there.

Long before *La Cousine Bette* Balzac demonstrated in *Ferragus* his predilection for complicated plot, one it is best to summarize before addressing the problem of perspective. In a disreputable section of Paris the young Baron de Maulincour catches sight of the beautiful Mme Jules Desmarets, wife of a successful stockbroker. His Platonic idol shattered, Maulincour follows her through the streets to her destination, and in the following days he attempts to learn the identity of the man she had been visiting. On the verge of doing so, he confides his suspicions to Jules, her husband; and the Baron suddenly finds himself poisoned, arsenic administered to his scalp by a mysterious foreign ambassador presented to him at a party. Jules now takes up Maulincour's pursuit and spies on his wife's activities. He discovers that she goes to visit her father, the escaped convict Ferragus, member of the Treize and the same man who, disguised, killed Maulincour. But this discovery is ill-timed. In order to protect his identity, Ferragus has arranged the apparent suicide of his mistress, Ida; and, the shocked victim of her husband's lack of trust, Madame Jules falls mortally ill. After her death the heartbroken Jules leaves Paris, but not before seeing, near the Paris Observatory, a despairing Ferragus, a faded image of Colonel Chabert. The narrative respects the law of chronology, thus engaging us in the mystery as it unfolds; and we meet the "typical" Balzacian narrator who follows characters into the dark recesses of Parisian streets and of secret private lives.

Near the end of *Ferragus,* just after Madame Jules's burial, the narrator briefly intervenes: "Ici semble finir le *récit* de cette *histoire;* mais peut-être serait-elle incomplète si, après avoir donné un léger croquis de la vie parisienne, si, après en avoir suivi les capricieuses ondulations, les effets de la mort y étaient oubliés" (891; 49; my emphasis). This comment abruptly dismisses any thought the reader might have that the narration of the story has indeed run its course, and for a moment we are disoriented. But the remark is meant instead to re-orient the reader, to teach us to see the novel from the writer's point of view. Although we may have followed the story ("histoire") to learn the fates of the characters, we must now turn our attention to the far more serious matter of the narration ("récit"). When the narrator thus announces an imminent shift, we are at that moment invited to share, as readers, in the author's own preoccupation: to witness the transformation of a story into a formally unified narrative.

Ferragus can, therefore, be read as a celebration of local color, "un léger croquis de la vie parisienne," ordered by the plot, the narration of which first unravels a complicated, but relatively insignificant puzzle and then incorporates it into the larger scheme of the novel's overall design. Balzac's emphasis on the artist's intelligence behind the narrative invites us to detach ourselves from the ongoing drama and read more critically. Its melodramatic violence lessened by the enlargement of context, Madame Jules's death becomes a single element in a larger composition and not an extravagant finale. In an afterword eliminated from most editions of the novel, Balzac openly states his interest in the portrait of Paris which the distinction between "récit" and "histoire" enabled him to create: "dans le récit de [cette aventure] les digressions étaient en quelque sorte le sujet principal pour l'auteur" (904). Because his conception of the novel was not restricted to the simple chronological unfolding of characters' lives, Balzac could organize *Ferragus* in such a way as to feature a series of entertaining prose sketches of the city. The narrator does not lead the heroes Ferragus and Jules to a deeper knowledge of themselves in the pages following the scene of Madame Jules's burial; he simply describes for us "les effets de la mort" in order to complete the novel's esthetic design. Without the dénouement heralded by the narrator's intervention, *Ferragus* could not be considered one of the mature Balzac's works: one in which the narration— "récit"—shapes the story—"histoire"—and the form of the novel may claim the full attention of author and reader alike.

In *Ferragus,* before the intervention, the narrator adopts successively the perspectives of the characters Maulincour and Jules, who would solve the mystery of Madame Jules's visits to the disreputable Rue Soly. But once Jules discovers that Ferragus is his wife's father, the mystery is solved; Madame Jules's death tragically results from her physical and emotional shock at Jules's intervention; and the "histoire" appears to be at its end. It is at this point that the narrator announces his intention to continue the story, to complete the narration, thereby eclipsing the limited perspective of the two characters. Thus, the structure of the novel is defined by distinct shifts in perspective; *Ferragus* is not related by an impassive, omniscient narrator contemplating an imaginary world from a fixed distance. The characters themselves are fully implicated into the elaboration of the novel's form because it is through their eyes that we sometimes follow the story. At times the narrator would force us to adopt the bourgeois prejudices and the chauvinistic and misogynistic sentiments he expresses through them, because these qualify his perspective and, therefore, our own as we read. Balzac, it seems, would redefine the art of reading as a discipline of those faculties enabling us to perceive narrative form and of those emotions interfering with an esthetic appreciation of the whole—the very challenge encountered by the narrator of *Louis Lambert* as he related his biography.

The narrator of *Ferragus* is clearly the instrument of the author, although this is not always true of the narrative voice in Balzac. In "Facino Cane," for example, we find one of the rare autobiographical reflections Balzac allowed himself, an almost lyrical celebration of his special gift for observation:

Chez moi l'observation étant déjà devenue intuitive, elle pénétrait l'âme sans négliger le corps; ou plutôt elle saisissait si bien les détails extérieurs, qu'elle allait sur-le-champ au-delà; elle me donnait la faculté de vivre de la vie de l'individu sur laquelle elle s'exerçait, en me permettant de me substituer à lui comme le derviche des *Mille et Une Nuits* prenait le corps et l'âme des personnes sur lesquelles il prononçait certaines paroles.
(VI, 1019; 257)

One cannot mistake the opening passage of *Ferragus* for an authorial pronouncement:

Il est dans Paris certaines rues déshonorées autant que peut l'être un homme coupable d'infamie; puis il existe des rues nobles, puis des rues simplement honnêtes, puis de jeunes rues sur la moralité desquelles le public ne s'est pas encore formé d'opinion; puis des rues assassines, des rues plus vieilles que de vieilles douairières ne sont vieilles, des rues estimables, des rues toujours propres, des rues toujours sales, des rues ouvrières, travailleuses, mercantiles. . . . Ces observations, incompréhensibles au-delà de Paris, seront sans doute saisies par ces hommes d'étude et de pensée, de poésie et de plaisir qui savent récolter, en flânant dans Paris, la masse de jouissances flottantes, à toute heure, entre ses murailles; par ceux pour lesquels Paris est le plus délicieux des monstres: là, jolie femme; plus loin, vieux et pauvre; ici, tout neuf, comme la monnaie d'un nouveau règne; dans ce coin, élégant comme une femme à la mode. (793-94; 13)

The passage, which continues until the introduction of the characters Clémence and Auguste de Maulincour, is anything but naturalistic; conspicuously missing is the convincing visual detail; and everywhere the narrator records the reputations of the streets, which are, after all, no more than received ideas. The narrator does not study the streets; he reflects public opinion. The narrowness of his vision heightens the fundamental distinction between Balzac's use of a narrator and his authorial vision; the one is an instrument,[3] the other is a poetic consciousness. This distinction is more readily apparent in those narratives recounted by a single character who cannot be confused with Balzac, such as *Le Lys dans la vallée* and *Sarrasine*.

What is this, the "traditional" Balzacian narrator? Although the narrator in *Ferragus* is not an identifiable character, his vision is neither impersonal nor impartial. He does not hesitate to refer to himself, using the editorial "nous," or to address the reader directly as "vous"; these conventions of the Balzacian narrative voice distinguish it from the more remote narrator in Flaubert. But Balzac's narrator, although he adopts a familiar tone, is elusive, changeable and very much part of the narrative he relates, not its omniscient source. The popular contrast of the narrators in Balzac and Flaubert, at least as it is commonly expressed, is misleading in that it creates the image of a static narrative perspective in Balzac, which is rarely, if ever, the case. In this sense, Balzac's narrator is just as impersonal as Flaubert's, just as much an instrument of the artist; but it is necessary to stress that the impersonality resides in the use of the narrative voice and not in its tone or in the biases it is given to express. The use of the narrative voice in both Balzac and Flaubert draws our attention to the form of their novels, and it is perhaps necessary for critics to redefine the basis for distinguishing between the two authors. For example, Jonathan Culler's remarks on the stance of the narrator in Flaubert may be taken to indicate the pervasiveness of Balzac's influence, rather than Flaubert's greater sophistication as a novelist:

> Impersonality depends not on what is said but on the fact that no identifiable narrator exists. And hence the efforts of critics to undermine Flaubert's doctrine of impersonality by citing all the instances where opinions are expressed seem to miss the point. What is rejected is a consistency in point of view which could lead to the identification of a knowledgeable Balzacian narrator or series of narrators limited in their points of view and characterizable by those very limitations.[4]

The unidentifiable narrator in the opening passage of *Ferragus* introduces a set of hypothetical conditions from which the dramatic action of the novel naturally arises, in itself proof of Balzac's discretionary use of the narrative voice:

HISTOIRE DES TREIZE: FERRAGUS 73

Balzac finally completes the evolution of his formal metaphor [Paris as courtesan] into the formulation of a plot paradigm, a hypothetical case from which he will subsequently launch the opening dramatic scene of his book.... This hypothetical case or paradigm of plot is composed of four principal motifs—a lady, an observer, a time and a place—and, with the single exception of the "ideal" time of nine o'clock, each of its ingredients may be traced directly to their sources in the emerging form of Paris/courtesan.[5]

The narrator in *Ferragus*, unlike the one in "Facino Cane," does not wholly give over his attention to the scenes and lives he observes. If anything, he is overwhelmed by prejudices, and this weakness is asserted to be total and involuntary: "Enfin, les rues de Paris ont des qualités humaines, et nous impriment par leur physionomie certaines idées contre lesquelles nous sommes *sans défense*" (793; 13); "La rue de la Paix ... ne réveille aucune des pensées gracieusement nobles *qui surprennent une âme impressible* au milieu de la rue Royale" (793; 13); "ne demandez raison de *la tristesse nerveuse qui s'empare de vous* qu'à la solitude, l'air morne des maisons" (793; 13); "Comment ne pas dépenser quelques minutes devant les drames, les désastres, les figures, les pittoresques accidents *qui vous assaillent* au milieu de cette mouvante reine des cités" (795; 14) (my emphasis).

As a result, the narrator does not present a broad canvas of Parisian society and geography that would permit us to observe the characters impassively, as happens, for example, in George Eliot. The narrative voice is neither impersonal nor detached in these pages—which is not to say that the opening passage of *Ferragus* betrays a deficiency of vision. Instead, like the Preface of the *Treize*, it opens and sustains a mood more by rhetoric than by substance. The involuntary and subjective impressions of the narrator convey his sensitivity rather than the details he might conceivably have noticed; it is the intensity of vision and vulnerability of the observer that matter and only secondarily his general surroundings. *Ferragus* does not begin with a panorama of the streets of Paris, but with an evocation of the frame of mind in which they will be observed, first generally by the narrator and then by the characters Maulincour and Jules.

The narrator's imaginary foray into the streets of Paris is above all a physical and psychological penetration of the city; it creates an atmosphere of suspicion that makes Maulincour's persecution of Madame Jules and Ferragus's persecution of Maulincour seem inevitable. That the perspective in the opening passage is a formal necessity and not a direct pronouncement by the author is suggested internally by the themes of transformations, especially those verging on the grotesque, and of formal boundaries, and ultimately by its poetic effect.

The themes of transformations and boundaries emphasize the narrator's unstable field of reference and circumscribed vision. The transformation of

Paris through the personification of the streets ("Il est dans Paris certaines rues déshonorées autant que peut l'être un homme coupable d'infamie" [793; 13]), and the animation of the city ("Toutes les portes baillent, tournent sur leurs gonds comme les membranes d'un grand homard, invisiblement manœuvrées par trente mille hommes ou femmes [794; 13]) dramatize the inseparability of the environment and its population, of setting and character. The reciprocal influence of the streets and their inhabitants puts the narrator's authority on questionable ground. He is necessarily part of "la vie toujours active [du] monstre" (794; 13). The boundaries of the city symbolically contain him; he is drawn to its center as if by centripetal force: "A qui n'est-il pas arrivé de partir, le matin, de son logis pour aller aux extrémités de Paris, sans avoir pu en quitter le centre?" (795; 14).

This irresistible magnetism makes the narrator victim of his faculty of vision. His surroundings compel him to exercise it, and rather than differentiate him from the multitude, it provokes in him the most conventional responses. In the end the narrator only articulates the common consensus: "Oui donc, il est des rues ou des fins de rue, il est certaines maisons, inconnues pour la plupart aux personnes du grand monde, dans lesquelles une femme appartenant à ce monde ne saurait aller sans faire penser d'elle les choses les plus cruellement blessantes" (795; 14). The vision of the narrator is absolutely dependent upon his immediate context; consequently, his perspective is actually quite provincial: "Ces observations [sont] incompréhensibles au-delà de Paris" (795; 13).

The themes of constant transformation and inescapable restriction, of changeability and captivity, bring to mind the theme of a lover's jealousy; it is, therefore, appropriate that those who observe Paris regard her as their mistress: "Paris est une créature; chaque homme, chaque fraction de maison est un lobe du tissu cellulaire de cette grande courtisane de laquelle ils connaissent parfaitement la tête, le cœur et les mœurs fantasques" (795; 13). "Voyager dans Paris est, pour ces poètes, un luxe coûteux" (795; 14). The vision of these poets is both responsive and creative; it is primarily an attitude of receptivity, anticipating Maulincour's and Jules's reaction to the circumstantial evidence against Clémence. Thus, the narrator's conclusions are not logical, but poetic; dramatic, not distanced, preparing the imminent adventure:

Mais si, par hasard, [une femme] est venue [dans ces défilés du pays parisien] à neuf heures du soir, les conjectures qu'un observateur peut se permettre deviennent épouvantables par leurs conséquences.... Elle est à la merci du premier homme de sa connaissance qui la rencontre dans ces marécages parisiens. Mais il y a telle rue de Paris où cette rencontre peut devenir le drame le plus effroyablement terrible, un drame plein de sang et d'amour, un drame de l'école moderne. (795-96; 14)

The narrator is anything but a detached observer.

The opening passage of *Ferragus* illustrates the distinction between the theme of observation and Balzac's vision, for the narrator is clearly the vehicle of a storyteller who directs us to read *Ferragus* with a certain detachment, and at the same time preserves the tone of an intimate conversation with his reader. However, the opening passage does not prepare the events that follow in the way, for example, that the Pension Vauquer implicates and necessitates the existence of its owner and residents, and hence the story of *Père Goriot*. The description of the boarding house appeals to the senses—sight, touch, smell; the opening of *Ferragus* introduces the reader to the assumptions that will motivate the characters, that is, their conventional interpretation of appearances.[6] The narrator does not invite us to visualize the streets of Paris; he wants our interest in the scene to coincide with Maulincour's. At one point he directly identifies the reader with Maulincour and with himself:

Tantôt la créature que vous y suivrez, par hasard ou à dessein, vous paraît svelte; tantôt le bas, s'il est bien blanc, vous fait croire à des jambes fines et élégantes ... par moments ce n'est plus une femme, c'est un démon, un feu follet qui vous entraîne par un ardent magnétisme jusqu'à une maison où la pauvre bourgeoise, ayant peur de votre pas menaçant ou de vos bottes retentissantes, vous ferme la porte cochère au nez sans vous regarder. (797-98; 14)

Although the narrator's articulation of the tyranny of social convention may strike a responsive chord, it does not automatically follow that his remarks are founded upon fact.[7] Even though Balzac's vision of society may be remarkably consistent, this consistency alone does not constitute a philosophy or a systematic method of inquiry; it is an artist's vision, not incompatible with science, but of a different order. There is no evidence at this point that *Ferragus* belongs to a larger context than the story the narrator is engaged in telling. The narrator observes and interprets within the confines of the scene; he does not step back to survey his story until much later, after Madame Jules's death, and even then the expanded field of vision restricts our attention to *Ferragus* alone as a portrait of Paris.

In this context it is significant that the kind of sensibility evinced by the narrator is quite specifically transferred to the character, Maulincour, even before details of his appearance and history are supplied: "En un moment son cœur bondit, une chaleur intolérable sourdit de son diaphragme et passa dans toutes ses veines, il eut froid dans le dos, et sentit dans sa tête un frémissement superficiel" (796; 14). The consciousness of the character and that of the narrator are essentially one, and we need not know the particulars concerning Maulincour—here designated merely as "un jeune homme"—before that connection has been made. That it is a question of consciousness is later graphically illustrated by Maulincour's death; the physical vulnerability of the brain to an externally introduced substance is a symbolic extension of his extreme sensitivity to impressions. The "frémissement *superficiel*" prefigures his entire fate: a susceptibility to external forces—the socially determined vision, the locally administered poison. In *Ferragus* Balzac seems to discard the avatars of his narrative voice once the possibilities of their limited perspective have been exhausted: thus, Maulincour's death occurs just before Jules begins his investigation; Ferragus disappears from the novel upon the narrator's intervention, returning only as a sort of after-image in the final paragraphs of the book; and when the narrator himself has completed his portrait of the city, the novel ends. Maulincour is only the first casualty of this process.

One might interpret this silencing of prospective narrative voices as a kind of revenge by the author-creator on inordinately ambitious narrator-creatures. And yet the theme of thwarted paternal influence—the direct or indirect revolt against a father—and in *Ferragus* the orphan Jules unknowingly defies his father-in-law—has ramifications on the level of perspective. It is a drama of succession, legitimate or not, and a bid for immortality. Seen in this light, the process of narrating the seemingly insignificant anecdote of *Ferragus* dramatizes a psychology of sorts, a quest for power and authority. We remember that the identification of character and narrator, illustrated here through Maulincour and Jules, originates, thematically, in the Preface to the *Treize*. The informant's arrangement to preserve the history of the Treize is humorously figured as a usurpation of a higher power, the gift to mankind of a new Homer. That the informant succeeded in momentarily supplanting God is proved by the very existence of the novels and by his controlling influence: after all, he revealed the history to the narrator on his own terms. In *Ferragus* the theme of the illegitimate arrogation of power is sounded again on two levels: thematically, in Maulincour's and later Jules's intrusion on Ferragus's self-appointed domain, and in Ferragus's attempted adoption of a new identity; and formally, in the subordination of the immediate interest of the story—Ferragus's adventure—to the larger design of the novel. The motivations of the characters and the act of narration itself involve the appropriation of another's talent, life or story for one's own purpose: for the informant, to survive through the written word; for Maulincour, Jules and Ferragus, to satisfy a passion; for Balzac, to create a formally unified novel, a portrait of Paris.

Maulincour's point of view would appear to dominate the novel from his emergence as a character to the ballroom scene, in which he is poisoned by Ferragus and excites Jules's suspicions against Clémence. From the first, Maulincour does not intend simply to account for the mystery of Madame Jules's appearance in a disreputable section of Paris; he fully expects to possess his fallen idol: "Auguste pouvait se livrer à toutes les félicités de l'amour heureux, et son imagination lui ouvrit alors l'immense carrière des plaisirs de la possession" (812; 20). Omniscience, presumably the narrator's prerogative, is his ambition because omniscience leads to complete control. Maulincour, like de Marsay in *La Fille aux yeux d'or* after him, adopts the attitude of an Oriental despot: "Il tranchait déjà du sultan, et pensait à demander impérieusement à Mme Jules de lui révéler tous ses secrets" (822; 23). The gravity of his invasion of her privacy, as well as the indignity of it, are fully expressed in Ferragus's letter to the Baronne de Maulincour: "Il avait espionné l'homme le plus inoffensif du monde pour en pénétrer *tous les secrets*, quand, de ces secrets, dépendait la vie ou la mort de trois personnes" (830; 26; my emphasis). Maulincour's efforts are further characterized as an attempt to usurp Clémence's life, first by Ferragus ("Te perdre ma fille, dit Ferragus, te perdre pour la curiosité d'un misérable Parisien!" [875; 43]), and later by Jules ("Elle m'a été enlevée là, par la funeste curiosité de ce monde qui s'agite et se presse, pour se presser et s'agiter" [898; 51]).

The theme of intrusion also introduces the scene immediately following the ball; in one sentence Balzac implicates the narrator, the reader and Jules in a deliberate invasion of Clémence's privacy:

Pour développer cette histoire dans toute la vérité de ses détails, pour en suivre le cours dans toutes ses sinuosités, il faut ici divulguer quelques secrets de l'amour, se glisser sous les lambris d'une chambre à coucher, non pas effrontément, mais à la manière de Trilby, n'effaroucher ni Dougal, ni Jeannie, n'effaroucher personne, être aussi chaste que veut l'être notre noble langue française, aussi hardi que l'a été le pinceau de Gérard dans son tableau de *Daphnis et Chloë*. (838; 29)

The tenor of this passage recalls an earlier narrative digression with its implicit reference to Maulincour:

Une bien belle chose est le métier d'espion, quand on le fait pour son compte et au profit d'une passion. N'est-ce pas se donner les plaisirs du voleur en restant honnête homme? ... Il faut aller, sur la foi d'une indication, vers un but ignoré, manquer son coup, pester, s'improviser à soi-même des élégies, des dithyrambes, s'exclamer niaisement devant un passant inoffensif qui vous admire.... Puis besoin est d'un cœur gros d'amour ou de vengeance ... pour jouir alors de tous les accidents de Paris en leur prêtant un intérêt de plus que celui dont ils abondent déjà. Alors, ne faut-il pas avoir une âme multiple? n'est-ce pas vivre de mille passions, de mille sentiments ensemble?
(812-13; 20)

In both cases the observer's movement is shown to conform to the movement of the person being pursued—"Il faut aller ... vers un but ignoré," "pour en suivre le cours dans toutes ses sinuosités": spying is a form of attachment and not of detachment. The observer enjoys the privilege of heightened sensitivity—"n'est-ce pas vivre de mille passions," "se glisser ...

à la manière de Trilby"—an illicit excitation that nonetheless respects a certain notion of propriety, of convention. Finally, the narrator, Maulincour and Jules all engage in a multiplication of self that is essentially creative: "aussi hardi que l'a été le pinceau de Gérard," "s'improviser à soi-même des élégies, des dithyrambes . . . avoir une âme multiple." The literary and art-historical references draw attention to the literally "formal" discipline the observer, be he narrator or character, must impose upon himself in order to pursue his subject. Despite the striking contrast between the inner sanctum of the bedroom and the sordid Rue Soly, both Jules and Maulincour are artful observers, each in his own setting. Consequently, in the shift of perspective from one character to the other the effect is one of continuity and progression:

> Balzac's penetration into the room, and the reader's, is justified within the structure of the novel by the fact that the husband, Jules, has just caught the virus of suspicion passed along to him by Auguste de Maulincour, so that our penetration of the holy ground coincides with a parallel penetration of a psychological element foreign to its inner calm.[8]

Like Maulincour, Jules immerses himself in the business of spying—"la mer sans rivage des suppositions" (862; 38); and whereas Maulincour tried to displace Ferragus in order to dominate Clémence, Jules struggles to retain what he had thought was a complete claim to her affection: "Tu n'avais ni sœur, ni père, ni mère, ni compagne, et je n'étais alors ni au-dessus ni au-dessous de personne dans ton cœur: j'y étais seul" (842; 31). Again like his predecessor, Jules wants nothing less than complete knowledge, hence complete control: "'Ah! je veux tout savoir!' s'écria-t-il [Jules] dans un accès de rage" (850; 34). Just as Maulincour appears to attach himself to a surface in order to spy on Ferragus—he "se recula pour se coller en espalier sur le mur de l'autre côté de la rue" (789; 15)—so does Jules: "Il se colla aux vitres qui, dans son cabinet, se donnaient sur la rue" (862; 38). Maulincour is physically prevented from learning Ferragus's identity as Madame Jules's father; Jules is not. But in return for the privilege of an informed perspective, Jules is forced to adopt a posture that is symbolically awkward, tiring and voyeuristic: "Aussi Jules fut-il obligé, pour se maintenir là [in Madame Gruget's closet], et pour y bien voir, de rester dans une position assez fatigante, en se perchant sur un marchepied que la veuve Gruget avait eu soin d'apporter" (874; 42). It is as if the character, attempting to usurp the prerogative of the narrator—omniscience—is forced to assume a punishing and unnatural position in return for a momentary privilege.

The scene that Jules witnesses, the encounter of Ferragus and his daughter, is the "key" to the novel, in that the identity of Ferragus as parent and member of the Treize is finally confirmed. Again, the tension originating in a character's attainment of tenuous authority makes itself felt: the paternal love that is the source of the adventure resembles the jealousy of Maulincour and Jules, a passion impinging on Clémence's freedom of action —"Mon Dieu, mon père, tromper, tromper, quel supplice!" (877; 44)—and claiming her entire affection—"Ah! tu sais ce qu'est un amant, mais tu ne sais pas ce qu'est un père" (875; 43). Like Maulincour and Jules before him, Ferragus acts in covert, illicit fashion: he had secretly controlled the Desmarets's fortune ("Un de ses [Jules's] anciens camarades attribuait à Mme Jules la fortune de son mari, qu'il expliquait par une haute protection chèrement achetée" [808; 18]); although necessarily absent from their life except, peripherally, in his meetings with Clémence, he assumed a central position in it: "J'ai su que, depuis quatre ans, mon père et ses amis ont presque remué le monde pour mentir au monde. Afin de me donner un état, ils ont acheté un mort, une réputation, une fortune, tout cela pour faire revivre un vivant, tout cela pour toi, pour nous" (885-86; 47). Ferragus, like the Treize of which he is a member, acts indirectly, discreetly, in a socially marginal way. His identity as a pariah is dramatically illustrated by the automatic withdrawal of the passers-by surrounding him at the moment of his first appearance in the novel:

Soit que ses vêtements mouillés exhalassent une odeur fétide, soit qu'il eût à l'état normal cette senteur de misère qu'ont les taudis parisiens, de même que les bureaux, les sacristies et les hospices ont la leur, goût fétide et rance, dont rien ne saurait donner l'idée, les voisins de cet homme quittèrent leurs places et le laissèrent seul.

(817; 22)

The marginal presence of Ferragus is felt even more in the novel's form than it is in the novel's imaginary society.

In the implicit succession of perspective from Maulincour to Jules, culminating in the revelation of Ferragus's relationship to Clémence, the source of thematic tension in which the plot originates has been exhausted, the apparent contradiction eliminated. Now that the continuous points of view have led to Ferragus, the father and motivating force behind all of the preceding events, we have reached the climax not only of the plot, but also of the drama of perspective. Two conditions will now influence the progression of the narrative: first, the guiding intelligence of Ferragus has been eclipsed and will no longer control the course of events; and second, the unmasking of his name and past prompts public recognition of his identity, an identity of relation (parent to child). The forthcoming transferral of perspective from Jules to an impersonal, "omniscient" voice must accommodate these two unexpected complications.

What had constituted the base of Ferragus's vision all along has been his willful suppression of his past history as a criminal, a fact irrevocably impressed not only into public memory, but also physically into his flesh, by means of a brand. In other words, his vision was anchored in a denial of a symbol representing historical experience, his own former self—a rejection of the denotative power of symbol and its influence. Thus, as Jules looks on from his post in the closet just before his wife arrives, he witnesses this scene:

> Jules aperçut en effet un homme occupé à panser un cordon de plaies, produites par une certaine quantité de brûlures pratiquées sur les épaules de Ferragus. . . . Je redeviendrai donc quelque chose de social, un homme parmi les hommes, et je vaux bien le marin qu'ont mangé les poissons [Ferragus plans to adopt the identity of an ambassador thus killed]. Dieu sait si c'est pour moi que je me fais comte!
> —Pauvre Gratien, toi, notre plus forte tête, notre frère chéri, tu es le Benjamin de la bande, tu le sais. (874-75; 42-43)

The Treize, in their first overt appearance in the trilogy, conspire to eradicate a socially applied, socially meaningful sign—a stigma—that is Ferragus's identifying mark. In a sense, for characters to engage in such activity —erasing a sign, attacking an authorized symbol—is to subvert the author's creation in principle. It is as if, because of his secret rebellion against the figure-making process, Ferragus will no longer dominate the plot of the novel. It is also with Madame Jules's arrival—"Pauvre père, comment allez-vous?" (875; 43)—that the male rivalry for possession of her will end. If Maulincour, Jules and Ferragus are like sons ready to usurp a father's power, Ferragus's or the author's, it is also true that the female characters are like oppressed, silenced daughters. Appropriately, the theme of blood relationship, and specifically of daughterhood, literally erupts into the text:

> En ce moment, un cri terrible retentit dans la chambre où était M. Jules Desmarets.
> —Ma fille, ma pauvre fille! . . . Qui sauvera ma fille, demanda la veuve Gruget. . . .
> —Et comment? demanda machinalement M. Jules stupéfait d'avoir été reconnu par sa femme. (877-78; 44)

Madame Gruget's daughter Ida, Ferragus's mistress, has been driven to commit suicide for her knowledge of his secret paternity; and, as if part of a chain reaction, Madame Jules becomes ill in a way implicating suicide: having disobeyed her doctor's orders in going to see Ferragus, "Elle a voulu se tuer" (880; 45). The pathological cause of her death, an amenorrhea,[9] symbolizes not only her protective reticence ("je meurs victime d'une discrétion nécessaire" [883; 46]), but also that artificial reticence imposed on her by the narrative voice in its several guises, all of which are masculine. That the voice of the narrator now becomes her own—immediately after her death Jules reads her lengthy testament—may well be a form of poetic justice rendered the female characters. It is as if the authorial consciousness governing the novel belatedly acknowledges its own necessary feminine component, its own universality. It is the theme of relation, not difference, that surfaces in the letter; Madame Jules is clearly her father's daughter:

"Après avoir aimé comme nous aimions, il n'y a plus que Dieu.... Je te prie de brûler tout ce qui nous aura appartenu, de détruire notre chambre, d'anéantir tout ce qui peut être un souvenir de notre amour" (886-87; 47). The riddle of Ferragus's identity solved, the narrator intervenes: "Ici semble finir le récit de cette histoire" (891; 49), the distinction between narration and story reminding of the work's formal dimension. What makes *Ferragus* more than a mystery novel is its ending, which integrates the "mystery" of the "histoire" into the design of the "récit." Because the narrator records Jules's ordeal through the close of the novel, the continuity of the narrative is not broken by the shift of emphasis. The narrator now launches into a long, almost excruciatingly detailed description of Jules's encounter with the Parisian bureaucracy in his effort to obtain permission to cremate his wife's remains. The setting, of course, will be the Père-Lachaise cemetery: "C'est une infâme comédie! c'est encore tout Paris avec ses rues, ses enseignes, ses industries, ses hôtels; mais vu par le verre dégrossissant de la lorgnette, un Paris microscopique..." (898; 51).

The detail lavished on this next-to-the-last scene has its justification: it is part of that "léger croquis de la vie parisienne" (891; 49) in whose gruesome aspects the narrator has delighted all throughout the novel. It might be argued that the many sketches of the city in *Ferragus* exist at the expense of the plot, though delightfully so: "dans le récit de [cette aventure] les digressions étaient en quelque sorte le sujet principal pour l'auteur" (904). But Paris is not merely a colorful backdrop for the melodramatic plot; it is a symbol of integration and assimilation: "A Paris, les différents sujets qui concourent à la physionomie d'une portion quelconque de cette monstrueuse cité s'harmonisent admirablement avec le caractère de l'ensemble" (866; 40). It is Paris that in the opening scene dictates the norms for judgment which spur Maulincour to action; it is a labyrinth, "un dédale" (843; 31), in which every character is lost or disoriented—morally, physically, spiritually. None of the characters is completely innocent, none is immune to social influence. The line between social determinism and personal responsibility is not clearly drawn; as Jean Paris remarks, "les deux séries, conjointes et contraires, de l'*innocence* et de la *culpabilité* se développent... parallèlement tout au long du livre, l'adjonction des divers personnages n'ayant pour effet que de renforcer le dilemme, de le *ramifier* ...."[10] Maulincour, Jules and Ferragus come to see Paris as the monstrous source of pain and illusion. As the bereaved husband learns of bureaucratic stalling on his request, the city comes to symbolize for him a crucible of contradictions: "Rien ne lui semblait plus naturel que d'anéantir ce réceptacle de monstruosités" (891; 49). Like Derville in *Le Colonel Chabert* and Rastignac in *Le Père Goriot*, he is seized with horror at the sight of "civilization":

Il embrassa d'un coup d'œil furtif ces quarante mille maisons, et dit, en montrant l'espace compris entre la colonne de la place Vendôme et la coupole d'or des Invalides: "Elle m'a été enlevée là, par la funeste curiosité de ce monde qui s'agite et se presse, pour se presser et s'agiter." (898; 51)

As Jules looks out upon the city with rage and despair, a burial takes place in Neuilly, in a cemetery "entouré de murs en ruines, champ plein de monticules; ni marbres, ni visiteurs" (899; 52). The carefully concerted contrast between the burials of Madame Jules and now Ida reminds us that indeed an underlying esthetic consciousness has directed the narration. Now it is permissible for the defeated Ferragus to inscribe his identity, "Moribundus Pater" (900; 52), on the funerary urn he has obtained for Jules, formally announcing his relation to its contents in the simplest and most eloquent of terms.

In the final scene the narrator brings us back to his mood and setting of the beginning of the novel; again he strikes the pose of the *flâneur* in Paris:

Qui n'a pas rencontré sur les boulevards de Paris, au détour d'une rue ou sous les arcades du Palais-Royal, enfin en quelque lieu du monde où le hasard veuille le présenter, un être, un homme ou femme, à l'aspect duquel mille pensées confuses naissent en l'esprit! A son aspect, nous sommes subitement intéressés ... sans que nous nous expliquions bien précisément la cause de notre émotion. (900; 52)

Again we are invited to identify with this inquisitive, impressionable spectator whose own "émotion," "pensées" or sensitivity is the subject of his expressed concern. Again the monstrous incongruity of the spectacle—this time a human being—need not obsess him; it is only a "rêve passager" (901; 52) that bears limited scrutiny, reflection. This time the paradox his vision seizes upon does not involve social reputation, but a kind of unnaturally perpetuated life; as he inspects those "créations errantes" (901; 52) haunting public places, the narrator remarks: "Il est impossible de savoir si l'on a oublié de les enterrer, ou si elles se sont échappées du cercueil; elles sont arrivées à un état quasi fossile" (901; 52). The spectacle of the dying Louis Lambert or Baron de Maulincour could have as easily inspired these words: intellectual deterioration and physical deterioration seem to be for Balzac one and the same.

The narrator takes us to the Paris Observatory and describes a specific site:

... l'espace enfermé entre la grille sud du Luxembourg et la grille nord de l'Observatoire, espace sans genre, espace neutre dans Paris. En effet, là, Paris n'est plus; et là, Paris est encore. Ce lieu tient à la fois de la place, de la rue, du boulevard, de la fortification, du jardin, de l'avenue, de la route, de la province, de la capitale; certes, il y a tout cela; mais ce n'est rien de tout cela: c'est un désert.... tous les vices et tous les malheurs de Paris ont là leur asile ... la Science y étudie les marées et les longitudes:

M. de Chateaubriand y a mis l'infirmerie Marie-Thérèse, et les Carmélites y ont fondé un couvent. (901-02; 53)

Despite the variety of sights, asylums, visitors, residents, this section of Paris —or rather the narrator's view of it—generates none of the inner tensions animating the Paris of the opening scene, that consuming, fiery, agitated beast. Here the proliferation of detail does not give life to a figure or imaginary monster; the conflicting observations cancel each other out: "c'est un désert." The narrator's frustration is visible—"ce n'est rien de tout cela" —and yet he has simply stated that his vision of the city can only be metaphorical: "là, Paris n'est plus; et là, Paris est encore." Even in this bleak setting poetry is possible, images given permanence in language.

As in the beginning of the novel, replete with figures designated vaguely —"un jeune homme," "une femme élégante"—so here we are introduced to an unnamed figure: "la créature la plus saillante de ces groupes, qui, s'il était permis d'assimiler les Parisiens aux différentes classes de la zoölogie, appartiendraient au genre des mollusques" (902; 53). It is of course Ferragus, metaphorically humbled for having once usurped the identity of "le marin qu'ont mangé les poissons" (875; 43). We see him, formerly among the "rois inconnus" (792; 12) of society, presiding over a game of bowls, immobile, leaning against a tree:

Vous l'eussiez pris pour le génie fantastique du cochonnet. Il ne disait rien, et les joueurs de boules ... ne lui avaient jamais demandé compte de ce silence obstiné; seulement, quelques esprits forts le croyaient sourd et muet. Dans les occasions où il fallait déterminer les différentes distances entre les boules et le cochonnet, la canne de l'inconnu devenait alors la mesure infaillible, les joueurs venaient alors la prendre dans les mains glacées de ce vieillard, sans la lui emprunter par un mot, sans même lui faire un signe d'amitié. Le prêt de sa canne était comme une servitude à laquelle il avait négativement consenti. Quand il survenait une averse, il restait près du cochonnet, esclave des boules, gardien de la partie commencée. La pluie ne le surprenait pas plus que le beau temps, et il était, comme les joueurs, une espèce intermédiaire entre le Parisien qui a le moins d'intelligence, et l'animal qui en a le plus. (902-03; 53)

Ferragus has not even the energy to draw figures with his cane, in imitation of Colonel Chabert; he has lost the will—or the ability—to speak, is stripped of every possible characteristic that could have made of him an artist figure. A "création errante," like Lambert the "création," Ferragus is described as a biological anomaly caught in an intermediate state of evolutionary development, a regression. Ferragus is neither man nor beast; he has fittingly retired to that "espace sans genre, espace neutre dans Paris" where he is simply an "être." Having removed the brand from his back, he no longer has identifying traits; even gender is denied him. Thus, the ending subtly transforms him into a monstrous figure, the personification of the city of Paris haunting and luring the narrator in the first pages of the novel. We have come full circle.

One small detail of this scene recapitulates the entire drama of the novel. Reminiscent of his initial appearance in the novel, when he directed his gaze briefly upon passers-by in a doorway—"Il y eut enfin tout un drame dans le mouvement de ses paupières flétries" (817; 42)—this brief notation epitomizes Ferragus's decline: "Il était béant, sans idées dans le regard, sans appui précis dans la démarche: il ne souriait jamais, ne levait jamais les yeux au ciel, et les tenait habituellement baissées vers la terre, et semblait toujours y chercher quelque chose" (901; 53). It had been Ferragus's previously unfathomable vision that had lent coherence to the mysterious turns of plot; it had been his ability to anticipate and thwart conventional responses to events that had dictated their outcome. His attempted change of identity was, like Maulincour and Jules's quest, a usurpation of society's prerogative to assign reputations. In the final scene Ferragus's vision has deteriorated to a mere fixation—more precisely a fixation on this "lieu sans nom" (901; 53) that is Paris and yet is not Paris. He looks for a recognizable sign—or rather a sign of recognition—that he cannot and will not find. Like the balls skimming the surface of the ground, he has left no permanent trace of his passage. The convict no longer exists; the Comte de Funcal, his adopted self, now has no reason for being. In losing Clémence, Ferragus lost the source and sustenance of his being—"Est-ce MOI enfin, moi qui ne respire que par ta bouche, moi qui ne vois que par tes yeux, moi qui ne sens que par ton cœur, est-ce moi qui ne saurais pas défendre avec des ongles de lion, avec l'âme d'un père, mon seul bien, ma vie, ma fille?" (876; 43)—and the need for his paternal foresight.

At last Jules passes by:

Jules, croyant reconnaître cette figure, voulut s'arrêter et sa voiture s'arrêta précisément. En effet, la postillon, serré par des charrettes, ne demanda point passage aux joueurs de boules insurgés, il avait trop de respect pour les émeutes, le postillon.

—C'est lui, dit Jules en découvrant enfin dans ce débris humain Ferragus XXIII, chef des Dévorants. Comme il l'aimait! ajouta-t-il après une pause. Marchez donc, postillon!" cria-t-il. (903; 53)

Jules and the coachman, stopped by a harmless insurrection, make us pause at the edge of the world circumscribed by the novel. In making that gesture of recognition Ferragus had once so urgently craved, Jules pays brief, reverent, but passing tribute to his wife's father, now a "débris humain." Holding himself at a physical remove, Jules makes a detached, disinterested observation—"Comme il l'aimait!"—reminding us also of the progressively detached perspective in the novel. In the end we are left with ambiguous presences, neither tragic nor imposing; Ferragus is not Lear, Jules is not

Job. Although the narrator characterizes the setting as a desert and Ferragus as sub-human, he does not tell us whether the scene is the final stage of a spiritual pilgrimage or simply a picturesque accident. There is no point of reference; the narrative voice is impassive, the figures muted. The pathos of Ferragus's loss of identity reminds us of the arbitrary nature of conventional symbolism, of the accidental and indelible nature of social identity; it also cautions us against a literal reading of the novel, since that loss is ambiguous. Such an ending does not imply the wholeness of experience, but rather its discontinuity; it does not require further elaboration in the form of another narrative. *Ferragus* is complete in and of itself.

Although the use of narrative perspective in *Ferragus* involves three distinct phases, the novel as a whole does not preclude the consistency of Balzac's authorial vision. The treatment of the central themes illustrates an identifying trait of Balzac's esthetic: the revelation of a conflict inherent in two different levels of meaning, the mimetic and the symbolic. The various actions of the Treize are specific, ingenious and possible; the male and female characters are convincingly portrayed; the sketches of Paris are entertaining and picturesque. It is when the narrative illustrates symbolic truths —the inescapable, unremitting solitude of the individual; the inalterable difference between men and women; the failure of the city, of civilization, to control instinctive drives—that disruption occurs, distorting naturalistic situations beyond belief and reducing harrowing spiritual adventures to a mundane context. Everything confirms Baudelaire's characterization of Balzac the artist as realist and visionary.

In the *Histoire des Treize* the conflict in the levels of meaning leads to the grotesque scenes of Maulincour's death and Jules's awkward spying from a closet, Montriveau's attempt to brand Madame de Langeais's forehead, and Paquita's death. In their immediate context these scenes are unintelligible and disturbing. But they are truly Balzacian. In the *Treize* the continual passage of the three themes from the descriptive to the symbolic level creates correspondences between the novels in the form of analogous situations. But each instance of this type of recurrent imagery is not in itself a structure; it reposes on the inner structure of the individual novel, not on a collective foundation.

This is true also of another kind of recurrent imagery, the reappearing character. At least two of the characters in *Ferragus*, de Marsay and Ronquerolles, appear in *La Duchesse de Langeais* and *La Fille aux yeux d'or*. But the roles they play are not extensions of those given them in *Ferragus*. Like Clémence, Ida and Madame Gruget, the Duchesse de Langeais and the heroines of *La Fille* take on the traditional symbolic dimensions Balzac accords his female characters, but each character is distinct. The adventures of Montriveau and de Marsay are discrete episodes of personal history, although the three stories of the *Treize* all culminate in a terrible loss. The setting for all three is the same, but the Paris of *Ferragus* is not that of the other two novels. No single identifiable narrator guides us through these dissimilar adventures, though the narration of each is visibly controlled. The theme of vision, which opens *Ferragus*, is superseded by Balzac's own —the conception of the novel as a single formal entity. It is a severe, and severely comic, vision in which the universality of human behavior is demonstrated not by a pattern of progression from one novel to the next, but by the representation—the "répétition"—of the Human Comedy, shown from many perspectives, studied in many forms. As Proust once mused:

> Imaginons aujourd'hui un littérateur à qui l'idée serait venue de traiter vingt fois, avec des lumières diverses, le même thème, et qui aurait la sensation de faire quelque chose de profond, de subtil, de puissant, d'écrasant, d'original, de saisissant, comme les cinquante cathédrales ou les quarante nénuphars de Monet. Amateur passionné de peinture, il [Balzac] avait parfois joie à penser que lui aussi avait une belle idée de tableau, d'un tableau dont on raffolerait. Mais toujours c'était une idée, une idée dominante, et non une peinture non préconçue comme le croit Sainte-Beuve.[11]

One need not know *Ferragus* before reading *La Duchesse de Langeais* or *La Fille aux yeux d'or,* but it reveals no less than they the preoccupations of the artist who wrote them.

Chapter IV

HISTOIRE DES TREIZE: LA DUCHESSE DE LANGEAIS

In his book on Rodin, Rilke describes a great theme of the sculptor in words that apply also, appropriately, to Balzac: "There is something of the longing which makes great poets in all vice, in all lustful sins against nature, in all the desperate and vain attempts to find an eternal meaning for life. Here is humanity's hunger reaching out beyond itself; stretching out hands towards eternity."[1] In *La Duchesse de Langeais*[2] this pursuit of "eternal meaning" leads neither to mystical revelation, as, ambiguously, in *Louis Lambert,* nor to the fulfillment of sexual and emotional desire. Instead, the journey's destination is a poem: the poem in prose that is the narrative, and the conclusion pronounced by the hero Montriveau with reference to the eponymous heroine: "ce n'est plus qu'un poème" (1037; 103). Shown as "la sœur Thérèse" at the opening and close of the novel, the Duchesse de Langeais represents more than a dubious tribute to Saint Teresa: she embodies the common longing for transcendence of the self experienced, in their different spheres, by mystic and lover—both truth-seekers ready to find meaning beyond need of language.

Neither Montriveau nor "la sœur Thérèse" can be called an aspiring mystic; unlike Louis Lambert, they contain their desire in the realm of poetical discourse prescribed by the narrator. Montriveau cannot tolerate ambiguity or compromise in speech; like the cruelly deceived Colonel Chabert, he makes the error of confusing conventional language with literal representation of fact. As the Duchess professes love all the while refusing to express it physically, Montriveau plans retaliation: a crude, and aborted, attempt to brand her forehead with a convict's stigma, as if literally to render his judgment against her. Thus confronted, the Duchess in turn recognizes her obligation to relate words to action, thought to expression, if not in the simplistic sense understood by Montriveau. Each character introduces the other to the complexity of symbol, the Duchess discovering the necessity of common reference, Montriveau in the end embracing the non-literal, his "poème." The theme of the conflict between the sexes takes on the cosmic dimensions suggested by Rilke's words as the characters evolve a more comprehensive and tolerant understanding of symbolic expression. What Louis Lambert experiences as a conflict—sexual desire and the desire for "eternal meaning"—in *La Duchesse de Langeais* is one and the same yearning.

The use of flashback in the narration of the story frees the narrator from the restriction of adopting the uninformed perspective of a character, as in *Ferragus*, and allows him to engage in the active reconstruction of an episode presumably buried in Montriveau's memory. Thus, although there is a symbolic kinship between Montriveau and Louis Lambert, the narrator of *La Duchesse de Langeais* emphasizes a consciousness of art and not of genius: the later work is indeed the "œuvre plus ou moins poétique" (XI, 692; VII, 323) shunned by Lambert's biographer. The narrator of *La Duchesse de Langeais* emphasizes thematically as well the importance of memory: as Montriveau holds the dead "sœur Thérèse" in his arms, he contemplates the same truth to which Chabert woke at Eylau: that reduction of Life to Death, resisted only by remembering fully who we are. Like Chabert, Ferragus and Louis Lambert, Montriveau must learn that possession of what one loves—knowledge, privilege, children, the beloved—is never absolute. Unlike them, he refrains from authorship, laying down his branding iron and seeking neither pen nor lawyer nor forged papers to establish his identity; and perhaps Balzac symbolically rewards him for this restraint by leaving his faculties intact at the novel's end.

Although the dramatic effect of *La Duchesse de Langeais* depends largely upon the unorthodox use of chronology, the reconstructed plot suggests its colorful mixture of Gothic horror and Human Comedy. The General Armand de Montriveau, returned from Napoleon's army in Egypt, falls passionately in love with the young Duchesse de Langeais in Paris. Although attracted to the General, she is unwilling to commit herself to him; and in a moment of rage and frustration he kidnaps her with the aid of the Treize and threatens to brand her as a criminal. Love triumphs, and he declines to do so; and after the event she repents of her detachment and sends messages to him openly declaring her love, among them the stationing of her carriage, bearing the family coat of arms, at his door. When Montriveau does not answer, the Duchess flees in despair to a Carmelite convent on an island off the coast of Spain. Montriveau tracks her down and vows to return with the Treize to abduct her; but when at last they enter her cell, they find only her mortal remains. The narrative begins with Montriveau's first encounter with "la sœur Thérèse" in the convent parlor, returns to the setting of the Faubourg Saint-Germain ("L'Amour dans la paroisse de Saint Thomas-d'Aquin") and the earlier episode of the kidnapping ("La Femme vraie"), and concludes with the final rescue of the cloistered Duchess ("Dieu fait les dénouements").

Balzac originally gave *La Duchesse de Langeais* an epigraph taken from Saint Teresa of Avila's *Way of Perfection* which describes the vehemence and purity of spiritual friendship. Although the epigraph disappeared from the Furne edition of *La Comédie humaine*, the chapter heading "La sœur Thérèse" in itself alludes to the Spanish saint and, therefore, indirectly to the Christian mystical tradition and to the theme of the grandeur of Spain. Geographically and spiritually, we are a world removed from the sordid, materialistic Paris we found in *Ferragus*, but that is of no matter. We are literally a world removed from *Ferragus*: we have begun another novel.

The very first lines of *La Duchesse de Langeais* describe a Carmelite convent in which the reformed rule introduced by Saint Teresa is strictly observed, with the assurance to us worldly readers that this fidelity to tradition "est vrai, quelque extraordinaire qu'il puisse paraître" (905; 54). The convent is a relic of a former age, strangely intact, and its inhabitants are oblivious to the march of history: "Si le nom de l'empereur vint bruire jusque sur cette plage, il est douteux que son fantastique cortège et les flamboyantes majestés de sa vie météorique aient été comprises par les saintes filles agenouillées dans ce cloître" (905; 54).

But this tribute to the enduring success of Saint Teresa's reform is qualified by the narrator's insinuation that the convent is remarkable precisely because it is an anachronism. This is an assessment he will make again in reference to the Faubourg Saint-Germain. The respectful, wondering tone with which he describes the color of the sea and the chapel's Gothic exterior is inspired not so much by an appreciation of their beauty as by a desire to magnify the mock-heroic dimensions of the hero's transgression of holy ground. In the typical pattern of Balzac's dramatic expositions, an unnamed character, "un général français" (908; 55), emerges from the setting, having found "sous ses murailles et dans ces chants [the liturgical music sung in the chapel] les légers indices qui justifièrent son frêle espoir" (908; 55). It is not that the passions of history and of the senses have been forcibly excluded from within the convent walls; it is rather that they have almost imperceptibly infiltrated an environment visibly opposed to them— geographically, architecturally, spiritually. And as in the narrator's self-conscious approach to the bedroom in *Ferragus* (838; 29), the tone and the theme of insinuation warn us of the impending dramatic upheaval and flood of erotically charged language that will foreshadow the boudoir scenes of the second chapter.

It appears at first that Balzac calls upon the image of Saint Teresa only to turn it against her, but this is not entirely so. The narrator attributes certain aspects of mystical love—the singlemindedness of devotion, the all-consuming longing of the soul—to the Duchesse de Langeais and Montriveau's romance, and we cannot help but marvel with him: "L'amour arrive rarement à la solennité; mais l'amour encore fidèle au sein de Dieu, n'était-ce pas quelque chose de solennel, et plus qu'un homme n'avait le droit d'espérer au dix-neuvième siècle, par les mœurs qui courent?" (918; 59). He does not confuse the ardor of spiritual feeling and erotic passion; if he did, the humor and irony of the situation would be lost. But it is only much later in the novel that the narrator explicitly makes the distinction: "L'extase religieuse est la folie de la pensée dégagée de ses liens corporels; tandis que, dans l'extase amoureuse, se confondent, s'unissent et s'embrassent les forces de nos deux natures" (1009; 92). In the first chapter he is openly playing on the ambiguity of meaning his context gives the allusion to mysticism; he withholds the precise definition, in order that his readers may follow the narration "sans que la réflexion nuise à leurs plaisirs" (972; 79). The "daring" evocation of Saint Teresa is one of many incongruities: the shift of the setting to Spain, the convent as anachronism, the improbability of Montriveau's adventure and the discovery of a truly grand passion in such a jaded age and in such an unlikely setting.

Montriveau, still "le général" (909; 55), is quick to perceive the guiding intelligence of the Duchess, "la sœur" (909; 55), behind the musical offerings performed in thanksgiving for "cette petite Restauration insulaire" (909; 55). Instead of inspiring awe and piety, the music provides purely esthetic pleasure for the French soldiers and officers, two of them "vrais *dilettanti*, qui regrettaient sans doute en Espagne le théâtre Favart" (909; 55). Into her interpretation of the *Te Deum* "la sœur introduisit des motifs qui respirèrent toute la délicatesse du goût parisien, et auxquels se mêlèrent vaguement les pensées de nos plus beaux airs nationaux" (910; 56), thereby reducing to a particular and nationalistic context that which should have been universal, anonymous, sublime. The narrator adds to our amusement, our feigned outrage at the playful imitation of sacrilege, by detecting in the phrasing of the music an echo of a song associated with a domestic, and profane, setting—"le vague rappel d'un air délicieux de mélancolie, l'air *Fleuve du Tage*, romance française dont souvent il [Montriveau] avait entendu jouer le prélude dans un boudoir à Paris à la personne qu'il aimait" (910; 56).

Like Montriveau, who counterfeits first illness, to buy time, and then piety, to gain an interview with Sœur Thérèse, the narrator grows bolder and more ambitious, and he gives a splendid performance. The communication he relates is entirely non-verbal: the underlying themes of the sacred music ("elle [Sœur Thérèse] lui raconta ses longues mélancolies et lui dépeignait sa lente maladie morale" [913; 57]), the meaning of the echo of Montriveau's spurs on the marble floor of the chapel (912; 56). In the course of the narration he makes the erotic overtones of the music explicit:

> Ce chant de joie, consacré par la sublime liturgie de la Chrétienté romaine pour exprimer l'exaltation de l'âme en présence des splendeurs du Dieu toujours vivant, devint l'expression d'un cœur presque effrayé de son bonheur.... (912; 56)
>
> Toutes ces richesses sacrées semblèrent être jetées comme un grain d'encens sur le frêle autel de l'amour à la face du trône éternel d'un Dieu jaloux et vengeur. (912-13; 57)

The narrator delights in the jarring of contexts from the sacred to the profane, the ineffable to the sensual, the solemn to the frivolous:

> En effet, la joie de la religieuse n'eut pas ce caractère de grandeur et de gravité qui doit s'harmonier avec les solennités du *Magnificat*; elle lui donna de riches, de gracieux développements, dont les différents rythmes accusaient une gaieté humaine. (913; 57)
>
> Elle [the voice of Sœur Thérèse] faisait à l'âme l'effet que produit aux yeux un filet d'argent ou d'or dans une frise obscure. (915; 57)

Like the narrative voice in the opening passage of *Ferragus*, the narrator in *La Duchesse de Langeais* intercepts signals from the setting and transmits them to the reader. He too refers to the poetic sensitivity that enables him to be a reliable and discriminating witness: "S'il faut un cœur de poète pour faire un musicien, ne faut-il pas de la poésie et de l'amour pour écouter, pour comprendre les grandes œuvres musicales?" (914; 57). Again like the narrator in *Ferragus*, he involves the reader in the scene by the use of forms of direct address: we are invited to visualize the scene, to draw upon our experience:

> Jetez ce paysage au milieu de la Méditerranée, sous un ciel brûlant; accompagnez-le de quelques palmiers, de plusieurs arbres rabougris.... (906; 54)
>
> Eh! bien, étendez cette espèce de rage sur cinq années; mettez une femme, un cœur, un amour à la place de ce rien; transportez la passion dans les plus hautes régions de sentiment.... (911; 56)
>
> Quand les airs eurent, par degrés, cessé leurs vibrations oscillatoires, vous eussiez dit que l'église, jusque-là lumineuse, rentrait dans une profonde obscurité. (913; 57)

However, the effects of the appeals to the reader's attention in the two novels are opposite. In *Ferragus* the reader is drawn into Maulincour's fundamental error by the obstructed vision of the narration; in *La Duchesse de Langeais* the reader is made accomplice to the flouting of convention performed both by the unrepentant characters and by the narrator. In *Ferragus* the issue is only the fall of a Platonic idol; here everything is at stake:

> Les grandeurs infinies de cette situation pouvaient agir sur l'âme du général, il était précisément assez élevé pour oublier la politique, les honneurs, l'Espagne, le monde

de Paris, et monter jusqu'à la hauteur de ce dénouement grandiose.... Combien de sentiments dans la situation des deux amants seuls réunis au milieu de la mer sur un banc de granit, mais séparés par une idée, par une barrière infranchissable! (918; 59)

It is in the interview that the protagonists actually confront that insurmountable barrier, a motif suggested as a theme of Sœur Thérèse's music (915; 58) and symbolized by the music itself, an incorporeal translation of physical passion. Thus, Montriveau, representing those forces restoring Roman Catholicism to political power in Spain, enters a room pervaded by the essence of spirituality, by a sense of the awful finitude of mortal existence: "Quelque chose de grand comme la tombe le saisit sous ces frais planchers. N'était-ce pas son silence éternel, sa paix profonde, ses idées d'infini?" (917; 58). Light pours in on one side, behind the grille, dimly reflecting upon the works of art on the other:

Le jour ne venait dans cette salle que par deux fenêtres situées dans la partie affectée aux religieuses, en sorte que cette faible lumière, mal reflétée par un bois à teintes brunes, suffisait à peine pour éclairer le grand Christ noir, le portrait de sainte Thérèse et un tableau de la Vierge qui décoraient les parois grises du parloir. (917; 58)

The grille divides the parlor into two symbolic zones: one of death, transparency and contemplation; the other of life, art and action. The male and female principles are divided: on one side the Carmelite without age or past and the mother superior who hovers at her side like the presence of death (reminding us of Madame Gruget in *Ferragus* and the duenna in *La Fille aux yeux d'or*), on the other the illustrious general intent this time on a personal victory. The simplicity of speech and humility of Sœur Thérèse, who twice reminds her visitor to call her by her adopted name, underscore the selfish motives of the general. Answering in Spanish to her superior, she admits her acquaintance with the "cavalier" (919; 59) and obediently turns to leave when ordered to do so. On Montriveau's side lies all the vanity of a self-interested pursuit, of French military glory and, interestingly, of the French language; on the side of Sœur Thérèse, all the virtues of renunciation, obedience and truthful speech. In true Romantic spirit, the encounter represents the clash of two nations: the glittering, artificial world of French culture, the stark and imposing splendor of Spain. For a moment the "burning symphonies" (914; 57) of the chapel scene are forgotten.

But the symbolic equilibrium is only precarious. Sœur Thérèse upsets the balance by a shameless play on words—"Ma Mère, dit-elle d'un ton de voix horriblement calme, ce Français est un de mes frères" (920; 59)—and initiates a conversation with Montriveau that tells more by its tone than by its presumed substance: "De quelle valeur étaient donc les mots, les regards, les gestes dans une scène où l'amour devait échapper à des yeux de lynx, à des griffes de tigre!" (920; 59). In sharp contrast to her previous words and bearing, Sœur Thérèse launches into a speech animated by shallow and contradictory pieties, full of devotional rhetoric:

> —Vous voyez, mon frère, ce que j'ose faire pour vous entretenir un moment de votre salut, et des vœux que mon âme adresse pour vous chaque jour au ciel. Je commets un péché mortel. J'ai menti. Combien de jours de pénitence pour effacer ce mensonge! mais ce sera souffrir pour vous. . . . Si les doctrines, si l'esprit de la sainte à laquelle nous devons cet asile ne m'avaient pas enlevée loin des misères terrestres, et ravie bien loin de la sphère où elle est, mais certes au-dessus du monde, je ne vous eusse pas revu.
> (920; 59)

Naturally, Montriveau interrupts at the first opportunity; and it becomes obvious that Sœur Thérèse too attaches little importance to her words, being above all mindful of the exigencies of the situation: "Et, ajouta-t-elle après une pause, modérez-vous mon frère. Notre Mère nous séparerait impitoyablement, si votre visage trahissait des passions mondaines ou si vos yeux laissaient tomber des pleurs" (921; 59-60). Appearances must be observed, even when one is sending one's soul to its eternal perdition. It is only natural that the lovers converse in a language unknown to the mother superior; their unspiritual friendship is foreign to the religious setting. Their adoption of French tells us that we are not really far from Paris after all. And in the spirit of Parisian manners, Sœur Thérèse parodies the words of the saint after whom she calls herself—of whom she herself is a travesty:

Sœur Thérèse:

Je vous aime bien mieux que je ne vous ai jamais aimé. Je prie Dieu tous les jours pour vous, et je ne vous vois plus avec les yeux du corps. Si vous connaissiez, Armand, le bonheur de pouvoir se livrer sans honte à une amitié pure que Dieu protège! Vous ignorez combien je suis heureuse d'appeler les bénédictions du ciel sur vous. Je ne prie jamais pour moi; Dieu fera de moi suivant ses volontés. Mais vous, je voudrais, au prix de mon éternité, avoir quelque certitude que vous êtes heureux en ce monde, et que vous serez heureux en l'autre, pendant tous les siècles. (922; 60)

Saint Teresa:

C'est une chose merveilleuse que de voir combien cet amour est cordial et véhément; combien de larmes il fait répandre; combien d'oraisons il coûte; quel soin on prend de recommander à Dieu la personne aimée; quel désir presse le cœur de la voir heureuse; combien de mécontentements et de peines on ressent si, l'ayant trouvée en avant, on l'aperçoit après, tournée en arrière. On est toujours dans la crainte que cette âme qu'on chérit tant, ne prenne un mauvais chemin, et que, venant à se perdre, on en soit séparé à jamais. C'est, comme j'ai dit, un amour sans peu ni beaucoup de propre intérêt, tout ce qu'on veut, c'est de voir cette âme riche des dons du ciel.[3]

The dialogue as such constitutes another entertaining verbal irony, revealing the nature of the conflict between Montriveau and the Duchess. He is literal-minded, she speaks in figures:

Si vous avez été vraie jadis dans vos remords, vous ne devez pas hésiter à me suivre aujourd'hui.
—Vous oubliez que je ne suis pas libre.
—Le duc est mort, répondit-il vivement.
La sœur rougit.
—Que le ciel lui soit ouvert, dit-elle avec une vive émotion, il a été généreux pour moi. Mais je ne parlais pas de ces liens, une de mes fautes a été de vouloir les briser tous sans scrupule pour vous.
—Vous parlez de vos vœux, s'écria le général en fronçant les sourcils. Je ne croyais pas que quelque chose vous pesât au cœur plus que votre amour. (921-22; 60)

In another exchange, when she deliberately misconstrues his meaning, Montriveau dismisses her argument simply by identifying it as so many words:

—Antoinette, veux-tu me suivre?
—Mais je ne vous quitte pas. Je vis dans votre cœur, mais autrement que par un intérêt de plaisir mondain, de vanité, de jouissance égoïste. . . .
—Phrases que tout cela! (923; 60)

Finally, when Montriveau returns the volley of her words, accusing her of shallowness and threatening suicide, Sœur Thérèse abandons argument altogether and returns to her adopted language: "Ma Mère, cria la sœur Thérèse en espagnol, je vous ai menti, cet homme est mon amant!" (923; 60). For once, her words ring true; her exclamation is at once a retreat to the arms of religion, solitude and death, and a last unmistakable cry of longing: "Ah! elle m'aime encore! s'écria-t-il en comprenant tout ce qu'il y avait de sublime dans le cri de la religieuse, il faut l'enlever d'ici . . ." (923; 60).

In the scene opening the novel, and especially in these final words, Balzac brings together the symbolic and mimetic dimensions of his story. Forces greater than mortal passion and will militate not against the lovers' reconciliation, but against their reunion. These forces are a double sign: thematically, of divine intervention; formally, of the narrator's. (The chapter title "Dieu fait les dénouements" is a friendly gesture from one sovereign to another.) Even the characters reflect this conjunction of image and form. Their subversion of traditional symbolism—the meaning of words and music, of the military uniform and the religious habit—represents the social necessity of clothing explosive feelings in conventional garb. But this necessity originates in both the impropriety and the inexpressibility of such emotions. The scene dramatizes the role of convention in society and in art; it introduces us to a vision in which irony, humor, fantasy and realism are all one.

The first chapter isolates the subject of the novel, the dramatic conflict of the protagonists—a statement of theme unencumbered by analysis and thrown into relief by its unusual context. The characters are identified simply by their first names and roles—general, nun, duchess, lover; their personal histories remain untold. The poetic effect precedes its prosaic cause. The opening scene is like a chord majestically struck on the organ, its vibrations felt and protracted in the succeeding pages of the novel. The "volcanic eruption" (911; 56) of emotions occurring there will be prolonged and qualified in the second and third chapters. Thematically, "La sœur Thérèse" reveals that the forces of history, in the persons of Montriveau and the Duchess, had somehow swerved from their anticipated course, and predicts that they will not easily, if at all, turn back again. But what is impossible for ordinary men is possible for the narrator: he will take us back in time. And thus, even though we are returned to the unmysterious world of manners and history, the spell of the novel remains unbroken. We are taken by surprise, not jolted, by the narrator's intervention: "Voici maintenant l'aventure qui avait déterminé la situation respective où se trouvaient alors les deux personnages de cette scène" (923; 61).

Immediately follows, in what is now the second chapter, a long "aperçu semi-politique" (923; 61) of the Restoration aristocracy of the Faubourg Saint-Germain—from "Ce que l'on nomme en France..." to "... du drame national appelé les Mœurs" (923-24; 61-65). The relationship of this passage to the first chapter does not become apparent until just after its close, when we are told that the Duchesse de Langeais is the personification of the Faubourg: "le type le plus complet de la nature à la fois supérieure et faible, grande et petite, de sa caste" (934; 65). The events leading up to her flight to the Spanish convent and Montriveau's meeting with her there are, therefore, only the logical extension of the contradictions and tensions inherent in her milieu and at a precise historical moment—and as formulated by Balzac. However, though the narrator uses certain rhetorical devices reminiscent of the beginning of *Ferragus*, the passage is not an example of the use of restricted perspective to set a dramatic tone. Instead, it is an historical interpretation of the forces of convention, now relocated in a Parisian setting:

> Le Faubourg Saint-Germain s'est laissé momentanément abattre pour n'avoir pas voulu reconnaître les obligations de son existence qu'il lui était encore facile de perpétuer. Il devait avoir la bonne foi de voir à temps, comme le vit l'aristocratie anglaise, que les institutions ont leurs années climatériques où les mêmes mots n'ont plus les mêmes significations.... Ces idées veulent des développements qui appartiennent essentiellement à cette aventure, dans laquelle ils entrent, et comme définition des causes, et comme explication des faits. (927; 62)

In other words, the first part of the chapter "L'Amour dans la paroisse de Saint-Thomas-d'Aquin" is an authorial reflection upon the meaning of the plot; it is quite unlike the opening of *Ferragus*, in which the myopic narrator uncritically sets forth the closed system of social identities. The narrator in *La Duchesse de Langeais* is omniscient in that he is detached from the events in the novel and distinguishes its historical thesis from the ongoing drama. This omniscience, which is an analytical perspective with respect to the novel's structure, is visible in *Ferragus* at the moment the narrator distinguishes between "récit" and "histoire." However, no matter what the narrator's distance from the story, Balzac's voice is always the same, and the narrator's definition of the Faubourg Saint-Germain recalls both the opening passage of *Ferragus* and the Preface to the *Histoire des Treize*:

Ce que l'on nomme en France le faubourg Saint-Germain n'est ni un quartier, ni une secte, ni une institution, ni rien qui se puisse nettement exprimer. La place Royale, le faubourg Saint-Honoré, la Chaussée d'Antin possèdent également des hôtels où se respire l'air du faubourg Saint-Germain. Ainsi, déjà tout le faubourg n'est pas dans le faubourg. (923; 61)

The first sentence, a definition by process of elimination, calls to mind the use of delimiting characteristics to describe the Treize in the Preface: "Ce monde à part dans le monde..." (791; 11).[4] The narrator refers to an intangible quality—here the influence of the Faubourg Saint-Germain— and not to physical detail, just as the narrator of the opening scene in *Ferragus* describes not the streets of Paris, but their reputation. Moreover, the theme of inexpressibility—the Faubourg is nothing "qui se puisse nettement exprimer"—announces a poetic, and not scientific, exposition of the subject. Like the rhetoric of the Preface and of the first scene of *Ferragus*, it calls upon the reader's sensitivity to the complex and tentative balance of words and phrases which seemingly embodies the referent. In sketching the background that makes Montriveau's interview with Sœur Thérèse unexceptionable and necessary, the omniscient narrator must make the spirit of their original encounter almost palpable to the reader—not the physical setting, which is in any case to be abandoned. Besides, Balzac's conception of the aristocracy precludes a strictly naturalistic approach to the subject: "une aristocratie est en quelque sorte la pensée d'une société, comme la bourgeoisie et les prolétaires en sont l'organisme et l'action" (925; 62).[5] The accuracy of the description of the Faubourg is a matter of opinion; its relationship to the other parts of the novel is a matter of form. Thus, the importance of the passage on the Faubourg lies in its reflection of "La Sœur Thérèse" and its anticipation of succeeding scenes in the novel.

Reminiscent of his insinuation into the inflexible structures of a Gothic chapel and of a system of belief, the narrator's approach to the Faubourg

Saint-Germain contrasts with the fixity of the subject. Like the Rock of Gibraltar setting, the Faubourg does not move; like the Carmelite rule, it will not bend. Just as Montriveau and Sœur Thérèse observe the appearances of piety without actually believing, so the aristocracy of the Faubourg preserves its traditions as a matter of form only:

> Penser est une fatigue, et les riches aiment à voir couler la vie sans grand effort. Aussi est-ce en comparant le fond des plaisanteries par échelons, depuis le gamin de Paris, jusqu'au pair de France, que l'observateur comprend le mot de monsieur de Talleyrand: *Les manières sont tout,* traduction élégante de cet axiome judiciaire: *La forme emporte le fond.* (1013; 94)

The Restoration, by definition an anachronism, is, like the convent, a vestige of a former era: "Si l'oligarchie française n'avait pas une vie future, il y aurait je ne sais quelle cruauté triste à la géhenner après son décès, et alors il ne faudrait plus que penser à son sarcophage; mais si le scalpel des chirurgiens est dur à sentir, il rend parfois la vie aux mourants" (923; 64). The narrator's ambivalence and the incongruity of the Restoration itself are translated, theme and style, into the portrait of the Duchesse de Langeais at the end of the passage:

> C'était une femme artificiellement instruite, réellement ignorante; pleine de sentiments élevés; mais manquant d'une pensée qui les coordonnât: dépensant les plus riches trésors de l'âme à obéir aux convenances; prête à braver la société, mais hésitant et arrivant à l'artifice par suite de ses scrupules.... Ne serait-ce pas toujours un portrait inachevé que celui de cette femme en qui les teintes les plus chatoyantes se heurtaient, mais en produisant une confusion poétique, parce qu'il y avait une lumière divine, un éclat de jeunesse, qui donnait à ces traits confus une sorte d'ensemble? (935; 65)

This description is an accumulation of paradoxes, like the introduction to the Treize in the Preface. But the forces of history, as interpreted by the narrator, convince us that such a character is possible; in turn, the possibility of such a character lends interest to, and is given substance by, the personal history that follows. Besides, we have already met the Duchess as Sœur Thérèse, and the narrator's second portrait is not simply a rhetorical flourish. If she is the "material expression" (959; 74) of the spirit of the Faubourg, she is also the Parisian incarnation of the spirit of Sœur Thérèse.

However, the ordering of the narrative subtly dramatizes the theme of the Duchess' tragedy: that Montriveau's words and gestures "n'apportaient aucun souvenir et ne réveillaient aucune image" (976-77; 80)—the sad heritage of a marriage of convenience. The reader, faced with an otherwise unintelligible passage, can reflect back upon the first chapter and the historical exposé to divine its meaning; the Duchess has no such privilege.[6] Madame de Langeais is incapable of reflection, thematically and symbolically; upon viewing Montriveau for the first time, "elle prit son lorgnon et l'examina fort impertinemment, comme elle eût fait d'un portrait qui reçoit des regards et n'en rend pas" (940; 67). The irony of her adoption of the contemplative life is not lost on the reader. When, in the course of relating a conversation, the narrator says, "Ces paroles représentent imparfaitement celles que fredonna la duchesse avec la vive prolixité d'une serinette" (976; 80), he is only transposing on the formal level the theme associated with the character: the imperfect correspondence of words and their referents.

The narrator's use of euphemism in the second chapter also recalls "La Sœur Thérèse." The "admirable jésuitisme" (919; 59) which made the continuation of the interview possible recurs in the "secret et jésuitique oukase" (979; 81) which enables the Duchess to become intimate with Montriveau while remaining within the bounds of propriety. Like those sensations whose expression is "interdite à la parole" (909; 55), those inspired by the erotic overtones of the sacred music, the sexual relations of the characters are also associated with the theme of inexpressibility: "mais pour l'honneur du faubourg Saint-Germain, il est nécessaire de ne pas révéler les mystères de ses boudoirs, où l'on voulait tout de l'amour moins ce qui pouvait attester l'amour" (978; 81). The conflict between the literal-minded Montriveau and the insincere Duchess reappears in the second chapter, again associated with the theme of adopted names (Madame de Langeais was originally Antoinette de Navarreins) and the theme of physical disorientation:

> Eh! mon Dieu, que nous font la France, le trône. la légitimité, le monde entier? Ce sont des billevesées auprès de mon bonheur. Régnez, soyez renversés, peu m'importe. Où suis-je donc?
> —Mon ami, vous êtes dans le boudoir de Mme la duchesse de Langeais.
> —Non, non, plus de duchesse, plus de Langeais, je suis près de ma chère Antoinette! (871; 78)

The general once again finds himself in alien territory: "elle lui refit *Le Génie du Christianisme* à l'usage des militaires" (968; 77).[7]

In this light, it is significant that Madame de Langeais's involvement with Montriveau begins not with their formal introduction, but with a dream she had had the previous night: "S'être trouvée dans les sables brûlants du désert avec lui, l'avoir eu pour compagnon de cauchemar, n'était-ce pas chez une femme de cette nature un délicieux présage d'amusement?" (946; 69). The nightmare produces an uncanny effect in the way that "La Sœur Thérèse" prepares the reader's surprise at recognizing the protagonists in a different setting: "La duchesse, déjà frappée par l'aspect de ce poétique personnage, le fut encore bien plus en apprenant qu'elle voyait en lui le marquis de Montriveau, de qui elle avait rêvé pendant la nuit" (946; 69). The dream also anticipates the kidnapping scene of the third chapter, in which the Duchess at last connects her gestures to emotions, words to meaning, form to content.

This scene, the climax of the novel, is one of those grotesque moments in Balzac when the symbolic and mimetic levels of meaning cross each other. Occurring midway in *La Duchesse de Langeais*, it recalls the emotional violence of the opening scene, it parodies the boudoir scenes in the second chapter, and it is itself balanced later by the episode in which Madame de Langeais sends her carriage to Montriveau's door. The placement of the scene within the novel and within the *Treize* is stunningly effective. The branding iron is a throwback to *Ferragus*; the mystery surrounding the location of Montriveau's chamber foreshadows the even greater mystery of Paquita's boudoir.

However, the scene is above all remarkable for its symbolic violence. It is not simply that the Gothic parody of the novel is stretched to its limits or that Madame de Langeais's humiliation, carried to the point of her puffing on Montriveau's cigars, seems in its abruptness a rather crude form of poetic justice. It is the transformation of a metaphor into action, a substitution of the literal for the figural, that is disconcerting.[8] At the end of the preceding chapter Montriveau had received the following advice from his friend Ronquerolles, which, true to character, he interprets literally:

> Sois inflexible comme la loi. N'aie pas plus de charité que n'en a le bourreau. Frappe. Quand tu auras frappé, frappe encore.... Ah! quand la douleur aura bien attendri ces nerfs, ramolli ces fibres que tu crois douces et molles; fait battre un cœur sec, qui à ce jeu, reprendra de l'élasticité; quand la cervelle aura cédé, la passion entrera peut-être dans cette machine à larmes, à manières, à évanouissements, à phrases fondantes; et tu verras le plus magnifique des incendies, si toutefois la cheminée prend feu. Ce système d'acier femelle aura le rouge du fer dans le forge! une chaleur plus durable que toute autre, et cette incandescence deviendra peut-être de l'amour. Néanmoins, j'en doute. (982-83; 83)

It is the reader, too, who is ridiculed by this sudden flouting of the conventions of reading. It is as if Balzac mocks our capacity to understand a figure of speech. In this convulsive moment in the text readers and characters alike are thrown into another context, in which they are overwhelmed by the literal meaning of words. Montriveau, at home, for once demonstrates the seriousness of his intentions in concrete form, the branding iron. Madame de Langeais for the first time associates words with meaning, emotions with action; the reader connects to Ronquerolle's words an actual fictional occurrence.

A lesser writer than Balzac, caught in such dramatic straits, would stand open to the charge of sensationalism. In light of Balzac's fiction generally, however, we can detect the author's "but de profonde moralité" in this melodramatic incident. Montriveau's recourse to the branding iron immediately establishes a symbolic relation between the Duchess and Ferragus: the latter erases his stigma, only to lose himself, and the former welcomes the one intended for her, only to become, in Balzac's words, "la femme vraie" (1003; 90). For the one the brand represents a public marking in accordance with social convention, the legal system; for the other it represents a private verdict rendered, in Montriveau's eyes, on the level of simple, unmediated justice. Symbolically speaking, for society to mark a man physically—that is, superficially—is within its province, whether it commits error or not; but for a man to assume absolute moral authority and thus mark others is both a confusion of codes (imposing the personal or ideal upon the social) and a usurpation of power. Balzac consistently punishes those characters who fail to make vital distinctions when wielding powerful symbols: not only is Montriveau unable to carry out his intended act, but he also, in the end, loses the Duchess to an unforgiving God ("Dieu fait les dénouements"—a God made in the author's own image). Moreover, Ferragus, Chabert and Louis Lambert, all of whom receive similar treatment in this respect, find their inability to master distinctions in symbolic expression related to their corresponding inability to possess their beloved: Ferragus loses his daughter, Chabert is repudiated by his wife, Louis Lambert resorts to self-destruction rather than marry Pauline. It is as if Balzac's fictional mythology insists again and again on the need to integrate acceptance of the self and of one's sexuality in the individual search for meaning. Montriveau's branding iron, metaphorically illustrating his desire, enables him to demonstrate—and the Duchess to contemplate—this Balzacian precept. As for the Duchess, her acknowledgement of the significance implied by her actions saves her from physical disfigurement and transforms her into her "true" self. Even if her symbolic punishment has the same effect as that meted out to Lambert and Ferragus, she at least is allowed to bow out of her novel gracefully.

Appropriately, we find this most discordant of scenes integrated esthetically into the novel. The description of Montriveau's room recalls the convent parlor of the first chapter: like "la pensée fixe du cloître" (917; 58), "l'âme et la pensée de [Montriveau] . . . planaient" (991; 86). Next to the bed an open doorway, hidden by a curtain reminiscent of the grille, separates the lovers from the Treize, who are heating the branding iron in the next room. The blindfold with which Montriveau intends to cover the Duchess' eyes reminds us of the headband of the veil worn by Sœur Thérèse (921; 60). The Duchess' words, "Mais je suis un peu curieuse" (1000; 89), spoken as Montriveau goes to kiss her, echo the Spanish chaplain's remark in the first chapter: "Je leur [to the Carmelites] ai dit l'objet de la messe, elles sont toujours un peu curieuses" (916; 58). Madame de Langeais's flight to a foreign and inaccessible location seems to be involuntarily repeated here: "La frayeur de la duchesse fut si grande qu'elle ne put jamais s'expliquer par où ni comment elle fut transportée" (991; 86). Montriveau warns her of the kidnapping in words borrowed from the English—"Ne touchez pas à la hache" (989; 85)—and again in Italian (990; 85); in the convent in Spain his native tongue, too, had been a foreign language.

Not only the chapter "La Sœur Thérèse," but also "L'Amour dans la paroisse de Saint-Thomas-d'Aquin" is evoked by the kidnapping scene. Montriveau relaxes in an armchair, wrapped in his robe, reversing the roles the characters played in the Duchess' boudoir: "Ne criez pas, madame la duchesse, dit-il en s'ôtant froidement son cigare de la bouche, j'ai la migraine" (991; 86). His exaggerated delicacy leads him to burn incense to clear the air, a gesture symbolically as evanescent and insubstantial as her previous shows of affection. Like Madame de Langeais in her natural setting, Montriveau is a virtuoso, adopting "l'air d'un maître de cérémonies" (999; 89). He delivers his words with an actor's flair for phrasing: "Ecoutez-moi bien, dit-il, en faisant une pause pour donner de la solennité à son discours" (993; 86); and at one point he gives himself a silent cue: "il se dit à lui-même: 'Je suis perdu, si je me laisse prendre à des disputes de mots'" (996; 88). His dissertation on social justice echoes the long speeches on religion and marriage formerly given by Madame de Langeais. For once, Montriveau is speaking her language and, like her, channeling sexual desire into a socially sanctioned form of expression, the branding iron. Moreover, the prophetic nightmare of the second chapter becomes an actual experience: "La terreur qu'Armand lui inspirait fut augmentée par une de ces sensations pétrifiantes, analogues aux agitations sans mouvement ressenties dans le cauchemar" (993; 86). These references to the other parts of the novel invite the reader to retaliate against the symbolic violence of the scene by perceiving its relationship to the whole, a splendid battle from which text, author and reader alike emerge victorious.

The convergence of themes in the kidnapping scene is further intensified by its central position in the *Histoire des Treize*. Montriveau's words explicitly refer to *Ferragus* and invoke its central theme—the irrevocability of social judgment: "Vous aurez enfin sur le front la marque infamante appliquée sur l'épaule de vos frères les forçats" (998; 88). The secrecy with which Madame de Langeais is conveyed to his apartment, as well as the slightly exotic touch of the incense, call to mind de Marsay's visits to Paquita in *La Fille aux yeux d'or*. At the same time the three motifs of the *Histoire des Treize* appear with all their inherent ambiguity. The Treize wait behind the curtain, ready to avenge Montriveau, and yet they do not

—a sign of their ultimate powerlessness. Two lovers confront each other, having finally reached a stage in which mutual understanding is possible, and yet, inexplicably, the barrier between them does not fall. The civilizing influence of Paris is reflected in the mimicry of its manners and the analysis of its caste system; but the precise location of the room is unknown, and the event taking place there is ultimately the rejection of a conventional and particularized background.

After this moment of symbolic upheaval and suspension, prolonged by the state of confusion—"un état de stupeur morale" (1004; 90)—in which the Duchess finds herself, the narrator signals that a turning point both in the story and in the narrative has been reached: "Quand une femme est en proie aux tyrannies furieuses sous lesquelles ployait Mme de Langeais, les résolutions définitives se succèdent si rapidement, qu'il est impossible d'en rendre compte.... Dès lors, les faits disent tout. Voici donc les faits" (1009; 92). The familiar language of the narrative intervention puts us back on familiar territory, and we leave the kidnapping scene behind. The narrator provides comic relief to that episode by presenting the scene in which Madame de Langeais publicly declares her love for Montriveau by sending her carriage to his door.

The reunion of the Navarreins family inspires a series of satirical sketches of such supremely outlandish characters that the narrator feels obliged to remark on the general eccentricity of the upper classes "pour empêcher les critiques de taxer de puérilité le commencement de la scène suivante" (1012; 93). (One can almost sense Proust waiting in the wings.) After leading Montriveau through an inferno of sorts, the narrator greets the reader with the wholly dispensable information that the general's uncle, the Comte de Montriveau, would eat twelve dozen oysters daily without the slightest ill effect (1014; 94). Comic, too, on the larger scale of human folly, is the misunderstanding between the Duchess and her family, whom she defies like a latter-day Antigone. Whereas her gesture to Montriveau comes nobly from the heart—and, not incidentally, from a clear-sighted recognition of her role as pawn to the family fortunes—her relatives are interested only in her violation of form: "Pour tout concilier, que venons-nous vous demander? De tourner habilement la loi des convenances au lieu de la violer" (1019; 96).[9] Another source of humor in the scene is the contrast between the Princesse de Blamont-Chauvry's historical perspective on the evolution of courtly manners and the Duchess' immediate and exclusive grasp of the sole words of wisdom of practical interest to her: "—Chère tante, je puis donc aller chez lui déguisée? —Mais, oui, ça peut toujours se nier, dit la vieille" (1022; 97).

This moment of revelation for the Duchess also shows us why she had been unable to meet Montriveau on common ground. After the abduction she had moved, symbolically speaking, from the level of conventional discourse—signs whose meaning derives primarily from context—to the level of the denotative or representational—language in whose field of direct reference lies meaning. The former requires interpretation as a response; the latter, corresponding action. Thus, in sending her carriage to her lover's door, Madame de Langeais commits the fatal (as we shall see) error of confusing codes—using a conventional sign (the carriage) to convey a message of a different order (her unconventionally profound love of Montriveau). When her aunt reminds her that in social parlance action need not correspond to language ("ça peut toujours se nier"), the Duchess glimpses a course of action that does not compromise her emotion. If her love is authentic, she need not fear appearances that suggest, falsely, the presence of ambiguity or hypocrisy at the source. This is the lesson learned with respect to his identity by Colonel Chabert, albeit much more painfully.

Thus, the family reunion in the wake of this scandal literally encircles the Duchess in her native symbolic territory, conventional language, and foils her attempted escape. It is by controlling memory, as the Navarreins know, that one resists extinction; and an aristocratic caste tenuously in power is not above expedient editing. Thus, the one intrinsically significant gesture the Duchess had made is ably denounced and erased from the public memory. This deliberate elimination of the sole visible proof of her love for Montriveau—proof that she had indeed crossed the "ligne droite et tranchée" (1002; 90) between passion and love—repeats the failure of communication earlier symbolized in his failure to apply the branding iron to her forehead. Both characters had recourse to symbols to express their anguish to their unresponsive partner. Both bowed to the truth that the Duchess' social identity was inalterable and inescapable—and perhaps also to the truth that in contemporary society the heroic gesture or the noble emotion is no longer possible.[10] When Montriveau's unpremeditated delay lets their last opportunity for reconciliation slip by, the Duchess leaves Paris for the convent in Spain—renouncing that identity and, therefore, life also. At this point the narrator intervenes once more, as if closing a parenthesis between the opening scene and the dénouement of the novel:

Les sentiments qui animèrent les deux amants quand ils se retrouvèrent à la grille des Carmélites et en présence d'une Mère Supérieure doivent être maintenant compris dans toute leur étendue, et leur violence, réveillée de part et d'autre, expliquera sans doute le dénouement de cette aventure. (1030-31; 100)

The second and third chapters of *La Duchesse de Langeais* comprise the nucleus of analysis around which the novel is structured, if we consider the novel as a study of manners, a form of social criticism. In these chapters we perceive the narrative's foundation in history and its role as a dramatic extension of that history, through the characters; at the same time two symbolic disturbances, the kidnapping scene and the carriage episode, reveal the cracks in that foundation and the frailty of those characters. This unfolding of events follows upon the great emotional convulsion of the first chapter and, in reprospect, establishes its necessity; and the theme of the power of circumstances over effort, figured in the image of the Duchess fleeing from Paris, foreshadows the ending. But if the historical exposition and the analysis of the characters in their native setting are imbedded in the narrative, it is because Balzac clearly wished to give primacy to the poetic effect of the chapter "La Sœur Thérèse." Thus, the central chapters of the novel contain the internal logic of the story and are enhanced by their secondary position; but it is the poetic logic of the novel's form announced by "La Sœur Thérèse" that triumphs in the end—and in the ending, a return to the convent setting.

The dénouement of *La Duchesse de Langeais* is an acknowledgement of the supreme difficulties of expression and of the necessity of convention in speech and manners, of form in art. All the themes of the novel are gently drawn together. The light touches of Balzac's humor—de Marsay dressed as a Carmelite, a comic reference to *La Fille aux yeux d'or*; the uncontrollable curiosity which leads the nun keeping vigil over the Duchess' body to search through the deceased's personal belongings—brighten the somber images of separation, death, powerlessness—and silence. Montriveau, after contemplating the Duchess' remains in his cabin, exchanges these words, the final words of the novel, with his friend Ronquerolles:

Ah! ça, dit Ronquerolles à Montriveau quand celui-ci reparut sur le tillac, c'était une femme, maintenant ce n'est rien. Attachons un boulet à chacun de ses pieds, jetons-la dans la mer, et n'y pense plus que comme nous pensons à un livre lu pendant notre enfance.
—Oui, dit Montriveau, car ce n'est plus qu'un poème.
—Te voilà sage. Désormais aie des passions; mais de l'amour, il faut savoir le bien placer, et il n'y a que le dernier amour d'une femme qui satisfasse le premier amour d'un homme. (1037; 103)

This ending inscribes upon our memories an image preserving that necessary tension between theme and form, between those conflicting movements constantly streaming through the novel and shaping it: the forces of history and the forces of symbolism, the gravity of reference and the flight of poetry, the conventions of literary tradition and the autonomy of form. Ronquerolles speaks with the assurance and facility of the public man, the social creature; Montriveau, with the simplicity and concision of a mind returning from an immense and private emotion, an interior journey. Montriveau's words preserve the Duchess in an image, the poem; Ronquerolles's diminish the importance of her death and welcome its absorption into history. His words are a closure, bringing the reader back to the *Histoire des Treize* and returning Montriveau to the realm of familiar and reassuring experience.

But this final affirmation of realism is only a convention, not a distillation of the novel. *La Duchesse de Langeais* cannot be so easily simplified; too much has happened. The reader, in his own sphere, has experienced the Duchess' trauma and Montriveau's illumination. We have been compelled, by the fragmented chronology of the narrative and the symbolic violence of its scenes, to contemplate the ordering of images as a single experience of our own, as readers: to see the novel not as a story, but as a form.

But not all of the poetic effects of *La Duchesse de Langeais*, a novel Balzac dedicated to Liszt, are universal. One belongs to it alone. The unchronological presentation of the story creates the theme of a diminuendo, a theme struck like a chord by the "burning symphonies" of the opening scene, sustained by the melodies played by the Duchess on her piano in Paris, and concluded by the strains of Gregorian chant that captivate Montriveau just before he goes to retrieve his eternally silent lover. The last lines may remind us of the limitations of form, but it is the poetry that we will remember.

Chapter V

HISTOIRE DES TREIZE:
LA FILLE AUX YEUX D'OR

In the third novel of the *Histoire des Treize, La Fille aux yeux d'or*,[1] we find a highly remote narrative perspective and a stylized narration bordering on psychological allegory or masque in its slow dramatic progression. The novel is especially known for the opening scene in the first chapter, "Physionomies parisiennes." As if from a promontory raised to the heights of metaphor, the narrator bids us contemplate the horrifying, vast spectacle below: his unsparing vision of a city built on the shifting moral and economic sands of greed, corruption, irredeemable vice. Then, abruptly, he relates a sensational tale: a young dandy and member of the Treize, Henri de Marsay, conducts an illicit affair with a beautiful Creole slave, Paquita, at the home of her owner, the Marquis de San-Réal. After falling in love with her, de Marsay invites her to escape with him; but Paquita fearfully insists that her enslavement to an "infernal génie" (1100; 126) is absolute. Once he realizes that tyrant to be a woman, and outraged by it, de Marsay resolves to murder Paquita with the help of the Treize; but he does so, only to find that lover's vengeance already exacted by his half-sister and mirror image, the Marquise de San-Réal. Both illegitimate children of an English lord, they experience the shock of recognition followed by a brief moment of physical attraction, firmly repressed: the Marquise vows to flee to a convent, and de Marsay resumes his casual existence. The narrator presents the urban panorama as a prose poem, making only the following overt transition before embarking on de Marsay's story: "Si ce coup d'œil rapidement jeté sur la population de Paris a fait concevoir la rareté d'une figure raphaëlesque, et l'admiration passionnée qu'elle y doit inspirer à première vue, le principal intérêt de notre histoire se trouvera justifié" (1054; 109).

The striking contradiction between de Marsay's physical beauty and the material and spiritual decay surrounding him expresses on the thematic level the same anomalous coexistence of the two parts of the novel on the level of form. Despite the apparent incongruity, Balzac presents the vision

HISTOIRE DES TREIZE: LA FILLE AUX YEUX D'OR 107

of Paris and story as integral parts of a single narrative, and it is as such, as a unified work, that we must approach the novel. However bizarre its plot and structure, *La Fille aux yeux d'or* is anchored in the same vision of universal humanness, of a shared striving for "an eternal meaning for life" (Rilke), that governs Balzac's works generally. Thus, what we would call the Freudian overtones of the text[2] still pertain to the theme of a fundamental human aspiration and its relation to poetical discourse. That the work begins with a passage exclusively metaphorical in its vision, not yet unfolding a story according to a chronological sequence of events, qualifies the all-too-facile shock the anecdote seems intended to administer.

Like Colonel Chabert, Montriveau and the Duchesse de Langeais, the characters in *La Fille aux yeux d'or* misinterpret different levels of meaning, mistaking the symbolic for the conventional and the conventional for the symbolic: despite appearances, Paquita actually remains faithful to both her lovers by recognizing their basic similarity. When de Marsay and the Marquise acknowledge this "fidelity to the blood" (1108; 129), they apprehend their identity as a function of taboo, not so much homosexuality as incest, stressing the theme of blood relationship. Thus, theme and form predicate the discovery of hidden connection:

What is crucial is not difference but similarity, not division—and it is here that the deep meaning of the mystery plot is located—but connection. In the context of the sexual drama of which Paquita is the central, mediating figure, what is continually brought out is the physical resemblance of the two lovers, a motif not simply designated to reflect the fact that they are blood relations, but also powerfully charged with sexual connotations, shading into two of the profoundest themes of the text, those of androgyny and incest.[3]

The equally profound connection on the level of perspective, unifying the two superficially dissimilar parts of the narrative, is further suggested by the presence of an artist-figure, the Marquise, who attacks a "fantaisie" (1109; 129), Paquita, with her dagger and writes letters in blood. As if incarnating the figure of the Reaper implicit in the first paragraph of the novel, the Marquise appears at the novel's close to prove one cannot kill a "fantasy" or poem whose "organic" life is actually metaphorical. Thus, the ending of the novel, like those of the works studied in the preceding chapters, affirms the intrinsic value of poetical discourse and returns the character to the realm of conventional signs—that level of socially effective discourse where moral and economic distinctions cannot be abstracted, hidden or suspended, as in fantasy or fiction.

The apparent fragmentation of the narrative thus bears no real resemblance to the same phenomenon in *Louis Lambert*, where different modes of discourse impede the "poetical" ordering of the narration. The only speculation at work in *La Fille aux yeux d'or* is poetical in nature; this the narrator states in the first lines of the novel. But the division between social panorama and story seems to be a requirement of Balzac's chosen theme, for in *Eugénie Grandet* these are smoothly coordinated, the story flowing from the narrator's description of Saumur. Although *La Fille aux yeux d'or* is not so harmoniously organized as the later work, it is nonetheless remarkable for its formal innovation and thematic complexity.

In the first paragraph the narrator sets the tone of the novel by openly declaring his esthetic bias. It is the grotesque aspect of the Parisian populace that has caught his eye:

> Un des spectacles où se rencontre le plus d'épouvantement est certes l'aspect général de la population parisienne, peuple horrible à voir, hâve, jaune, tanné. Paris n'est-il pas un vaste champ incessamment remué par une tempête d'intérêts sous laquelle tourbillonne une moisson d'hommes que la mort fauche plus souvent qu'ailleurs et qui renaissent toujours aussi serrés, dont les visages contournés, tordus, rendent par tous les pores l'esprit, les désirs, les poisons dont sont engrossés leurs cerveaux; non pas des visages, mais bien des masques: masques de faiblesse, masques de force, masques de misère, masques de joie, masques d'hypocrisie; tous exténués, tous empreints des signes ineffaçables d'une haletante avidité? Que veulent-ils? de l'or, ou du plaisir?
> (1039; 104)

The primary horror is not economic injustice, but the absence of beauty; the structure of society will interest the narrator only insofar as it accounts for this singular, awe-inspiring phenomenon. In the second sentence the demonic, driving rhythm of the prose transforms an appeal for the reader's informed consent ("Paris n'est-il pas . . .") into a compelling vision of near-mythic proportions; this magnification of perspective reveals the emblematic quality of the masks people wear, no simple commonplace. Lacking individual traits, the faces dispassionately herald the events on the pages below, placed, as it were, like impersonal masks of comedy and tragedy above the stage on which the spectacle occurs. Similarly, the introduction of the motif "or et plaisir" is stylized: stated, not proffered. The narrator's question is rhetorical; like his counterpart in *Ferragus* ("Il est dans Paris certaines rues . . ." [793; 137]), he interprets for us. The urgency and finality of his words correspond to the intensity of his vision and not to a moralistic revulsion at the sight of the populace.

Nevertheless, it is the theme of judgment, indirectly stated and devoid of religious overtones, that communicates the horror of the vision. The demythologized reaper, "la mort," presides over Paris, now reduced to the dimensions of a single "vaste champ," no longer the site of the many Elysian Fields. The image is so unlike that evoked in Hugo's poem "Mors" (1854) that the contrast is instructive. As Hugo's reaper works her way across her field,

HISTOIRE DES TREIZE: LA FILLE AUX YEUX D'OR 109

> Les peuples éperdus semblaient sous la faulx sombre
> Un troupeau frissonnant qui dans l'ombre s'enfuit;
> Tout était sous ses pieds deuil, épouvante et nuit.
> Derrière elle, le front baigné de douces flammes,
> Un ange souriant portait le gerbe d'âmes.[4]

Death leads her flock to that dreaded, but majestic confrontation with a terrible and ultimate truth; she performs a ritual slaughter whose inevitability and absoluteness provide their own consolation. But the symbolic dimensions of the field of Paris are cruelly restricted. Death periodically stamps the mechanical process of life with its seal; the metaphorical presence of nature ("champ," "moisson") underscores the grotesque, unnatural rhythm of that continual gesture. There will be no Last Judgment, no rectification; Paris is already the site of the resurrection of the dead, "ce peuple exhumé" (1039; 104). There can be no progress, no release; there is only the constant repetition, the unending spectacle. Everything that rises—"une moisson d'hommes," "les désirs, les poisons" and, later, capital itself ("le mouvement ascensionnel de l'argent" [1046; 106])—converges upon the level of corruptible appearances; transcendence is impossible. This world is the Paris of *Ferragus*, "ce réceptacle de monstruosités" (891; 49); it is the Faubourg Saint-Germain of *La Duchesse de Langeais*, the setting of the aristocracy's doomed and artificial revival. So uncompromising and pessimistic is this vision that it is difficult to consider the hopeful *Séraphîta* as much more than an intellectual curiosity.

The forceful tones and imagery of "Physionomies parisiennes" impress upon us the horror—the esthetic crime—of that inexorable deformation and consumption of human lives for the sake of a social hierarchy. The narrator's impersonality, his visionary pessimism and the specificity of context all underscore his tragic awareness of what has become a social ritual—the sacrifice of beauty—and thus prepare us for the ceremonial unfolding of de Marsay's adventure, which will culminate in the loss of his youth. The first paragraphs of the novel also prepare the eventual playful transformation of the poetical vision of the city into a metaphorical fantasy, and of the narrative as a whole into an improbable exotic tale. The sight of the most oppressive and revolting of societies will not deter the narrator from pursuing his subject. His vision, at once serious and imaginative, triumphs over the grotesque spectacle it reveals.

Thus, he continues:

> Quelques observations sur l'âme de Paris peuvent expliquer les causes de sa physionomie cadavéreuse qui n'a que deux âges, ou la jeunesse, ou la caducité: jeunesse blafarde et sans couleur, caducité fardée qui veut paraître jeune. En voyant ce peuple exhumé, les étrangers, qui ne sont pas tenus de réfléchir, éprouvent tout d'abord un mouvement de dégoût pour cette capitale, vaste atelier de jouissances, d'où bientôt eux-mêmes ils

ne peuvent sortir, et restent à s'y déformer volontiers. Peu de mots suffiront pour justifier physiologiquement la teinte presque infernale des figures parisiennes, car ce n'est pas seulement par plaisanterie que Paris a été nommé un enfer. Tenez ce mot pour vrai. . . . Cette nature sociale toujours en fusion semble se dire après chaque œuvre finie: "A une autre!" comme se le dit la nature elle-même. Comme la nature, cette nature sociale s'occupe d'insectes, de fleurs d'un jour, de bagatelles, d'éphémères, et jette aussi feu et flamme par son éternel cratère. (1039-40; 104)

Almost imperceptibly the narrator adopts the language of paradox; we are assured that the vision is no hallucination, no exaggerated fiction ("Quelques observations . . . peuvent expliquer"; "Peu de mots suffiront pour justifier . . ."). But in fact the narrator does not point to external evidence— the Paris of history, the visual image; he refers instead to his own resourcefulness with language, his ability to provide those substantiating words and observations. Empirical reality, when eventually evoked, will serve only to bear the reflection of his own chosen word-symbols, gold and pleasure. In a similar way the lifeless, camouflaged faces only reflect his jaundiced vision: this is not a scientific analysis of social ills. The narrow circumscription of his subject—"la teinte presque infernale des figures parisiennes"— seems to provoke the almost xenophobic distinction between that which is Parisian and that which is not. Indeed, foreigners coming to Paris are not expected to analyze their perceptions; they need only surrender to the city's irresistible charm. So the reader, coming to the text, need only fall under the spell of the narrator's art. Otherwise, all is false and contradictory. When the narrator goes on to justify his observations "physiologiquement," he immediately resorts to figural speech; Paris becomes an "enfer," and the narrator's authority lies in the absolute truth of his language: "Tenez ce mot pour vrai." Like the vast field of Paris with its harvest of men and women, the inferno constitutes the reality; in the realm of poetry it is a reality of metaphor.

Thus, it is not social nature alone that exists in a state of perpetual fusion within its proper sphere; so also does the creative thought of the narrator. And just as he opposes social nature to nature itself, so does he carefully distinguish the linguistic nature of his observations from the empirical nature of his subject. Correspondingly, there is a double movement of metaphor in the opening passage: first, from nature metaphors— "champ," "moisson"—to grotesque images—"masques," "physionomie cadavéreuse"; and second, from the latter, which represent the physical appearance of the Parisians, to those which transform the representation into a picture of a moral furnace consuming "ephemeras," days and trifles, in its fire. Society transforms nature into a man-made spectacle; art transforms society into stylized images. In art, as in society, there is nothing that cannot be introduced, assimilated, used to effect: "personne n'y est de trop, personne n'y est absolument utile, ni absolument nuisible. . . . Tout y est toléré" (1040; 104). In art, as in society, it is the closed context—text, morality, geography—that defines the source and issue of creative energies and determines their precise effect:

> Qui donc domine en ce pays sans mœurs, sans croyance, sans aucun sentiment; mais d'où aboutissent tous les sentiments, toutes les croyances et toutes les mœurs? L'or et le plaisir. Prenez ces deux mots comme une lumière et parcourez cette grande cage de plâtre, cette ruche à ruisseaux noirs, et suivez-y les serpenteaux de cette pensée qui l'agite, la soulève, la travaille. Voyez. Examinez d'abord le monde qui n'a rien. (1040-41; 104)

Paris becomes a plaster cage, a mysterious hive, ultimately a closed system of values. But the self-containment of the subject does not prevent the narrator, like Prometheus, from appropriating the source of illumination: "Prenez ces deux mots comme une lumière et parcourez cette grande cage .... Voyez." But even as he liberates language from its referential context, the narrator still affirms the authority, the accuracy of his vision. Unlike Plato's philosopher, he has not discovered light outside the cave, but inside it, in the illuminating power of language. He communicates to the reader a truth that is both poetic and literal, for it is in following his words, holding them before our eyes like lanterns, that we can share his vision—that we, too, can see. Language, therefore, is the light of the mind: specifically, the poetic language of the artist. The narrator's words do not explain, justify, document; they are the very source and substance of his vision. "Enfer," "or," "plaisir": these are the luminous entities that draw images of Parisian faces like rootless natural ephemera, moths and butterflies, into their light. The spectacle the narrator would have us see is already before us, enacted on the printed page.

In our journey through "cet enfer, qui, peut-être, un jour, aura son DANTE" (1044; 106), "or" and "plaisir," these luminous, disembodied figures, replace the solemn, pensive shade of a Virgil; and we witness the magical transformation of social nature through metaphor, a process not unlike the awakening of nature by the lyrical voice in Rimbaud's prose poem "Aube." And yet the almost supernatural power of metaphor to resurrect "ce peuple exhumé" is no source of renewal, no blessing or celebration. All that is revealed is the oppressive interrelationship of the classes, of the images themselves. The "monstre nommé Spéculation" (1041; 104), the overseer of the proletarians, is but the etymological half-sister of the spectacle itself (both from the Latin *specere*, to see), prefiguring the introduction of Lord Dudley's children at the end of the chapter. The narrator alludes separately to Venus and to Vulcan, husband and wife in the *Odyssey*,[5] and one wonders if the workers themselves are not the monstrous, because human, offspring of this mythological pair. The proletarians

... jettent, grands seigneurs d'un jour, leur argent le lundi dans les cabarets, qui font une enceinte de boue à la ville; ceinture de la plus impudique des Vénus, incessamment pliée et dépliée, où se perd comme au jeu de la fortune périodique de ce peuple; aussi féroce au plaisir qu'il est tranquille au travail. (1041; 105)

Venus, deprived of a divine and singular identity, falls, irretrievable, from Olympus; the "enceinte," her "ceinture," is reduced from its traditional connotation of containment to one of intermittent opening. In another subversion of traditional associations, gold dissolves into "une enceinte de boue," alchemy denied. But this demythologizing vision, with all its deliberate vulgar literalness, leads obliquely to a comment upon the impurity of the city's natural resources, its air and water:

Si l'air des maisons où vivent la plupart des bourgeois est infect, si l'atmosphère des rues crache des miasmes cruels en des arrière-boutiques où l'air se raréfie, sachez qu'outre cette pestilence, les quarante mille maisons de cette grande ville baignent leurs pieds en des immondices que le pouvoir n'a pas encore voulu sérieusement enceindre de murs en béton qui pussent empêcher la plus fétide boue de filtrer à travers le sol, d'y empoisonner les puits et de continuer souterrainement à Lutèce son nom célèbre. (1050; 108)

The creative logic of language takes the "enceinte" as its premise, proceeds from the metaphor to empirical fact ("la plus fétide boue") and arrives at the etymological and historical source, *Lutèce* (from the Latin *lutum*, mud). In another progression of sorts, the theme of dissolution, evoked by the image of the damp, unstable ground, qualifies the character of the intellect of those who walk upon it:

Le petit bourgeois persiste à vivre et vit, mais crétinisé; vous le rencontrez la face usée, plate, vieille, sans lueur aux yeux, sans fermeté dans la jambe, se traînant d'un air hébété sur le boulevard, la ceinture de sa Vénus, de sa ville chérie. (1045; 106)

Aussi leurs figures [of businessmen and professionals] offrent-elles cette paleur aigre, ces colorations fausses, ces yeux ternis, cernés, ces bouches bavardes et sensuelles où l'observateur reconnaît les symptômes de l'abâtardissement de la pensée et sa rotation dans le cirque d'une spécialité qui tue les facultés génératives du cerveau, le don de voir en grand, de généraliser et de déduire. (1048; 107)

Le plaisir est comme certaines substances médicales; pour obtenir constamment les mêmes effets, il faut doubler les doses, et la mort ou l'abrutissement est contenu dans la dernière.... Aussi Paris a-t-il ses thériakis, pour qui le jeu, la gastrolâtrie ou la courtisane sont un opium. (1050; 108)

If social nature is best characterized by its solvency on all its planes—material, spiritual, financial—it is poetically appropriate that the fetid mud, no solid ground, dissolve into a sea and that the City of Paris set sail upon it:

Paris n'est-il pas un sublime vaisseau chargé d'intelligence? Oui, ses armes sont un de ces oracles que se permet quelquefois la fatalité. LA VILLE DE PARIS a son grand mât tout de bronze, sculpté de victoires, et pour vigie Napoléon. Cette nauf a bien son tangage et son roulis; mais elle sillonne le monde, y fait feu par les cent bouches de ses tribunes, laboure les mers scientifiques, y vogue à pleines voiles, crie du haut de ses huniers par la voix de ses savants et de ses artistes: "En avant, marchez! suivez-moi!" (1052; 108)

In the tradition of Rabelais, the joyful, riotous image of an artistic and intellectual quest triumphs over the forces of physical and spiritual decay. The launching of the ship is none other than the flight of the imagination. If social nature, in imitation of nature itself, "semble se dire après chaque œuvre finie: 'A une autre!' " (1040; 104), then the narrator only follows their lead when, having completed his portrait of Paris, he takes up the narration of a single adventure. He launches de Marsay's story, a vessel sailed by art and analysis, truer lights than gold and pleasure, and always kept afloat by its foundation, that vast populated field, now dissolved into the reader's memory. The unexpected metamorphosis of the narrative is, like the City of Paris itself, only one more inspired transformation, one more creative act.

The sudden contraction of scope from the general "physionomies parisiennes" to the particular ones of Henri de Marsay and Paul de Manerville in no way affects the narrator's propensity for stylization. All that is changed is his subject. Thus, Paquita, identified by de Marsay's friend Paul, becomes the symbol of the narrative itself in its irreducible form, an emblematic figure: "Elle vient quelquefois ici, c'est *la Fille aux yeux d'or*" (1064; 113). Paul next confirms the intimate relationship of the narrative as a whole—*La Fille aux yeux d'or*—and the first part of "Physionomies parisiennes," whose emblem is the vessel City of Paris, when he describes the Marquise de San-Réal, glimpsed in Paquita's company, as another ship: "Une taille cambrée, la taille élancée d'une corvette construite pour faire la course, et qui se rue sur le vaisseau marchand avec une impétuosité française, le mord et le coule bas en deux temps" (1064; 113).[6]

De Marsay answers Paul with an image of his own, evoking the themes of monstrosity, prostitution, art and Antiquity associated with the Parisian populace and thereby reinforces the connection between the vision of the city and the adventure:

Elle [Paquita] est l'original de la délirante peinture appelée *la femme caressant sa chimère*, la plus chaude, la plus infernale inspiration du génie antique; une sainte poésie prostituée par ceux qui l'ont copiée pour les fresques et les mosaïques.... Me voilà, aujourd'hui, attendant cette fille dont je suis la chimère, et ne demandant pas mieux que de me poser comme le monstre de la fresque. (1065; 113)

Like the featureless Parisians implicitly transformed into tragicomic masks, the characters become figural, assuming roles and places assigned them by the invisible artist. The narrator's vision, his insistent stylization, triumphs over representation in the simplistic, naïve sense. Like Paquita and her duenna, the two parts of the chapter "Physionomies parisiennes," though strikingly different, "ont l'air d'être cousues ensemble" (1068; 115), not only by virtue of the simple designation of the chapter as such, but also by the narrator's use of metaphor. The repetition of the image of the ship— the City of Paris, the Marquise as corvette—anchors the symbol of poetic flight and poetic closure firmly in the center of the narrative. De Marsay's admiring reference to *"la femme caressant sa chimère"* mirrors our own contemplation of the landscape of the reaper and of the theatrical setting of the spectacle; and if the settings are like tableaux, then the action resembles a solemn, gradual procession culminating in the Marquise's anticipated return. Indeed, the narrator already identifies her, along with de Marsay, as one of the English Lord Dudley's many illegitimate offspring:

Pour rendre cette aventure compréhensible, il est nécessaire d'ajouter ici que lord Dudley trouva naturellement beaucoup de femmes disposées à tirer quelques exemplaires d'un si délicieux portrait. Son second chef d'œuvre en ce genre fut une jeune fille nommée Euphémie . . . ramenée à Madrid avec une jeune créole des Antilles, avec les goûts ruineux des colonies; mais heureusement mariée à . . . don Hijos, marquis de San-Réal qui . . . était venu habiter Paris, et demeurait rue Saint-Lazare. (1057-58; 111)

Thus, on the levels of anecdote and form the chapter "Physionomies parisiennes" prefigures the dramatic unfolding of the entire novel. By changing course in the middle of the chapter, the narrator indeed shifts his sight and takes the reader in a new direction; but when we stop to admire the contrast, we learn that he had charted a single journey all along—the narrative itself.

The novel's second chapter, "Singulière Bonne Fortune," repeats the pattern of contrasts set in "Physionomies parisiennes": its first part is largely composed of dialogue; its second, of description. The narrator, like his vision of Paris, recedes into the background. He does not need to draw our attention to the novel's design, as he did in *Ferragus*, because context —the esthetic or spectacular nature of Paris—and content—the existence and identities of Lord Dudley's children—have been clearly defined. There will be no distraction but the spectacle itself. As the prefigured adventure now takes on dramatic relief, the gravity of the almost ritual enactment is offset by the presence of humorous, colorful characters and improbable, exotic settings. The dimensions of the narrative, to the relief of the reader, now seem reduced to more comfortable, conventional proportions. The narrator exchanges Gargantua's high-powered microscope for the opera glasses of an ordinary theater-goer. Or so it seems.

A Figaro,[7] de Marsay's manservant Laurent arranges his master's access to the Hôtel de San-Réal. "Nous aurons Paquita!" (1069;1550), he exclaims with the same familiarity—and hence lack of seriousness—that had prompted Paul de Manerville to say of "la fille aux yeux d'or": "Nous ne connaissons que ça, mon cher!" (1064; 113). It appears that the rational, familiar, masculine universe will prevail over the feminine world of the Hôtel, with its mysterious door, Cerberean watchdogs and strangely inseparable inhabitants ("ces deux femmes ont l'air d'être cousues ensemble" [1068; 115]). Masculine vanity supplants the intellectual curiosity inspiriting the Rabelaisian quest:

> Mais en triomphant aussi facilement, de Marsay devait s'ennuyer de ses triomphes; aussi depuis environ deux ans s'ennuyait-il beaucoup. En plongeant au fond des voluptés, il en rapportait plus de gravier que de perles. . . . Sans le reflet magique de cette perle introuvable, il ne pouvait plus avoir que, soit des passions aiguisées par quelque vanité parisienne, soit des partis pris avec lui-même de faire arriver telle femme à tel degré de corruption, soit des aventures qui stimulassent sa curiosité. (1070; 115)

De Marsay, like the reader, looks upon *La Fille aux yeux d'or* as a fine diversion. The title of the chapter guarantees de Marsay's success, and we are told that he is deserving of it: "De Marsay n'était pas un étourdi" (1066; 114). One hardly notices the subtle shift of emphasis from the familiar to the figural in the narrator's translation of the "tableau vivant" suggested by de Marsay's allusion to painting (*"la femme caressant sa chimère"*) into theater and of theater into a "pièce vivante," so deceptive are the tone and the information:

> Il [de Marsay] allait jouer cette éternelle vieille comédie qui sera toujours neuve, et dont les personnages sont un vieillard, une jeune fille et un amoureux: don Hijos, Paquita, de Marsay. Si Laurent valait Figaro, la duègne paraissait incorruptible. Ainsi, la pièce vivante était plus fortement nouée par le hasard qu'elle ne l'avait jamais été par aucun auteur dramatique! Mais aussi le hasard n'est-il pas un homme de génie? (1071; 115)

What is false in terms of the plot is symbolically true. Though Don Hijos is hardly the third protagonist in the comedy, *La Fille aux yeux d'or* is a timeless, living drama insofar as it is a successful work of art; and that Fate is indeed a genius who arranges the sole untransferable destiny, self-recognition, the revelation reserved for de Marsay in the dénouement.

The scene of de Marsay's toilette, "l'aspect général de la population parisienne" (1039; 104) given particular attention, repeats the narrator's warning of the encroachment of the symbolic upon the familiar and representational. De Marsay tells Paul:

> Toi, qui n'as qu'une femme et qui peut-être as raison de n'en avoir qu'une, essaie de faire le fat? . . . tu ne deviendras même pas ridicule, tu seras mort. Tu deviendrais un préjugé à deux pattes, un de ces hommes condamnés inévitablement à faire une seule et même chose. Tu signifierais *sottise* comme M. de La Fayette signifie Amérique; M. de Talleyrand, diplomatie; Désaugiers, chanson; M. de Ségur, romance. S'ils sortent de leur genre, on ne croit plus à la valeur de ce qu'ils font. (1072; 116)

De Marsay cannot suspect the literal truth of his words: as mere character in the narrator's play, he will forever signify *La Fille aux yeux d'or*; no matter how interesting he might conceivably be as a figure in his own right, he cannot leave his *genre*, his fictional existence in a particular narrative. It is around *La Fille aux yeux d'or*, even in the absence of the character, that de Marsay and Paris itself must gravitate:

> ... ils [de Marsay and Paul de Manerville] ne rencontrèrent nulle part la sublime Paquita Valdès pour le compte de laquelle se trouvaient cinquante des plus élégants jeunes gens de Paris, tous musqués, haut cravatés, bottés, éperonnaillés, cravachant, marchant, parlant, riant, et se donnant à tous les diables. (1073; 116)

Formerly accustomed to having "bourgeoises" stop to look at him, de Marsay is now the one who retraces his steps in order to see the object of his admiration:

> Le lendemain, de Marsay vint encore se promener au soleil sur la terrasse des Feuillants, et y vit Paquita Valdès: déjà pour lui la passion l'avait embellie. Il s'affola sérieusement de ces yeux dont les rayons semblaient avoir la nature de ceux que lance le soleil et dont l'ardeur résumait celle de ce corps parfait où tout était volupté.
> (1073; 116)

In a similar way, the scene at the Tuileries seems to trivialize, and paradoxically obscure, the rather obtrusive hint of the story's symbolic dimension. De Marsay contemplates disposing of the duenna: "Nous connaissons la Mythologie et la fable d'Argus" (1074; 117); and in his letter to Paquita, only several paragraphs later, he writes: "L'un des deux flacons contiendra de l'opium pour endormir votre Argus" (1075; 117). In their immediate context the conspicuous allusions reflect de Marsay's too facile mind and the exaggerated, farcical nature of his scheme; and yet Paris, populated by Venus and Vulcan, and de Marsay himself as Adonis (1054; 109), is indeed a mythological territory—the novel's symbolic geography.

But the full force of this persistent, stylizing vision is best demonstrated by the narrator's presentation of the interpreter who translates for de Marsay and Christemio:

> Il [Christemio] était suivi d'un homme que toutes les imaginations, depuis celles qui grelottent au Groenland jusqu'à celles qui suent à la Nouvelle-Angleterre [sic], se peindront d'après cette phrase: *c'était un homme malheureux*. A ce mot, tout le monde le devinera, se le représentera d'après les idées particulières à chaque pays. Mais qui se figurera son visage blanc, ridé, rouge aux extrémités, et sa barbe longue? qui verra sa cravate jaunasse en corde, son col de chemise gras, son chapeau tout usé, sa redingote verdâtre, son pantalon piteux, son gilet recroquevillé, son épingle en faux or, ses souliers crottés, dont les rubans avaient barboté dans la boue? qui le comprendra dans toute l'immensité de sa misère présente et passée? Qui? le Parisien seulement. L'homme malheureux de Paris est l'homme malheureux complet, car il trouve encore de la joie pour savoir combien il est malheureux. (1076; 117)

HISTOIRE DES TREIZE: LA FILLE AUX YEUX D'OR 117

Curiously, the narrator first appeals to the reader's imagination, as if for once stopping to acknowledge our presence, even to welcome our interpretation of an image, that of the "unfortunate man." Then providing an abundance of precise visual detail, he suddenly denies us the liberty of forming our own impressions by insisting upon his authority as creator of images in the text. He is like the narrator in *Ferragus*, who held his observations to be "incompréhensibles au-delà de Paris" (794; 13). Perfect understanding of his words is reserved for the happy few and certainly not for those unreflecting foreigners. As if to compound the insult to the non-Parisian reader, he concludes with an entirely unconvincing explanation of the unparalleled misery of the unfortunate man in Paris. The emphasis on local color seems only to bring out the narrator's provincialism, his apparent underestimation of the reader's intelligence; and this patronizing attitude resurfaces in de Marsay's insulting epithet "Chinois" (1077; 118), directed to Christemio, and again in his gratuitous comment, "Enfin, voici donc une aventure bien romanesque" (1077; 118). In Balzac those vividly imagined scenes translating cultural prejudices—such as this scene or the branding episode in *La Duchesse de Langeais*—offend the reader not only by forcing us, without apology, to become the "hypocrite lecteur," but also by provoking a response to the narrator's sheer indifference to our sensibilities. We are not his accomplices, his equals, in the creation of the text; we follow from a distance, "pas tenus de réfléchir" (1039; 104), mere spectators. This deliberate distancing provides us, as it were, with a defense mechanism against the raw symbolism of such episodes; and we, like de Marsay, gratefully dismiss them as curious moments in an "aventure bien romanesque."

This provocation prepares us for the scene that follows, the first of de Marsay's two carefully contrasted visits in this chapter to the Hôtel de San-Réal. The scene is almost oppressively literary, its references almost exclusively restricted to the European arts, including the narrator's fiction. De Marsay's disorientation foreshadows a significant event; similar moments occur in *Ferragus* and *La Duchesse de Langeais*:

Henri fut si rapidement emporté dans Paris, et ses pensées lui laissèrent si peu la faculté de faire attention aux rues par lesquelles il passait, qu'il ne sut pas où la voiture s'arrêta.
(1078; 118)

[Maulincour] alla dans Paris comme un homme ivre, et se trouva bientôt chez lui sans savoir comment il y était venu. (800; 15)

La frayeur de la duchesse fut si grande, qu'elle ne put jamais s'expliquer par où ni comment elle fut transportée. (991; 86)

The narrator states that "un homme qui lui [to de Marsay] parut être le mulâtre" (1078; 118) accompanies the hero to the Hôtel, thereby prohibiting an overly literal identification of the character; likewise, a figure reminiscent of Madame Gruget, but not explicitly identified as her, appears with Ferragus at the end of the first novel of the trilogy (903; 63). De Marsay relates the rooms to which he is taken to a literary memory: "Il reconnut cette sensation que lui procurait la lecture d'un de ces romans d'Anne Radcliffe où le héros traverse les salles froides, sombres, inhabitées, de quelque lieu triste et désert" (1078; 118). This recourse to literature itself reintroduces the unsettling theme of the determining influence of art over life (*"la femme caressant sa chimère"*), of public reputation over the self ("Tu signifierais *sottise* comme M. de La Fayette signifie Amérique..."). Even the narrator's description of the turban worn by Paquita's mother is an interpretation, not a representation: "Sur un canapé... se tenait une femme assez mal vêtue, coiffée d'un de ces turbans que savent inventer les femmes anglaises quand elles arrivent à un certain âge, et qui auraient infiniment de succès en Chine, où le beau idéal des artistes est la monstruosité" (1079; 118). Far more present than the turban itself is the "beau idéal" of the narrator, the exotic scene full of contrasts.[8]

This tendency to abstraction appears also in the narrator's description of the characters' emotions; they metamorphose into intangible peripheral presences, like the "éphémères" of social nature:

Ces idées, qui souvent flottent comme des vapeurs à l'alentour des âmes, y déterminent donc une sorte de maladie passagère. Dans le doux voyage que deux êtres entreprennent à travers les belles contrées de l'amour, ce moment est comme une lande à traverser.... (1079; 118-19)

The narrator seems to withdraw from the scene before him to an imaginary landscape, a linguistic creation. As the images become increasingly refined and figural, the scene seems to lose its relation to the "aventure bien romanesque" presumably unfolding, and it becomes, in a sense, mathematical:

Chez Henri, comme chez l'Espagnole, il se rencontrait une égale violence: et cette loi de la statique en vertu de laquelle *deux forces identiques s'annulent en se rencontrant* pourrait être vraie aussi dans le règne moral. Puis l'embarras de ce moment fut singulièrement augmenté par la présence de la vieille momie. L'amour s'effraie ou s'égaie de tout, pour lui tout a un sens, tout lui est présage heureux ou funeste. Cette femme décrépite était là comme un dénouement possible, et figurait l'horrible queue de poisson par laquelle les symboliques génies de la Grèce ont terminé les Chimères et les Sirènes, si séduisantes, si décevantes par le corsage, comme le sont toutes les passions au début. (1080; 119; my emphasis)

Like the preceding images, this second in a series of axioms[9] implies the subordination of naturalistic detail to symbolism and form. Paquita's mother, a forbidding and obtrusive presence, symbolizes the inescapable influence of the novel's form—truly the Argus previously invoked by de

Marsay. Not only is she a "dénouement possible," but "l'horrible queue de poisson" also—part of the metaphorical sea sailed by the City of Paris and the Marquise as corvette. She is, moreover, part of de Marsay himself as chimera. Paquita's mother more properly figures both the exposition ("Physionomies parisiennes") and dénouement (the third chapter, "La Force du sang"), implicit here in the middle of the narrative. The narrator, or rather the artist behind him, draws a circle defining the limits of his fictional world, the circle which as Dante he wishes us to see; and within its circumference references converge and multiply, proliferating like the Parisian population in its continual resurrection. If the text is "comme une lande à traverser," that metaphorical territory Paquita and de Marsay have entered, then the narration itself is "le sentier fleuri où l'on ne marche pas, mais où l'on roule sans néanmoins descendre" (1080; 119).

If her mother personifies the dénouement implicit in every part of the narrative, Paquita represents the light by which, at this moment, it is seen:

Elle [Paquita] parut alors si merveilleusement belle à Henri que toute cette fantasmagorie de haillons, de vieillesse . . . disparut aussitôt. Le salon s'illumina, il [de Marsay] ne vit plus qu'*à travers un nuage* la terrible, fixe, muette sur son canapé rouge . . . .
(1081; 119; my emphasis)

Otherwise unqualified by the narrator, Paquita embodies a series of superlatives: "les plus belles mains" (1081; 119), "la plus riche organisation que la nature se fût complu à composer pour l'amour" (1082; 119), "l'infini rendu palpable" (1082; 119). She is, in effect, "*la femme-écran*" (1095; 124) whose elimination will precipitate the dénouement. De Marsay, speculating on "le jeu présumé de cette machine, l'âme mise à part" (1082; 119), depersonalizes her even more in his thoughts. Paquita is also a "riche moisson de plaisirs promis" (1082; 119), recalling that "moisson d'hommes" of the first paragraph; and her mother, expressionless, hiding her emotions "sous ce masque [of impassivity]" (1083; 120), represents that horrifying aspect of Parisian existence paradoxically obscured by Paquita's luminous presence. The one with her passion for gold (1108; 129) and the other with her capacity to give pleasure incarnate the motif "or et plaisir."

Allusions to religion and mythology too return us to the poetic universe of "Physionomies parisiennes": Paquita's exclamation, "Sainte Vierge" (1082; 120); her "volupté surnaturelle" (1084; 120); the unhoped-for "sortilège" (1083; 120) that brings de Marsay to the boudoir. The mother, like a priestess, celebrates de Marsay and Paquita's symbolic marriage: "Paquita jeta un cri d'effroi, dit un mot à la vieille, qui prit d'autorité la main de Henri, celle de sa fille, les regarda longtemps, les leur rendit en hochant la tête d'une façon horriblement significative" (1083; 120). Finally, the way in which de Marsay's departure is described calls to mind the image of Zeus returning from the underworld in his chariot, leaving Persephone behind:

> [Paquita] prit un baiser qui leur donna de tels vertiges à tous deux, que de Marsay crut que la terre s'ouvrait . . . [Christemio] laissa le flambeau sous la voûte, ouvrit la portière, remit Henri dans la voiture, et le déposa sur le boulevard des Italiens avec une rapidité merveilleuse. Les chevaux semblaient avoir l'enfer dans le corps. (1084; 120)

These religious and mythological allusions are not the only ones that reinsert de Marsay's adventure at this point into the context of the novel as a whole. When de Marsay's language is at its most expressive, original and creative, it is revealed that his voice is not his alone, but a shared one:

> En un moment, il lui dit mille paroles insensées avec la rapidité d'un torrent qui bondit entre les rochers, et répète le même son sous mille formes différentes.
> "C'est la même voix! dit Paquita mélancoliquement, sans que de Marsay pût l'entendre, et . . . la même ardeur." (1083; 120)

Even the most urgent and inventive of utterances has its precedent; in life, as in the novel, every word and gesture can only repeat those that went before. Even in the most restricted of universes—the narrator's own creation—nothing is free from influence; everything is an allusion. Thus, the narrator may elevate his personal conceit, with all its nationalistic, misogynistic and racist overtones, to the level of the mythological dimension he has just evoked. The presentation of the Treize as myth will illuminate the stylized nature of the narrative:

> De Marsay exerçait le pouvoir autocratique du despote oriental. Mais ce pouvoir, si stupidement mis en œuvre dans l'Asie par des hommes abrutis, était décuplé par l'intelligence européenne, par l'esprit français, le plus vif, le plus acéré de tous les instruments intelligentiels. . . . Les femmes aiment prodigieusement ces gens qui se nomment pachas eux-mêmes, qui semblent accompagnés de lions, de bourreaux, et marchent dans un appareil de terreur. (1084-85; 120)

De Marsay, "l'esprit français" personified, dismisses Paquita's quite literal warnings as "imaginations de femme" (1078; 118); masculine replaces feminine in an arbitrary and infuriating reversal. The narrator has once again asserted his supremacy as the unyielding source of the novel's imagery, just as he did before when describing the "unfortunate man" of Paris. The pointed and unexpected exaltation of the Treize alienates us, reminding us of our dependency upon a narrator who is forever dictating the confines of our vision. The barrage of allusions creates an opaque, deflecting screen of images, obscuring, like Paquita, "*la femme-écran,*" the large lines of the story. Were it not for the narrator's intervention—"Pour bien comprendre sa [de Marsay's] conduite au dénouement de cette histoire . . ." (1084;

120)—we could not be sure that the constant crossing back and forth from the familiar to the symbolic, the personal to the mythological, conformed to an esthetic design. Like de Marsay, we see the *"Fille aux yeux d'or"* as an emblem—the italics are Balzac's—and an enigma:

> Il rêva de la *Fille aux yeux d'or*, comme rêvent les jeunes gens passionnés. Ce fut des images monstrueuses, des bizarreries insaisissables, pleines de lumière, et qui révèlent les mondes invisibles, mais d'une manière toujours incomplète, car un voile interposé change les conditions de l'optique. (1085; 121)

The passages relating de Marsay's second visit to the Hôtel de San-Réal, also part of the chapter "Singulière Bonne Fortune," are conspicuous for the stylization and repetition of those images peculiar to the novel, its own inner conventions. Not only is the description of the boudoir in itself a small masterpiece of fine detail,[10] but also the juxtaposed square and circle that define the room's contours repeat the theme of the monstrous union of opposites so prominent in the preceding scene. The narrator's description of the fluted folds of the curtain, the most specific of his observations, refers to Greek architecture; the curtain itself, because it changes "les conditions de l'optique," represents that veiled consciousness of de Marsay's most recent dreams:

> Ce boudoir était tendu d'une étoffe rouge, sur laquelle était posée une mousseline des Indes cannelée comme l'est une colonne corinthienne, par des tuyaux alternativement creux et ronds, arrêtés en haut et en bas dans une bande d'étoffe couleur ponceau sur laquelle étaient dessinées des arabesques noires. (1087-88; 121-22)

In the cold, shadowy room dominated by the mother's presence "tout eût glacé l'amour si Paquita n'avait pas été là" (1079; 118); here in the boudoir "tout aurait réchauffé l'être le plus froid" (1088; 122). The boudoir is a temple dedicated to Eros; Paquita "apparut à Henri agenouillée devant lui, l'adorant comme le dieu de ce temple où il avait daigné venir" (1088-89; 122). And it is also the famous conch shell (1089; 122) from which a radiant Venus steps forth—not the proletarian Venus of "Physionomies parisiennes"; but the repeated allusion in itself brings the two worlds, or rather the two chapters, together.[11]

The narrator returns to the theme of painting, first evoked by de Marsay in his conversation with Paul (*"la femme caressant sa chimère"*), by calling Paquita "un chef d'œuvre de la création" (1089; 122) and by evoking the "affinités inexplicables *caressées*" (1088; 122; my emphasis) by the white and pink of the boudoir's interior design. This implicitly affirms not only that de Marsay's transformation into the chimera is now complete, but also that the Marquise, creator of "ce réduit éclos par la baguette d'une fée" (1087; 122), is nothing less than an artist.[12]

The narrator misleads the reader, it seems, by implying Paquita's innocence. When de Marsay calls her an enigma, "Paquita ne comprit rien à ce que disait le jeune homme" (1099; 123); when she had dressed him in the Marquise's red dress and shawl, "elle riait d'un rire convulsif, et ressemblait à un oiseau battant des ailes; mais elle ne voyait rien au-delà" (1091; 123). This scene, at first glance, is unintelligible, but in fact an event of symbolic importance is taking place: Paquita knowingly arranges the chimera in the Marquise's picture, and de Marsay is willingly posing. We, like de Marsay, see nothing "au-delà" in this curious event; but Paquita, despite the narrator's words, sees much more. Because de Marsay would rule in this, the Marquise's domain, he takes up his position—"ne demandant mieux que de me poser comme le monstre de la fresque" (1065; 113)—in the most uncomfortable of ways, though he cannot realize the symbolic meaning of his borrowed costume. Here, as in *Ferragus* when Jules hides in Madame Gruget's closet, we are made to witness another grotesque posturing, another usurpation of an artist's, or master designer's, prerogative. De Marsay's search for the word solving the charade (1090; 122) and the psychological motivation for Paquita's action matter far less than the symbolic intrusion upon the Marquise's territory.

Nevertheless, the narrator invites us to become like de Marsay—to consider Paquita as a riddle, to supply the missing word: "Mais, chose étrange! si la *Fille aux yeux d'or* était vierge, elle n'était certes pas innocente" (1091; 123). But on the verge of "physiologically justifying" a paradox, he suddenly turns to figurative language, just as he did in "Physionomies parisiennes." The literal and reductive word is not pronounced. The narrator's evocation of "cette poésie des sens" (1091; 123), following this announcement of Paquita's loss of virginity and near-disclosure of her bisexuality, can only seem evasive:

Ce fut un poème oriental, où rayonnait le soleil que Saadi, Hafiz ont mis dans leurs bondissantes strophes. Seulement, ni le rythme de Saadi, ni celui de Pindare n'auraient exprimé l'extase pleine de confusion et la stupeur dont cette délicieuse fille fut saisie quand cessa l'erreur dans laquelle une main de fer la faisait vivre. (1091-92; 123)

We are left with a love affair that is more literary than erotic, and the context is narrowed down to the novel itself:

L'union si bizarre du mystérieux et du réel, de l'ombre et de la lumière, de l'horrible et du beau, du plaisir et du danger, du Paradis et de l'Enfer, qui s'était déjà rencontrée dans cette aventure, se continuait dans l'être capricieux et sublime dont se jouait de Marsay. (1091; 123)

It is as if the narrator wilfully deprives us of the pleasure of identifying the symbolic significance of the character on our own. His consciousness of the novel as a whole oppresses us in the way that "l'être inconnu qui planait comme une ombre au-dessus d'eux" (1089; 122) oppresses de Marsay and Paquita.

Even the comic relief is literary in nature and serves to emphasize the self-contained universe of the novel. At the end of the chapter Paquita's farewell to de Marsay parodies the traditional aubade: "Dieu! voici le jour. Sauve-toi. Te reverrai-je jamais? Oui, demain, je veux te revoir, dussé-je pour avoir ce bonheur, donner la mort à tous mes surveillants. A demain" (1092; 123). The narrator then invites comparison between his novel and *La Nouvelle Héloïse* (suggesting, in passing, de Marsay's tragic destiny as a new Abelard); Rousseau bequeathed his work to posterity

... par de grandes idées qu'il est difficile de dégager par l'analyse, quand, dans la jeunesse, on lit cet ouvrage avec le dessein d'y trouver la chaude peinture du plus physique de nos sentiments, tandis que les écrivains sérieux et les philosophes n'en emploient jamais les images que comme la conséquence ou la nécessité d'une vaste pensée; et les aventures de milord Edouard sont une des idées les plus européennement délicates de cette œuvre. (1092; 123)

The author's own vast idea in writing *La Fille aux yeux d'or* is not so much the revelation of the intimate connection between the structure of society ("Physionomies parisiennes") and the structure of the psyche (de Mersay's adventure) as the conception of this theme as an esthetic possibility. At the very moment the narrator seems to widen the context of the story to embrace philosophy, he chauvinistically celebrates "les idées les plus européennement délicates," the very context represented by de Marsay and the Treize and by the text itself—all products of European civilization. De Marsay, too, celebrates the novel's own private world, the one introduced in "Physionomies parisiennes": he lights his cigar "à la lanterne d'une bonne femme qui vendait de l'eau-de-vie et du café ... à toute *cette population parisienne qui commence sa vie avant le jour*" (1093; 123; my emphasis). The two visits to the Hôtel and the portrait of Paris all conclude on an axiomatic note, the repetition of which emphasizes the novel's unity. De Marsay's dreams after his second visit to Paquita are, like those he had before it, full of "images monstrueuses" (1085; 121), monstrous because they are the common denominator of innocence and experience: he "s'endormit du sommeil des mauvais sujets, lequel, par une bizarrerie dont aucun chansonnier n'a encore tiré parti, se trouve être aussi profond que celui de l'innocence. Peut-être est-ce un effet de cet axiome proverbial, *les extrêmes se touchent*" (1093-94; 124).

The pattern of the final chapter, "La Force du sang," repeats that of "Singulière Bonne Fortune": de Marsay again speaks with Paul de Manerville, again visits the Hôtel de San-Réal twice, and again returns to the mainstream of Parisian life. But in this chapter all is seen "sous un singulier jour" (1096; 124)—that critical perspective leading first to de Marsay's enlightenment, then to his sister's and ultimately to the reader's.

In the first part of "La Force du sang" the hero personifies the narrator of the preceding chapter, the self-styled indispensable intelligence: "Si l'on peut être fier de quelque chose, n'est-ce pas d'un pouvoir acquis par soi-même, dont nous sommes à la fois la cause, l'effet, le principe et le résultat?" (1095; 124). De Marsay defines himself in terms recalling the narrator's rhetoric in the Preface to the *Histoire des Treize*: "Ce monde à part dans le monde . . ." (791; 11). He thus identifies himself as a linguistic creation; his persona, as much as that of the narrator, is a rhetorical necessity. Repeating his former lesson on the nature of symbolism—"S'ils sortent de leur genre on ne croit plus à la valeur de ce qu'ils font" (1072; 116)—de Marsay implicitly asserts the supremacy of the fiction through which he lives:

> On nous parle de l'immoralité des *Liaisons dangereuses*, et de je ne sais quel autre livre qui a un nom de femme de chambre; mais il existe un livre horrible, sale, épouvantable, corrupteur, toujours ouvert, qu'on ne fermera jamais, le grand livre du monde, sans compter un autre livre mille fois plus dangereux, qui se compose de tout ce qui se dit à l'oreille, entre hommes, ou sous l'éventail entre femmes, le soir, au bal.
> (1097; 125)

De Marsay has now acceded to that superior level of intelligence shared by narrator and reader—the realization that he is only an actor in the play: "La vie est une singulière comédie" (1097; 125). Having seen "dans son ensemble" (1098; 124-25) the night spent in the boudoir, de Marsay recognizes the precise nature of his role; likewise, the reader, when he has finished the book, will be able to perceive the relationship of the parts—the vision and the adventure, and the three chapters—to the whole, to the single, coherent entity that is the novel.

De Marsay's return to the boudoir is not a simple demystification of his preceding visit, although it clearly begins as such:

> Le soir il vint au rendez-vous, et se laissa complaisamment bander les yeux. Puis, avec cette ferme volonté que les hommes vraiment forts ont seuls la faculté de concentrer, il porta son attention et appliqua son intelligence à deviner par quelles rues passait la voiture. Il eut une sorte de certitude d'être mené rue Saint-Lazare, et d'être arrêté à la petite porte du jardin de l'hôtel San-Réal. (1097-98; 125)

The introduction of Christian imagery spells, typically in Balzac, the end of enchantment, the advent of irony. "Saint-Lazare" in secular context recalls that mechanistic resurrection of the dead which, in Paris, is no miracle, but an everyday occurrence. The lovers, like the immodest Venuses, have descended from Olympus:

Agenouillée comme un ange en prière, mais comme un ange triste et profondément mélancolique, la pauvre fille ne ressemblait plus à la curieuse, à l'impatiente, à la bondissante créature qui avait pris de Marsay sur ses ailes pour le transporter dans le septième ciel de l'amour. (1098; 125)

When Paquita says to de Marsay, "Thy will be done," her words are pathetic: "Eh bien, si tu m'abandonnes à la fureur du monstre qui me dévorera, que ta sainte volonté soit faite!" (1099; 126). This unexpected revelation of a sentimental attachment diverts both de Marsay and the reader from their original purpose, the cold analysis. The scene is further complicated by the narrator's description of the lovers' second sexual encounter, in which Paquita, "la pauvre fille," suddenly becomes symbolic, and "le terrible de Marsay" (1098; 125), selfless and vulnerable:

Paquita répondait à cette passion que sentent tous les hommes vraiment grands pour l'infini, passion mystérieuse si dramatiquement exprimée dans Faust, si poétiquement traduite dans Manfred, et qui poussait Don Juan à fouiller le cœur des femmes, en espérant y trouver cette pensée sans bornes à la recherche de laquelle se mettent tant de chasseurs de spectres, que les savants croient entrevoir dans la science, et que les mystiques trouvent en Dieu seul. L'espérance d'avoir enfin l'Etre idéal avec lequel la lutte pouvait être constante sans fatigue ravit de Marsay qui, pour la première fois, depuis longtemps, ouvrit son cœur. Ses nerfs se détendirent, sa froideur se fondit dans l'atmosphère de cette âme brûlante, ses doctrines tranchantes s'envolèrent, et le bonheur lui colora son existence, comme l'était ce boudoir blanc et rose. (1101; 126)

At this point in the story the allusions need not astonish and delight the reader; following upon de Marsay's identification of the missing word of the charade, they can only denote an aspiration and not the attainment of an ideal. Paquita has come to represent a specter vainly sought or a truth beyond our grasp, like the hidden source of empirical reality and the God of the mystics. When Paquita tells de Marsay, "Je ne suis quelque chose hors de toi qu'afin d'être un plaisir pour toi" (1102; 173), she is not simply signaling her complete surrender to her lover's will. Her words also intimate that she is something innate, part of de Marsay's psyche, and that, because she is outside him, she is the projected illusion responsible for his happiness. De Marsay needs Paquita psychologically and spiritually, but he can possess her only physically and impermanently. His "doctrines tranchantes" cannot resolve this paradox; inadequate, they vanish from his mind; and in the end watchful reason succumbs to the mindless contentment of pleasure, lulled by the harmonious effect of the soft, suggestive colors.[13] De Marsay resembles the Argus-like duenna drugged by opium, slumbering elsewhere in the Hôtel.

And we have watched de Marsay experience a variety of emotions, from the determination to solve the enigma, to the sympathy elicited by Paquita's tearful confession, to the reverie induced by her cryptic pronouncement.

This scene, then, is built thus far on three successive movements progressing, on the level of meaning, from the literal to the thematic to the symbolic; and in the narrator's approach to Paquita, from demystification to characterization to stylization. She is initially the object of de Marsay's intended revenge, in every way inferior to him; then, when she confesses her love for him, she becomes his equal; finally, as that "Etre idéal" he would possess, she eclipses him in significance. This revelation of Paquita's significance on three different levels of meaning can occur only because the narrator has indirectly and successively adopted the perspectives of the three major characters: of de Marsay, for whom Paquita is "une aventure bien romanesque"; of Paquita herself, "la Fille aux yeux d'or," intrinsically involved in the events unfolding; and of the absent Marquise de San-Réal, who will later lament the loss of that ideal being, "ce qui nous a paru être l'infini" (1109; 129).

It is after this triple dislocation of perspective that the all-important identification of de Marsay and the Marquise occurs, as if dramatically to unveil the single truth, the central image, which inspired the narrator's several revelations of its importance: "Paquita, qui l'avait enlevé vigoureusement en l'air comme pour le contempler, s'était écriée: 'Oh! Mariquita! —Mariquita! cria le jeune homme en rugissant, je sais maintenant tout ce dont je voulais encore douter'" (1102-03; 127).

Upon hearing Paquita's exclamation, de Marsay, understandably, reverts to his original frame of mind, to his obsession with the unequivocal and literal. Paquita's words sustain, however, the three levels of meaning already evoked in the scene: de Marsay and the Marquise do literally resemble each other; their status in the adventure, as Paquita's lovers, is thematically equal; and, symbolically, they can be said to represent the sexual polarity of the single psyche. When de Marsay finally meets his half-sister face to face, he will only receive confirmation of Paquita's threefold revelation, which at this moment he is unable to comprehend. Significantly, Paquita provokes de Marsay's rage "sans connaître de quel crime elle était coupable" (1103; 119). Once again, as in the scene where Paquita dressed de Marsay in the Marquise's clothes, we learn that reason cannot fathom the symbolic truths disclosed by apparently incoherent words and gestures; rational and symbolic logic are of different orders, speak different languages. Only when they contemplate the violent act committed in the dénouement will de Marsay and the Marquise appreciate Paquita's "fidelity to the blood" (1108; 129), to Lord Dudley's progeny; only when we contemplate the narrative as a whole will we appreciate the unity and complexity of Balzac's imagery.

But because our, and de Marsay's, understanding is still clouded, the scene must end on a false note, with a renewed attempt on the narrator's part to demystify de Marsay's previous visit to the boudoir and the reappearance of the theme of masculine vanity. We return to the familiar context of aspects, surfaces and superficiality, calling to mind "l'aspect général de la population parisienne, peuple horrible à voir" (1039; 104). This time the aubade is almost tragic in tone:

> Elle attendit un mot de réponse, et reprit avec un accent plein de tendresse: "Adolphe, dis-moi donc une bonne parole. Voici bientôt le jour."
> Henri ne répondait pas. ... L'exclamation de Paquita fut d'autant plus horrible pour lui qu'il avait été détrôné du plus doux triomphe qui eût jamais agrandi sa vanité d'homme. ... Paquita, stupéfaite, n'eut dans sa douleur que la force de donner le signal du départ. (1104; 127)

De Marsay, who had once proclaimed, "Enfin, voici donc une aventure bien romanesque" (1077; 118), again articulates the reader's immediate and uninformed reaction to the turn of events: " 'L'aventure se complique d'une façon assez intéressante,' se dit Henri" (1105; 128). The remaining pages of the novel, of the chapter "La Force du sang," will give his words the most unexpected and devastating of meanings. When the Marquise appears in the dénouement, de Marsay will be shown to be not the detached observer he thinks he is, but an image artfully created by the narrator: he is both one of the "exemplaires d'un si délicieux portrait" (1058; 111), that is, of Lord Dudley, and a particular illustration of "l'aspect général de la population parisienne." Similarly, "La Force du sang" itself is revealed to be the shock produced not only by the sight of Paquita's massacred body, but also by the identification of her two lovers as brother and sister —a forceful statement of the oppressive interrelationship of imagery in the novel, one of its earliest themes. Moreover, the final words of the third chapter and of *La Fille aux yeux d'or* inscribe the tale within the moral universe of "Physionomies parisiennes," where knowledge prematurely corrupts beauty. This closure thus defines, as if speaking for the work itself in words borrowed from Paquita, "ce cercle d'airain qu'on avait décrit entre la création et moi" (1100; 126).

The narrator does not immediately draw our attention to the line firmly drawn by the novel's formal boundaries. Instead, he begins by stressing the familiarity of the world within it. The melodramatic violence of the murder seems to occur in the context of the novel's extravagant imagery. Waiting outside the Hôtel de San-Réal, de Marsay and Ferragus "entendirent des cris affaiblis qui eussent attendri des tigres" (1106; 128), recalling an earlier moment when Paquita had offered de Marsay a dagger "par un geste de soumission qui aurait attendri un tigre" (1090; 120). The ornamental presence of the Treize upholds the thematic convention of the trilogy, widening the context of the single narrative and thereby distracting the reader. We anticipate an entertaining, uninvolved climax to the story: "Attends-moi, je veux aller voir comment cela se passe là-haut, afin d'apprendre la manière dont se traitent leurs querelles de ménage" (1106; 128).

The murder scene, like so many before it, is at first sight unintelligible, patently ridiculous, and yet is strangely consonant with the work as a whole. Just as the men and women of "Physionomies parisiennes" are defined and consumed by the hierarchical system their lives serve to perpetuate, so Paquita is sacrificed, closed within the novel bearing her name. The life-blood of the character indelibly marks the setting that defines and consumes her existence:

Les mains de Paquita étaient empreintes sur les coussins. Partout elle s'était accrochée à la vie, partout elle s'était défendue, et partout elle avait été frappée. Des lambeaux entiers de la tenture cannelée étaient arrachés par ses mains ensanglantées, qui sans doute avaient lutté longtemps. Paquita devait avoir essayé d'escalader le plafond. Ses pieds nus étaient marqués le long du dossier du divan, sur lequel elle avait sans doute couru. Son corps, déchiqueté à coups de poignard par son bourreau, disait avec quel acharnement elle avait disputé une vie qu'Henri lui rendait si chère. Elle gisait à terre, et avait, en mourant, mordu les muscles du cou-de-pied de Madame de San-Réal, qui gardait à la main son poignard trempé de sang. (1106-07; 128)[14]

This grotesque image might be said to epitomize the lamentable taste of which Balzac is frequently accused, were it not for its symbolic appropriateness in the context of the narrative. For the contemporary reader this moment in *La Fille aux yeux d'or* is reminiscent of the scene in Kafka's "Metamorphosis" when Gregor Samsa, his insect jaws bloodied, careens widely about his bedroom, leaving smudge marks on walls and ceiling. Free to roam and experiment in the symbolic confines of his room, Samsa is a writer-figure liberated from the tyranny of conventional appearances.[15] In the same way, the Marquise makes Paquita an instrument of symbolic expression within the closed setting of the boudoir. And just as Samsa's family will eventually look, horrified, into his bedroom, so de Marsay gazes at the shocking spectacle in the boudoir; the boundaries of the writer's imaginary world open—become accessible—to others, even those it might scandalize.

We are now able to see that the opening vision of Paris and de Marsay's adventure proceed from the same sources, a single point of view. Not only imagery, but language confirms the unity of the novel. The description of the Marquise, with its classical allusions and animal imagery, is reminiscent of earlier descriptions of her brother, the "Adonis" (1054; 109):

Certains animaux, mis en fureur, fondent sur leur ennemi, le mettent à mort, et tranquilles dans leur victoire, semblent avoir tout oublié. Il en est d'autres qui tournent autour de leur victime, qui la gardent en craignant qu'on ne la leur vienne enlever, et qui, semblables à l'Achille d'Homère, font neuf fois le tour de Troie en traînant leur ennemi par les pieds. Ainsi était la marquise. (1007; 128-29)

> Les femmes aiment prodigieusement ces gens qui se nomment pachas eux-mêmes, qui semblent accompagnés de lions, de bourreaux, et marchent dans un appareil de terreur. Il en résulte chez ces hommes une sécurité d'action, une certitude de pouvoir, une fierté de regard, une conscience léonine qui réalise pour les femmes le type de force qu'elles rêvent toutes. Ainsi était de Marsay. (1085; 121)

And into the boudoir with de Marsay come not only a multitude of literary memories and familiar metaphors, but also the multitude from "Physionomies parisiennes": "elle était trop enivrée de sang chaud, trop animée pour la lutte, trop exaltée pour apercevoir Paris entier, si Paris avait formé un cirque autour d'elle" (1107; 129).

The "cirque," then, is also that impenetrable "cercle d'airain" that keeps the narrative form intact and insures its integrity. As the Marquise, narrator and reader all pause, the novel's own conventions and literary influences converge upon the scene, forming still another crowd of invisible onlookers. The novel itself seems generically inbred. The themes of heredity and incest so prominent in this next-to-last scene are far from gratuitous: it is through the images of Lord Dudley's children that we perceive the narrator's consciousness of literary tradition and the consistency of his stylizing vision.

Appropriately, then, the ending of the novel abounds in conventions: literary allusions, the references to orthodox religion, the Marquise's projected flight to a convent, the attribution of Paquita's death to tuberculosis. But the reader is rescued from the jaws of solemnity by the author's wit. The Marquise's parting words to Paquita—" 'Meurs sans confession! lui disait-elle; va en Enfer, monstre d'ingratitude; ne sois plus à personne qu'au démon' " (1107; 129)—are sublimely outrageous, coming from one who herself, in the confessor's eyes, has committed a multitude of sins. The repetition of the word *douleur*—"j'aurai voulu te faire éprouver toutes les douleurs que tu me lègues" (1107; 129), "Morte, ah! j'en mourrai de douleur" (1107; 129)—culminates in the solution to her dilemma, the humorous recourse to another literary convention: "Je me retourne en Espagne pour m'aller mettre au couvent de los Dolores" (1109; 129). Both comic and tragic, however, are the overtones of her lament: "je suis réduite à ne plus aimer que Dieu!" (1107; 129). Clearly, God is a convention who pales beside that ideal sought by the strongest, most passionate minds: "l'infini rendu palpable" (1082; 119). Thus, de Marsay advises his sister to remove "les traces de cette fantaisie" (1109; 129), and it is with sadness—a sort of metaphysical resignation—that the Marquise concludes: "rien ne console d'avoir perdu ce qui nous a paru être l'infini" (1109; 129). These are the words of a Louis Lambert or Frenhofer cured of his delusion.

In *La Fille aux yeux d'or*, a distinctly modern work, the replacement of nature by social nature, of the pastoral setting by an urban one, complicates the artist's task. The field, flowers, insects and "belles fleurs humaines" (1054; 109) of which the narrator speaks are not truly natural; in the city setting they are somehow foreign, grotesque, obtrusive. The many literary allusions and references to other parts of the novel reveal that the springs of creativity are not pure and spontaneous, but historically conditioned, limited and contaminated. Paquita's mother returns to haunt the dénouement she figures (1080; 119), as if to intimate that the most stylized of images embodies but an intensification of the narrator's vision and not a true contrast:

> ... elle a une passion qui fait capituler toutes les autres, et qui aurait anéanti son amour maternel, si elle avait aimé sa fille ...
> —Laquelle? dit vivement Henri en interrompant sa sœur.
> —Le jeu, dont Dieu te garde! répondit la marquise. (1108; 129)

Like the proletarians in "Physionomies parisiennes," Paquita's mother has been delivered up to the "monstre nommé Spéculation" that disfigures and consumes its subjects. Brought from the New World to the Old, abandoning nature for social nature, her beauty corrupted by urban civilization, she, too, has joined the "peuple exhumé" (1039; 104) of Paris. Because it is her "horrible figure" (1108; 129) that appears in the dénouement, she is, with the Parisians, the grotesque spectacle that originally caught the narrator's eye (1039; 104). The novel's other parent, Lord Dudley, like his daughter an "être inconnu qui planait au-dessus d'eux," his children (1089; 122), contributes to the story only the two "exemplaires d'un si délicieux portrait" (1058; 111) whose resemblance and common source are finally verified.

The strange and sharp contrast of classical allusions and Christian imagery, insistently repeated throughout the novel; the heightened consciousness of the accidental nature of social, sexual, national and racial identity; the thematic association of colonialism and capitalism; the bizarre and disturbing union of fantasy and stylization—all these suggest that *La Fille aux yeux d'or* may be nothing less than a glimpse, through Balzac, into the European collective historical consciousness: a meditation upon the traumatic displacement of Hellenistic civilization by the Christian one and the equally traumatic advent of the modern industrial era. Abruptly, then, the last lines of the novel return us to the familiar world of appearances:

> Huit jours après, Paul de Manerville rencontra de Marsay aux Tuileries, sur la terrasse des Feuillants.
> "Eh bien, qu'est donc devenue notre belle FILLE AUX YEUX D'OR, grand scélérat?
> —Elle est morte.
> —De quoi?
> —De la poitrine." (1109; 129)

De Marsay's evasiveness—his "discrétion active"—proves his reluctance to throw, as it were, pearls before swine. He now lives in "le réflet magique de cette perle introuvable" (1070; 104), the illumination of that visionary dénouement; his words—"De la poitrine"—stylize his lover's violent death by the sword into a conventional image of the reaper's daily work. In de Marsay's reply to Paul the narrator has at last physiologically justified his vision of the city, for none of the imaginary population of Paris, not even "la Fille aux yeux d'or," are immune to the infectious air (1050; 108) they breathe, the atmosphere in which they forever live—the magic reflection of the narrator's gaze. The vision of Paris and de Marsay's story are truly inseparable, "cousues ensemble" (1068; 115): together they are *La Fille aux yeux d'or*. The form of the narrative, with its visible and sensible divisions, the three chapters and the two contrasting parts, remains a paradox, but a paradox that is a single entity, a discrete reality, a singular gem. This should come as no surprise, and yet we *are* surprised and marvel at the writer's art—at its consistency, its lucidity, its transparency. As Virginia Woolf said of the works of the great novelists:

... different as these worlds are, each is consistent with itself. The maker of each is careful to observe the laws of his own perspective, and however great a strain they may put upon us they will never confuse us, as lesser writers so frequently do, by introducing two different kinds of reality into the same book.[16]

Chapter VI

EUGÉNIE GRANDET

In turning away from the harsh, melodramatic glare of the *Histoire des Treize* to the quietly luminous *Eugénie Grandet*,[1] we approach a world full of purposeful industry: the servant Nanon seated at her spinning wheel, Eugénie and her mother embroidering by the window, the miser Grandet secretly counting his gold in a room only he may enter. Patiently constructing his work detail by detail, the narrator, too, participates in what appears to be a collective enterprise of edifying labor:

Peut-être la profonde passion d'Eugénie devrait-elle être analysée dans ses fibrilles les plus délicates; car elle devint, diraient quelques railleurs, une maladie, et influença toute son existence. Beaucoup de gens aiment mieux nier les dénouements que de mesurer la force des liens, des nœuds, des attaches qui soudent secrètement un fait à un autre dans l'ordre moral. (1102; 570)

Had the narrator of *Louis Lambert* heeded this criticism, that "œuvre plus ou moins poétique" he scrupulously renounced might have successfully materialized, freeing the character Lambert from the oppression of his biographer's self-scrutiny. And yet, as Nicole Mozet points out, the success of *Eugénie Grandet* served to deflect serious consideration of other works in *La Comédie humaine*: "Balzac lui-même ... dénonçait la perfide entreprise de dénigrement qui se cachait derrière le concert des louanges décernées à cet unique roman: '*Eugénie Grandet*, avec laquelle on a assassiné tant de choses de moi.'"[2] And it is true that the relative dramatic quietude and muted social criticism of the novel invite favorable comparison with other, more extravagant works. As for the reader, he is not immediately cast, as happens in *Le Colonel Chabert*, in the role of the narrator's pupil, given exercises in careful reading before the arrival of the central character; nor is he drawn into the labyrinth of jealous vision (*Ferragus*), challenged to reconstruct a fragmented plot (*La Duchesse de Langeais*) or confronted with the unlikely juxtaposition of a vision and story (*La Fille aux yeux d'or*). The image of the narrator quietly absorbed in the painstaking art of portraiture is pleasing to us; his is a reasonable, undemanding effort that does not challenge our very being, defy us to reexamine our prejudices and hypocrisies, the values of society.

Only superficially does *Eugénie Grandet* resemble such an innocuous and technically facile book. The narrator's vision only seems imperturbable, "omniscient"; his journey leads us to the same revelation of futility and horror associated with the pursuit of gold and pleasure in Paris, of fictitious angels in the self-absorbed mind. A vision of life besieged unremittingly by difficulty and conflict pervades the novel in the way the ancient wooden doors, storefronts and rooftops in Saumur are stained with an invisible melancholy neither rain nor compassionate scrutiny can hope to wash out. In following the narrator through the streets of this provincial town, where secret attachments conspire against personal freedom and the possibility of independent insight, we discover a world of inscription and symbol made very much in the image of our own.

In a parallel to the beginning of *La Fille aux yeux d'or,* "Physionomies parisiennes," the first chapter of *Eugénie Grandet,* entitled "Physionomies bourgeoises," takes us through the narrow, forbidding streets of Saumur by way of introduction to provincial life. There is nothing of the spectacular, circus-like atmosphere of the vividly corrupt Paris streets and public places, nothing of the mythical aura surrounding the prospect of man's fall from Eden and senseless, headlong rush towards death. There is a cruelty of fate in Saumur that abjures the harsh, allegorical distinction; and hidden in every crevice of street, shop and soul, this fate diffuses evenly, impartially, its "principles of melancholy":

> Il se trouve dans certaines villes de province des maisons dont la vue inspire une mélancolie égale à celle que provoquent les cloîtres les plus sombres, les landes les plus ternes ou les ruines les plus tristes. Peut-être y a-t-il à la fois dans ces maisons et le silence du cloître et l'aridité des landes et les ossements des ruines; la vie et le mouvement y sont si tranquilles qu'un étranger les croirait inhabitées, s'il ne rencontrait tout à coup le regard pâle et froid d'une personne immobile dont la figure à demi monastique dépasse l'appui de la croisée au bruit d'un pas inconnu. Ces principes de mélancolie existent dans la physionomie d'un logis situé à Saumur, au bout de la rue montueuse qui mène au château, par le haut de la ville. Cette rue, maintenant peu fréquentée ... est remarquable pour la sonorité de son petit pavé cailloteux, toujours propre et sec .... (1027; 542)

The furtive movements of the few inhabitants, distrustful of the hypothetical visitor, the sharpness of the echo of his footsteps on the cobblestones, the starkness of the façades of these old and somber houses—surely this must be the legacy of some very recent war still harrowing to the memory. Saumur is the image of a devastated spirit. The stranger who happens upon its streets can expect no warm reception, no bright distraction for his eye; his is idle curiosity met with frank, impassive stare, chilled by icy, mute reproach. What is it that causes the heart to sink, to recoil as though spurned or orphaned? The houses of Saumur, fictional cousins of those in Hawthorne's Salem, inspire a certain melancholy, but do not divulge its cause. Their reticence daunts all but the most intrepid storyteller, and even he winds his way cautiously along the streets, each word a carefully measured stop. Cloister, plain, ruin—this metaphorical desolation engenders moth-like creatures vanishing into the recesses of houses built of wood and sorrow. The description of these houses continues:

... leurs divers aspects contribuent à l'originalité qui recommande cette partie de Saumur à l'attention des antiquaires et des artistes. Il est difficile de passer devant ces maisons, sans admirer les énormes madriers dont les bouts sont taillés en figures bizarres et qui couronnent d'un bas-relief noir le rez-de-chaussée de la plupart d'entre elles. Ici, des pièces de bois transversales sont couvertes en ardoises et dessinent des lignes bleues sur les frêles murailles d'un logis terminé par un toit en colombage que les ans ont fait plier, dont les bardeaux pourris ont été tordus par l'action alternative de la pluie et du soleil. Là se présentent des appuis de fenêtre usés, noircis dont les délicates sculptures se voient à peine, et qui semblent trop légers pour le pot d'argile brune d'où s'élancent les œillets ou les rosiers d'une pauvre ouvrière. Plus loin, c'est des portes garnies de clous énormes où le génie de nos ancêtres a tracé des hiéroglyphes domestiques dont le sens ne se retrouvera jamais. Tantôt un protestant y a signé sa foi, tantôt un ligueur y a maudit Henri IV.... L'Histoire de France est là tout entière. (1027-28; 542)

The initial impression of melancholy gives way to curiosity, for the narrator's eye for detail—he is part antiquarian, part artist—leads him to conduct a quiet inspection. Unknown artists have left their fragile, but enduring signatures before him—"figures bizarres" carved into the projecting beams, "délicates sculptures" barely visible on the window sills, "hiéroglyphes domestiques" on doors. The narrator gives evidence of an extreme sensitivity to the telltale signs of weight and oppression: the heaviness of wooden beams, the frailty of the wall, the thickness of the clay pot holding roses or carnations in defiance of misery, the warping of roof and shingles by the relentless alternation of rain and sun. The elements assert their power over human effort: it is the flower, though tended by the poor laborer, that weighs down upon the sill, the weather that weakens the house, time that renders even the most impassioned and deeply imprinted messages indecipherable. The History of France offers no solace or illumination, lends no sense of purpose to this perpetual erosion of artifact and spirit. This History is ingrained in the wood, as indifferently etched as the blue lines formed by slate: a physical presence rooted in the silence, sterility and invisible marrow of these haunting, and haunted, houses. The past is a sort of gravity shaping the contours of present matter and spirit; it cannot be withstood, and yet we cannot understand it. It is an inheritance of religious persecution and petty ambition, of political upheaval and anonymous labor. Its meaning appears to be utterly lost. What does it signify? What can possibly be retrieved?

We have become the "stranger" walking down the streets, for it is clear that the narrator is a knowledgeable guide steeped, perhaps from childhood, in this provincial desolation. Here the tyranny of Speculation shuns the excesses of sexual depravation, drink and gambling so common in the capital; in Saumur exploitation has been made legitimate. Speculation marries Respectability and becomes a member of the bourgeoisie. It is not the impoverished worker's room we enter or the *hôtel* of the idle nobleman. Instead, we are taken to the shops, dark and windowless, their merchandise unceremoniously set out on counters or hung from rafters: "Entrez? Une fille propre, pimpante de jeunesse, au blanc fichu, aux bras rouges quitte son tricot, appelle son père ou sa mère qui vient et vous vend à vos souhaits ..." (1029; 543). Automatically we are drawn into the commerce of everyday life in Saumur, into the tacit struggle to outwit the forces of nature: "Il y a un duel constant entre le ciel et les intérêts terrestres. Le baromètre attriste, déride, égaie tout à tour les physionomies" (1029; 543). The mark of history may fade on the merchant's heavily bolted door, but not the sign of his present allegiance: "ces mots: Voilà un temps d'or! se chiffrent de porte en porte" (1029; 543). A kind of magical alchemy serves the genius of capitalism: "Aussi chacun répondit-il à son voisin: Il pleut des louis, en sachant ce qu'un rayon de soleil, ce qu'une pluie opportune lui en apporte" (1029; 543). Indeed, as the narrator will later tell us, the coins thus metamorphosed from nature by Grandet are remarkably bright, as if newly minted, the imprint and ridges unworn. In Saumur's economy industry and inscription are inseparable; meteorology becomes a defensive strategy against the erosive forces of nature.

On a symbolic level we would expect to find in the narrator a natural ally of the Saumurois, for in committing his story to paper, he, too, would resist the passage of time, the indifference of history and nature. Surprisingly, he goes on to describe the insular mentality of the provincials and the utter lack of privacy their way of life affords. How does the narrator justify this territorial claim on curiosity and indiscretion? What connection exists between the mundane, unquestioned materialism of village life and the inescapable public scrutiny of every thought and movement?

Une ménagère n'achète pas une perdrix sans que les voisins ne demandent au mari si elle était cuite à point. Une jeune fille ne met pas la tête à sa fenêtre sans y être vue par tous les groupes inoccupés. Là donc les consciences sont à jour, de même que ces maisons impénétrables, noires et silencieuses n'ont point de mystères. . . . Il ne passe personne dans la rue qui ne soit étudié. Aussi, jadis, quand un étranger arrivait dans une ville de province, était-il gaussé de porte en porte. (1029-30; 543)

Were the narrator that stranger introduced in the first lines of the novel and now shunted quite deliberately from door to door, the story of Eugénie and her father could not be told. The narrator is instead an insider, and in his writer's economy it is expedient for him to study the secret inscriptions on the door of the Grandet *hôtel* and those in the hearts of its inhabitants. He has brought us inevitably to the threshold of his own domain, the territory of the imagination; and its yield, like the profitable wines so prized by the Saumurois, will rejoice the spirits of more than the consumers only (*Eugénie Grandet* was one of Balzac's financial successes). In Paris gold buys only pleasure, the soul being lost; in the provinces, which are more conservative, it buys only the soul: "les consciences sont à jour." For Balzac, Louis Lambert being one of his cautionary figures, this may be a necessary commerce, a necessary sort of cultivation; for *louis*—the inanimate kind—provide for our "intérêts terrestres," though we do not live by them alone. Publication is as inevitable as physiognomy, "de même que ces maisons impénétrables . . . n'ont point de mystères."

Thus, in *Eugénie Grandet*, unlike, for example, *Ferragus* or *Louis Lambert*, we never stop to question the authority of the narrator, whose identity is constant. The early evocation of a "physionomie d'un logis situé à Saumur" (1027; 542) purposefully develops into the image at the center of the story, an unshakable metaphorical presence:

Après avoir suivi les détours de ce chemin pittoresque . . . vous apercevez un renforcement assez sombre, au centre duquel est cachée la porte de la maison à M. Grandet. Il est impossible de comprendre la valeur de cette expression provinciale sans donner la biographie de M. Grandet. (1030; 543)

Personification of the house by metonymy ("physionomie d'un logis") now becomes personification by the invention of a character ("la biographie de M. Grandet"). And the narrator, precisely because he does not identify himself with the unwelcome city visitor, is perfectly equipped to supply the needed information: "M. Grandet jouissait à Saumur d'une réputation dont les causes et les effets ne seront pas entièrement compris par les personnes qui n'ont point, peu ou prou, vécu en province" (1030; 543).

M. Grandet's biography begins in 1789 with his marriage, which enabled him to acquire "pour un morceau de pain, légalement, sinon légitimement, les plus beaux vignobles de l'arrondissement, une vieille abbaye et quelques métairies" (1030-31; 543). This date marks the beginning not only of Grandet's financial success, but also of his interest as a character and genius for manipulation through language: "Depuis la Révolution, époque à laquelle il attira les regards, le bonhomme bégayait d'une manière fatigante aussitôt qu'il avait à discourir longuement ou à soutenir une discussion" (1035; 545). This sly, calculating intelligence distinguishes Grandet from his literary predecessor, Harpagon, and transforms him into an equally delightful caricature of avarice, if unmistakably Balzacian:

> Au physique, Grandet était un homme de cinq pieds, trapu, carré... ses yeux avaient l'expression calme et dévoratrice que le peuple accorde au basilic; son front, plein de rides transversales, ne manquait pas de protubérances significatives; ses cheveux jaunâtres et grisonnants étaient blanc et or.... Son nez, gros par le bout, supportait une loupe veinée que le vulgaire disait, non sans raison, pleine de malice. Cette figure annonçait une finesse dangereuse, une probité sans chaleur, l'égoïsme d'un homme habitué à concentrer ses sentiments dans la jouissance de l'avarice et sur le seul être qui lui fut réellement de quelque chose, sa fille Eugénie, sa seule héritière. (1035-36; 545)

This description, like the opening passage, is a microcosm of the novel: the brilliance hidden behind the "protubérances significatives," underestimated by the townspeople, will engineer the union of Grandet's fortune and of Eugénie with no loss of integrity—"une probité sans chaleur"—in essence, the plot of the narrative. The comparison of the miser to a basilisk is also beyond reproach: the root *basileus* (Greek, king) is also that of *basilica*, incorporating in a single image Grandet's sovereignty in his household and religious devotion to his fortune. A tropical American lizard, the basilisk also remotely prefigures the connection between the Grandet family and the American continent, in Charles's involvement with the slave trade. And finally, the legendary basilisk, with that calm, devouring and also fatal gaze, is a heraldic monster, an emblem of this tale of inheritance. After describing Grandet's costume, the narrator adds: "Saumur ne savait rien de plus sur ce personnage" (1036; 546), which need not disturb the reader. All has been said with respect to the major themes of the novel: the principles of melancholy, the symbol of the basilisk, the syntactic conjunction of Eugénie and Grandet's wealth state the mood, mythic overtones and impending drama of the narrative.

Although she dominates the popular imagination of the Saumurois, all that is known of Eugénie Grandet is her capacity as heiress: "Que ne disait-on pas d'une héritière dont on parlait à vingt lieues à la ronde et jusque dans les voitures publiques, d'Angers à Blois inclusivement?" (1038; 546). With this long, literally circuitous preamble to the introduction of Eugénie as character Balzac resurrects the technique he uses to introduce Colonel Chabert, but to different effect; Eugénie is like a figure woven in a tapestry whose presence becomes apparent only as the overall design emerges. The metaphorical shower of *louis*, industry exploiting nature; the inspired stuttering of Grandet, greed corrupting language; the conversion of religious values into material ones, symbolized by the basilisk—these themes, Saumur's dynamic laws, have already set in motion the drama of Eugénie's coming of age. The narrator therefore stresses the inherent significance of the opening description: "Il est maintenant facile de comprendre toute la valeur de ce mot, la maison à monsieur Grandet" (1039; 546).

Leaving behind the spectacle of Parisian manners and the shifting sands of philosophical speculation, the narrator has chosen to contemplate an unchanging, unquestioned system in which conservation, ritual, hierarchy —all characteristic of the Grandet household—are principles of conduct, not cause for anxiety. This is not to say that Grandet's immovable customs are not ludicrous, but rather to observe the presence of constant, predictable rhythms in the conduct of daily life—rhythms absent in Balzac's fictional Paris and in the description of Lambert's intellectual development. The narrator emphasizes the value of continuity in the elaboration of perspective as well; the description of Grandet's home restates the earlier motifs of deterioration, isolation, the presence of history in the evidence of inscription:

> Au-dessus du cintre régnait un long bas-relief de pierre dure sculptée, représentant les quatre Saisons, figures déjà rongées et toutes noires. . . . La porte, en chêne massif . . . était solidement maintenue par le système de ses boulons, qui figuraient des dessins symétriques. Une grille carrée, petite, mais à barreaux serrés et rouges de rouille, occupait le milieu de la porte bâtarde et servait, pour ainsi dire, de motif à un marteau qui s'y rattachait par un anneau, et frappait sur la tête grimaçante d'un maître clou. Ce marteau, de forme oblongue et du genre de ceux que nos ancêtres nommaient jaquemart, ressemblait à un gros point d'admiration; en l'examinant avec attention, un antiquaire y aurait retrouvé quelques indices de la figure essentiellement bouffonne qu'il représentait jadis. . . . Par la petite grille, destinée à reconnaître les amis, au temps des guerres civiles, les curieux pouvaient apercevoir . . . quelques marches dégradées par lesquelles on montait dans un jardin . . . . (1039; 547)

The Four Seasons, here emblematized, are both figural (images in procession larger than the life of the individual) and literal (recognizable and namable designs carved in wood). Of universal import, these are not "des hiéroglyphes domestiques dont le sens ne se retrouvera jamais" (1028; 542). Even the knocker on the door has its tradition, accessible to the knowledgeable observer. The narrator finds in the clown-like figure traced upon it yet another physiognomy announcing its presence, "un gros point d'admiration." A survivor of civil wars, the grille also mediates his interested gaze, just as once it had welcomed more urgent inspection, being "destinée à reconnaître les amis." Rather than mystify and discourage the onlooker, these objects proffer their significance to the one who has learned to read them.

Entering into the central room, the narrator continues to describe the interpenetration of Fable and History, of myth and mimesis: "Les sièges de forme antique étaient garnies en tapisseries représentant les fables de La Fontaine; mais il fallait le savoir pour en reconnaître les sujets, tant les couleurs passées et les figures criblées de reprises se voyaient difficilement" (1040; 547). Worn deep into the fabric of ordinary life, Literature, in the form of images from La Fontaine, has a pervasive, indelible influence: however unremarkable the scenes sewn into the tapestry, these images preserve the form of a solid structure and, studied patiently by one steeped in the traditions of his culture, yield their meaning. These chairs symbolize the narrative: a temporary resting place and frame for the reader's consciousness. Indeed, we have not traveled far. The interior of the Grandet household corresponds perfectly to its geographical location; indoors above the table we find the all-important barometer (1040; 547). On the opposite wall art acts again to preserve history and tradition, of the family this time, in the portraits of Madame Grandet's grandfather and Grandet's maternal grandmother (1040; 547). These are the patron saints—misers all—of "la maison à monsieur Grandet."

The beginning of *Eugénie Grandet* has no identifiable narrator, and yet its historical and visual detail has come to assume virtually mythological proportions. What Erich Auerbach writes of "la pension Vauquer" in *Le Père Goriot* is equally true of Grandet's house:

The motif of the unity of a milieu has taken hold of him [Balzac] so powerfully that the things and the persons composing a milieu often acquire for him a sort of second significance which, though different from that which reason can comprehend, is far more essential—a significance which can be best defined by the adjective demonic. In the dining-room with its furniture which, worn and shabby though it be, is perfectly harmless to a reason uninfluenced by imagination, "misfortune oozes, speculation cowers." In this trivial everyday scene allegorical witches lie hidden, and instead of the plump sloppily dressed widow one momentarily sees a rat appear. What confronts us, then, is the unity of a particular milieu, felt as a total concept of a demonic-organic nature and presented entirely by suggestive and sensory means.[3]

Instead of allegorical witches and rats, we find a basilisk with a fatal brilliant gaze; we are not in the room "où suinte le malheur, où s'est blotti la spéculation," but rather in "le théâtre de la vie domestique" (1040; 547) watched over by the portraits of Grandet's ancestors and made immortal by association with the Four Seasons and La Fontaine. The stage of this theater has been discreetly set, slowly materializing before our eyes; and if a principle of order seems to be missing, the poetic principle of melancholy governs the logic of the description, infusing naturalistic detail with the intensity of dramatic necessity. Why the narration moves from a description of Saumur to a portrait of Grandet to one of the Grandet home cannot be explained except as a dictate of poetic intuition; each unit is consistent with the whole, like a cell replicating the basic genetic code of the organism while itself performing a specialized function.

Having thus established the milieu composed of persons and things, the narrator introduces Eugénie:

> Dans la croisée la plus rapprochée de la porte, se trouvait une chaise de paille.... Une travailleuse en bois de merisier déteint remplissait l'embrasure, et le petit fauteuil d'Eugénie Grandet était placé tout auprès. Depuis quinze ans, toutes les journées de la mère et de la fille s'étaient paisiblement écoulées à cette place, dans un travail constant, à compter du mois d'avril jusqu'au mois de novembre. Le premier de ce dernier mois elles pouvaient prendre leur station d'hiver à la cheminée. (1041; 547)

One might call this, like Colonel Chabert's, an introduction by metonymy, for it is by means of contiguous displacement—streets, father, suitors, home, mother's chair, workbench, armchair—that we finally arrive before the character announced by the novel's title. And Eugénie—and her mother —still have no fixed locus, changing their station from window to fireplace according to the season, in imitation of the "action alternative de la pluie et du soleil" (1028; 542) that rules Saumur's economy. Grandet alone, source of light and nourishment, seems to possess the quality of absoluteness:

> ... si Eugénie voulait broder une collerette à sa mère, elle était forcée de prendre sur ses heures de sommeil en trompant son père pour avoir de la lumière. Depuis longtemps l'avare distribuait la chandelle à sa fille et à la Grande Nanon, de même qu'il distribuait dès le matin le pain et les denrées nécessaires à la consommation journalière. (1041; 547)

From this ritual we learn much about the novel: Grandet, giving out the daily bread, seems to have done so since time immemorial ("Depuis longtemps"); and prefigured here is the final image of the novel, "la Grande Nanon," the epithet conferring a kind of indestructability upon the character. In this feudal kingdom Eugénie, the rightful heiress, already has recourse to deception in the service of her personal interests, unafraid to "tromper son père pour avoir de la lumière." This phrase tells us the way in which Eugénie will lose innocence in pursuit of her cousin Charles and experience; for her a precondition of sight is willful disobedience of the father, which places her in the company of Jules, the Treize and Balzac's other rebellious figures. Unlike Louis Lambert and Colonel Chabert, whose illumination depends instead on the transcendence of physical limitation— "percer la couverture de chair qui mettait une barrière entre la vie et moi" —Eugénie equates illumination with forbidden knowledge and subverts her father's authority and values by inventing a religion of eros.[4] Given the same theme—"tromper son père pour avoir de la lumière"—a Hawthorne or Dostoevsky would have created a psychological drama full of religious, allegorical significance. That Eugénie's drama will unfold without the support of such mythic structures reveals the radical conservatism at the heart of Balzac's vision. As Northrop Frye observes: "There is a strongly conservative element at the core of realism, an acceptance of society in its present structure, an attitude of mind that helps to make Balzac typical of realism, just as the opposite revolutionary attitude helps to make Victor Hugo typical of romanticism."[5]

The association of intelligence with deceit, of family ties with greed, of nature with capitalism—these motifs impassively sound the theme of social corruption as an unshakable framework for the story; it is so early made clear that Eugénie will not be Antigone to her father's Creon—and even the latter comparison is a slight to Grandet's unimpeachable devotion to his ruling passion. Conservatism in Balzac may perhaps be defined as strict fidelity to observed detail, but it does not follow that vision in Balzac is a complacent one. The bridge between Balzac as realist and Balzac as visionary—for the latter subsumes the former—may lie in his narrators' persistent recognition that the most incontrovertible of facts, the most irresistible of influences, the most vivid of words or gestures, are ultimately accidental in a world built on illusion. In Balzac's universe the arbitrary reigns supreme —and its arbitrariness is seen as such. Grandet embodies this condition perfectly, and it is Eugénie's difficult inheritance.

This authorial pessimism thus revealed by the narrative perspective, the drama proper begins:

En 1819, vers le commencement de la soirée, au milieu du mois de novembre, la grande Nanon alluma du feu pour la première fois ... chacun se souvint que ce jour était l'anniversaire de la naissance de Mlle Eugénie. Aussi, calculant l'heure où le dîner devait finir, Me Cruchot, l'abbé Cruchot et M. C. de Bonfons s'empressaient-ils d'arriver avant les des Grassins pour fêter Mlle Grandet. Tous trois apportaient d'énormes bouquets cueillis dans leurs petites serres. La queue des fleurs que le président voulait présenter était ingénieusement enveloppée d'un ruban de satin blanc, orné de franges d'or. Le matin, M. Grandet, suivant sa coutume pour les jours mémorables de la naissance et de la fête d'Eugénie, était venu la surprendre au lit, et lui avait solennellement offert son présent paternel, consistant, depuis treize années, en une curieuse pièce d'or. (1044-45; 549)

Here, as in previous moments, the particular, familiar detail assumes the burden and richness associated with mythological allusion. Nanon performs a simple, elemental gesture of Promethean proportions; a sort of archetypal gravity is conferred upon her action by the qualification "pour la première fois." The interior of the house now warmed by fire—symbol of passion and enlightenment—the family celebrates the advent of a cold, forbidding season to be ambiguously redeemed by the birth of Eugénie's love for Charles. This new season actually commemorates an old, eternal war between the rival des Grassins and Cruchot families; the locution "Aussi ... s'empressaient-ils" implies the dramatic necessity of this regenerated conflict. The audience of "tout Saumur" (1044; 549) and the presence of universal recollection ("chacun se souvint") establish a context of collective memory, the living stage of myth; and like the Magi drawn by the star over Bethlehem to lay gifts before the manger, so the three Cruchots travel to the Grandet home to leave their precious gifts (the flower stem *"ingénieusement* enveloppée") in honor of "la naissance de Mlle Eugénie." On this first of two "jours mémorables"—Eugénie's saint's day in the spring is a kind of Easter—the Father wakens the daughter and prepares her for her worldly mission, a task first begun when Eugénie was ten years old—the same age at which Lambert leaves home to become a scholar. Indeed, Eugénie will soon be about her father's business, even in accumulating her "douzain de mariage" (1045; 549); for this, the narrator tells us, is "un antique usage encore en vigueur et saintement conservé" (1045; 549) in the provinces. Marriage will not endanger the integrity of a fortune built on the principle of conservation, tradition and a miser's definition of filial piety, one that embraces devotion directed both to himself and to the god he serves. Madame Grandet and her ancestors provide merely for Eugénie's peripheral needs—clothing, an increase of her fortune—but Grandet watches over what is essential. Avarice, elevated to a spiritual discipline, is as monstrous as it is, for its adherents, sublime.

Indeed, in the dialogue that follows, Grandet emerges as an ascetic Preacher, at moments diabolically worthy of Ecclesiastes:

—En vérité, madame Grandet, vous ne savez quoi vous inventer pour dépenser de l'argent. Le deuil est dans le cœur et non dans les habits. (1100; 569)
—Nanon, dit-il, en s'avançant dans le couloir, veux-tu bien éteindre ton feu, ta lumière, et venir avec nous?
—Mais, monsieur, vous aurez du beau monde.
—Ne les vaux-tu pas bien? ils sont de la côte d'Adam tout comme toi. (1049; 550-51)
—C'est vrai, monsieur, que ça [crows] mange les morts?
—Tu es bête, Nanon! ils mangent, comme tout le monde, ce qu'ils trouvent. Est-ce que nous ne vivons pas des morts? Qu'est-ce donc que les successions? (1080; 562)

Vanitas vanitatum, Grandet seems to say; in the sight of Mammon, as in the sight of eternity, all is equal, ephemeral, destined to return to dust.

It is no doubt from this perspective that the miser views the politics of ingratiation pursued by the Cruchots and the des Grassins, not to mention the suicide of his brother and destitution of his nephew. The narrator, who tells the scene with irreverent detachment, all the while leaving Grandet his mysterious superiority, implicitly speaks with the "omniscience" that is the miser's own. Thus, the comedy unfolds as if under Grandet's bemused gaze, revealing the comedy for what it is. The des Grassins and their son Adolphe, another trio of worshippers, offer Eugénie a present:

> ... une boîte à ouvrage dont tous les ustensiles étaient en vermeil, véritable marchandise de pacotille, malgré l'écusson sur lequel un E.G. gothique assez bien gravé pouvait faire croire à une façon très soignée.... Elle tourna les yeux sur son père, comme pour savoir s'il lui était permis d'accepter, et M. Grandet dit un "Prends, ma fille!" dont l'accent eût illustré un acteur. (1050-51; 551)

The gift is of such shoddy workmanship that the inscription is as an insult, unworthy of the hieroglyphs carved into the wooden doors of *hôtels* and unworthy of the inscriptions on the newly minted coins given Eugénie by her father. Eugénie's effusive reaction—"Je n'ai rien vu de si joli nulle part" (1051; 551)—betrays the horrible state of ignorance, esthetically speaking, in which her father has kept her; but he, of course, has not been duped: "Ils viennent s'ennuyer ici pour ma fille. Hé! ma fille ne sera ni pour les uns ni pour les autres, et tous ces gens-là me servent de harpons pour pêcher" (1052; 552).

Having established Grandet's realistic, cynical perspective as the correct light by which to read this scene, the narrator then describes the tableau before him, again in mythological terms:

> Cette gaieté de famille, dans ce vieux salon gris, mal éclairé par deux chandelles; ces rires, accompagnés par le bruit du rouet de la grande Nanon, et qui n'étaient sincères que sur les lèvres d'Eugénie ou de sa mère: cette petitesse jointe à de si grands intérêts; cette jeune fille qui, semblable à ces oiseaux victimes du haut prix auquel on les met et qu'ils ignorent, se trouvait traquée, serrée par des preuves d'amitié dont elle était la dupe; tout contribuait à rendre cette scène tristement comique. N'est-ce pas d'ailleurs une scène de tous les temps et de tous les lieux, mais ramenée à sa plus simple expression? La figure de Grandet exploitant le faux attachement de deux familles, en tirant d'énormes profits, dominait ce drame et l'éclairait. N'était-ce pas le seul dieu moderne auquel on ait foi, l'Argent dans toute sa puissance, exprimé par une seule physionomie? (1052; 552)

Like Pauline in *Louis Lambert*, Nanon, spinning by the hearth, tends to a cruelly deceived creature: Lambert and Eugénie both fall victim to their visions of heavenly or earthly paradise. While the other players in this scene are bent over their cards, Grandet, source of light, alone comprehends the game and its stakes. The allegorization of Money, the mythological hum of Nanon's spinning wheel, the manichean division of knowledge and ignorance, are so many lights and shadows cast upon a canvas of realistic detail. This moment of suspension invites us, like the narrator, to reflect upon the function of the literary work: the creation of a "scène de tous les temps et de tous les lieux." It is through the "simple expression" of the particular that the storyteller meets the universal:

> The novel does not have access to the primordial time of myths, but in so far as he tells a credible story, the novelist employs a time that is *seemingly historical* yet is condensed or prolonged, a time, then, that has at its command all the freedoms of imaginary worlds.
>
> More strongly than any of the other arts, we feel in literature a revolt against historical time, the desire to attain to other temporal rhythms than that in which we are condemned to love and work.... Traces of such a mythological behavior can also be deciphered in the desire to rediscover the intensity with which one experienced or knew something *for the first time*; and also in the desire to recover the distant past, the blissful period of the "beginnings."[6]

Here, as in Colonel Chabert's account of his escape at Eylau, myth and mimesis create a plausible image invested with the "magical power"[7] to transport us to an imaginary space where human gesture has solemn, universal significance and a freedom denied us in everyday life. The narrator attests to the universality of his drama; and yet in detailing the "façons despotiques" (1055; 552) of the hero, he has made it clear that the order of Grandet's household, his universe, is often arbitrary. When Nanon lights the fire "pour la première fois," when the narrator walks down the streets of Saumur in an effort to interpret the symbols of an irretrievable past, we have entered a fictional mythology fully conscious of its limits, neither constrained nor undermined by a voice full of doubt, as in *Louis Lambert.*

Thus, although Charles Grandet arrives in Saumur much in the same way that Lambert the "aérolithe" descends upon the Collège des Oratoriens, the interruption disconcerts only the reader and the characters, not the narrator and Grandet:

> ...son arrivée en ce logis et sa chute au milieu de ce monde peut être comparée à celle d'un colimaçon dans une ruche, ou à l'introduction d'un paon dans quelque obscure basse-cour de village.
> —Asseyez-vous auprès du feu, lui dit Grandet. (1054; 552)

Having entered the basilisk's den, warming himself by its fire, Charles has unknowingly subjected himself to the laws of this strange kingdom bordering on the fantastic and yet inscribed within the boundaries of the "seemingly historical," the naturalistically convincing. With Charles's arrival the narrative again suspends its own rhythms; the brief second chapter, "Le Cousin de Paris," is a kind of pause during which the provincials—and notably Eugénie—develop their own powers of observation and are not themselves mere objects of contemplation. Indeed, Charles is simply a restatement of an earlier theme: the stranger who arrives in Saumur, puzzled and ostracized, has here been given a particular identity. The narrator's original delight in minute detail resurfaces here, transposed in a lighter register; after describing Charles's elegant costume and the negligent dress of the Saumurois, the narrator pictures the characters engaged in similar relentless inspection:

> Le Parisien prenait-il son lorgnon pour examiner les singuliers accessoires de la salle, les solives du plancher, le ton des boiseries ou les points que les mouches y avaient imprimés et dont le nombre aurait suffi pour ponctuer L'Encyclopédie méthodique et Le Moniteur, aussitôt les joueurs de loto levaient le nez et le considéraient avec autant de curiosité qu'ils en eussent manifesté pour une girafe. (1058; 554)

La Fontaine and Molière have temporarily been abandoned in favor of lighter reading, and the markings in wood oppress us not with the weight of a disremembered past, but with the suggestion of journalistic prose. Eugénie, however, is thoroughly enchanted:

> Eugénie ... crut voir en son cousin une créature descendue de quelque région séraphique.... La vue de son cousin fit sourdre en son cœur les émotions de fine volupté que causent à un jeune homme les fantastiques figures de femmes dessinées par Westall dans les Keepsake anglais et gravées par les Finden d'un burin si habile qu'on a peur, en soufflant sur le vélin, de faire envoler ces apparitions célestes. (1058-59; 554)

Where all others see a zoological anomaly, Eugénie sees a heavenly being who, although seraphic, is decidedly a "créature," in contradistinction to Lambert, the "création" viewed by the narrator. The "fine volupté" that marks her sensual awakening is, unknown to her, esthetic in character; love is like a visual art that makes her at last conscious of her surroundings: "elle était travaillée par un poignant désir d'inspecter la chambre de son cousin ... afin de la rendre, autant que possible, élégante et propre" (1059; 554). In a way, Charles's arrival occasions her intellectual awakening as well: "Il lui avait plus surgi d'idées en un quart d'heure qu'elle n'en avait eu depuis qu'elle était au monde" (1060; 554). This ability to criticize the order established by an authority figure, Grandet, is the typical prelude to catastrophe: Paquita in the Marquise's boudoir, the Duchesse de Langeais in the Faubourg Saint-Germain, Ferragus in legitimate society—these figures who dare to defy a predetermined order or composition inevitably bring drama and disaster into their lives.

The incipient rebellion originates in the "inattention du père Grandet" (1063; 555), that is to say, his continued absorption in his reading. When the miser puts his brother's letter away, he automatically resumes his despotic, almost priestly role: "Je vais vous montrer le chemin" (1069; 558), he says to Charles as he takes him to the guest room, a practical and financial counsel. Most important, technically speaking, Grandet's brief adoption of the role of reader creates the circumstances through which Eugénie can distinguish herself from her surroundings, develop an identity as character. The narrator now turns to a figure who, superficially at least, seems much less interesting than her father. For that reason the narrator's powers of discernment constitute the drama of the third chapter, "Amours de province," balancing the stirrings of an inner life with the continued theatrical and financial coups of an imposing and memorable character.

As he brings to life a dormant, almost faceless figure, the narrator draws attention to the disproportion between the potential richness of Eugénie's inner life and the meanness of her milieu by means of the tone, the choice of metaphors and the theme of balance and proportion itself:

> Dans la pure et monotone vie des jeunes filles, il vient une heure délicieuse où le soleil lent épanche ses rayons dans l'âme, où la fleur leur exprime des pensées, où les palpitations de cœur communiquent au cerveau leur chaude fécondance, et fondent les idées en un vague désir; jour d'innocente mélancolie et de suaves joyeusetés! Quand les enfants commencent à voir, ils sourient; quand une fille entrevoit le sentiment dans la nature, elle sourit comme elle souriait enfant. Si la lumière est le premier amour de la vie, l'amour n'est-il pas la lumière du cœur? Le moment de voir clair aux choses d'ici-bas était arrivé pour Eugénie. (1073; 559)

Eugénie's initiation to the "things of this world," her emotional and sexual coming of age—"heure délicieuse," "chaude fécondance," "vague désir"—inspires comparison with the visual discoveries made by the infant, uncorrupted, living through his senses, ready to embrace all that he sees. The sun that inundates the soul with light metaphorically takes up residence in the heart; thus internalized, the image of light suggests a profound harmony between nature and human affection, between childlike delight in the world and adult acceptance of it. The contemporary reader may well fail to be enchanted by a passage marked by the familiar Romantic topos of the vision of the child, not to mention other such clichés: the sun as symbol of eros, the woman as radiant principle of love, the image of the solitary and contemplative figure who will later be likened to a writer (1075; 560). However, in the context of the narrative these themes have specific connotations. The image of the sun, for example, appears in the first pages of *Eugénie Grandet* as the symbol of commercial prosperity, incarnated by Grandet: "le rire équivoque du père Grandet était un vrai rayon de soleil" (1043; 548). As if corrupted by association with the town of Saumur, the sun emits a harsh, distorting light, its rays contaminated by the gleam of gold. Eugénie's vision respects the limits of the exclusively materialistic horizons such a sun reveals: "Le moment de voir clair *aux choses d'ici-bas* était arrivé pour Eugénie."

The image of the infant learning to see—a motif that will accompany the description of Grandet's death—evokes only immediately the favorable meanings of freshness and receptivity. An implicit regression from adult to infant qualifies the seemingly benevolent description: is it the utter newness of Eugénie's feelings or her completely formless reaction to them that the narrator would emphasize? The appearances of childlike absorption in one's thought is suspect in Balzac's fiction: in *Louis Lambert* it takes a pathetic and pathological form; in *Le Colonel Chabert*, a wounded and sinister one. Like the image of the sun, the child image will appear at critical moments in the novel, as if to brand Eugénie as her father's daughter, indelibly to confirm her in her destiny as heiress.

The narrator goes on to describe Eugénie's appearance and frames her in a meditative pose:

Eugénie se croisa bonnement les bras, s'assit à sa fenêtre, contempla la cour, le jardin étroit et les hautes terrasses qui le dominaient; vue mélancolique, bornée, mais qui n'était pas dépourvue des mystérieuses beautés particulières aux endroits solitaires ou à la nature inculte. Auprès de la cuisine se trouvait un puits entouré d'une margelle, et à poulie maintenue dans une branche de fer courbée, qu'embrassait une vigne aux pampres flétris.... De là, le tortueux sarment gagnait le mur, s'y attachait, courait le long de la maison et finissait sur un bûcher où le bois était rangé avec autant d'exactitude que peuvent l'être les livres d'un bibliophile.... Enfin les huit marches... étaient disjointes et ensevelies sous de hautes plantes comme le tombeau d'un chevalier enterré par sa veuve au temps des croisades. Au-dessus d'une assise de pierres toutes rongées s'élevait une grille de bois pourri, à moitié tombée de vétusté, mais à laquelle se mariaient à leur gré des plantes grimpantes. De chaque côté de la porte à claire-voie s'avançaient les rameaux tortus de deux pommiers rabougris.... Un immense noyer... inclinait ses branches jusque sur le cabinet du tonnelier. (1074; 560)

This is the landscape of Eugénie's soul: melancholic, limited in its sights (significantly obstructed by "le cabinet du tonnelier"), yet mysterious in its silence and abandon. The hidden depths of the well, the discreet tenacity of the ivy, the neatness of the stacked wood—these qualities mirror Eugénie's obscure virtues. Dislodged and overshadowed by tall plants, the garden steps conjure up an image of medieval valor and virtue—nobility, fidelity, piety. But this impression of monastic stillness is overturned by metaphor: a vine "embraces" the iron bar over the well; plants "se mariaient" at will to the decaying arbor; apple trees possibly laden with Edenic symbolism proffer their gnarled branches towards the sun; light falls upon the "Cheveux de Vénus" (1075; 560), a plant soon to be explicitly connected with Eugénie herself; and the rustling sound of leaves (1075; 560) seems to suggest her inner agitation. When the heroine steps forth from the garden into an archetypal, imaginary space, we discern no rupture between myth and mimesis, so intertwined are detail and allusion: *"Pour la première fois,* elle eut dans le cœur de la terreur à l'aspect de son père, vit en lui le maître de son sort, et se crut coupable d'une faute en lui taisant quelques pensées" (1077; 561; my emphasis).

With this descriptive passage the figure of Eugénie has assimilated all the wealth of her poetical inheritance: the characteristics of a provincial "type", the allusiveness of a literary creation, the meanings in the narrative up to this point. Thus, in the ensuing comical dialogue the narrator can pit Eugénie against her father as an equal. Indeed, in defying Grandet, Eugénie becomes more and more like him,[8] as if severing herself from an erroneous first attachment to her mother: "la vie des célèbres sœurs hongroises, attachées l'une à l'autre par une erreur de la nature, n'avait pas été plus intime que ne l'était celle d'Eugénie et de sa mère" (1084; 564). Like Grandet's, Eugénie's eye is immediately drawn to the sight of gold:

—Vous avez une bien jolie bague, dit Eugénie [to Charles], est-ce mal de vous demander à la voir? (1089; 565)

Eugénie avait aperçu, par le regard furtif qu'elle jeta sur le ménage du jeune homme ... les jolies bagatelles de sa toilette, ses ciseaux, ses rasoirs enrichis d'or. (1097; 568)

She, too, would involve Nanon in her schemes to outwit the rest of the family:

—Achètes-en [coffee for Charles].
—Et si monsieur me rencontre?
—Il est à ses prés. (1085; 564)

Quand le père Grandet eut fermé sa porte, il appela Nanon.
—Ne lâche pas le chien et ne dors pas, nous avons à travailler ensemble. (1119; 577)

Like Grandet, Eugénie learns to dissemble her calculations by affecting distracting mechanical activity:

Eugénie tirait ses points avec une régularité de mouvement qui eut dévoilé à un observateur les fécondes pensées de sa méditation. (1098; 568)

Grandet tourna ses pouces pendant quatre heures, abîmé dans des calculs dont les résultats devaient, le lendemain, étonner Saumur. (1100; 569)

Her native intelligence in this domain utterly astonishes Grandet, disarmed by the resemblance:

—Vous avez mille pièces cette année, mon père? dit Eugénie.
—Oui, *fifille*. . . .
—Eh bien, mon père, vous pouvez facilement secourir Charles.
L'étonnement, la colère, la stupéfaction de Balthazar en apercevant le *Mane-Teckel-Pharès* ne sauraient se comparer au froid courroux de Grandet qui, ne pensant plus à son neveu, le retrouvait logé au cœur et dans les calculs de sa fille. (1098-99; 569)

As Grandet will eventually conclude with a mixture of exasperation and self-congratulation: "Elle ne bougera pas, elle ne sourcillera pas, elle est plus Grandet que je ne suis Grandet" (1155; 590).

If Eugénie vies with her father for control of her destiny, Balzac vies with another literary giant in giving the miser center stage. As Grandet makes his rounds decrying the "pillage" (1091; 566) he finds made in Charles's honor, he must compete with a young rival for possession of Eugénie, as does Molière's Harpagon in pursuit of his beloved Mariane. Both Harpagon and Grandet begrudge even the necessary expenditures for food and clothing; miserliness in speech inspires in both a penchant for aphorisms; both demand filial obedience and punish its absence with the banishment of their child; and when both would initiate their daughters to the secrets of finance, they are met with defiance over a rival passion—love. The implicit presence of Molière enlivens the grotesque melodrama unfolding in the Grandet household, showing Grandet's parsimony to verge legitimately upon the ludicrous, an exaggeration born of literary precedent.

Unlike Harpagon, however, Grandet displays a genius for calculation that forbids the reader's ridicule or pity. After torturing Maître Cruchot (and the reader) with his stuttering, Grandet arrives at a stunning insight:

Eh bien, ca . . . ca . . . ca . . . calculez ce que que que dou . . . ou . . . ouze cents francs par an pen . . . pen . . . pendant quarante ans do . . . donnent a . . . avec les in . . . in . . . intérêts com . . . com . . . composés que que que vouous saaavez.

—Va pour soixante mille francs, dit le notaire.

—Je le veux bien! . . . Eh bien, reprit le vigneron sans bégayer, deux mille peupliers de quarante ans ne me donneraient pas cinquante mille francs. Il y a perte. (1081; 562)

And soon thereafter:

—Ma femme, dit-il sans bégayer, je les ai tous attrapés. . . . Les propriétaires de tous les bons vignobles gardent leur récolte et veulent attendre, je ne les en ai pas empêchés. Notre Belge était désespéré. J'ai vu cela. Affaire faite, il prend notre récolte à deux cents francs la pièce, moitié comptant. Je suis payé en or. (1098; 569)

Even his plan to restore his brother's good name, the project that will dominate the following chapter of the novel, is a brilliant "comédie" (1105; 571) that will make him "le lendemain, sans qu'il lui en coutât un denier, l'objet de l'admiration de sa ville" (1105; 571). Grandet is distinctly a 19th-century creation in that he, unlike his predecessor, cultivates a passion sustained by an understanding of contemporaneous economic structures. Avarice, as practiced by Grandet, is a sign of analytical prowess. He could not possibly say, as does Harpagon: "La charité, maître Simon, nous oblige à faire plaisir aux personnes, lorsque nous le pouvons" (L'Avare, II, ii).[9] In Grandet's economy moral rectitude is permissible only when it does not conflict with one's financial well-being: "Le deuil est dans le cœur et non dans les habits" (1100; 569).

In the third chapter the narrator has taken both Grandet and his daughter to the thresholds of their individual selves, to doors opening upon what is for each of them the ultimate meaning of life. Eugénie, in the garden, would find in love her destiny—a hope that will be proved illusory; Grandet "se voyait en perspective huit millions dans trois ans, et voguait sur cette longue nappe d'or" (1100; 570)—the only future he is capable of imagining. The narrator pauses to comment upon the psychology of avarice:

> Oh! qui a bien compris l'agneau paisiblement couché aux pieds de Dieu, le plus touchant emblème de toutes les victimes terrestres, celui de leur avenir, enfin la Souffrance et la Faiblesse glorifiées? Cet agneau, l'avare le laisse s'engraisser, il le parque, le tue, le cuit, le mange et le méprise. La nature des avares se compose d'argent et de dédain. (1105; 571)

Grandet's metaphorical slaughter of the lamb—not even a burnt offering to his god, for, ever parsimonious, he would salvage from it a meal—cannot truly be called sacrificial; it is a perfectly ordinary gesture, the meaningless ritual of systematic economic exploitation: "Où est l'homme sans désir, et quel désir social se résoudra sans argent?" (1104-05; 571). History defeats Allegory, checks the myth-making impulse: Balzac's characters simply cannot be abstracted from the complicated fictional world they inhabit, a refraction of the historical one. Balzac seems to leave his characters here as if poised over a metaphysical void, perhaps the result of his radical acceptance of social structures; we are promised only the continuation of the drama, both Grandet's and Eugénie's, as confirmed by the title of the next chapter: "Promesses d'avare, serments d'amour."

The chapter begins with a gesture symbolizing the "douce émotion" (1107; 572) shared by Eugénie and Charles: her simple offering, and his gracious acceptance, of a bowl of coffee. Although the story of their romance is a realistic variation of the "Sleeping Beauty" tale,[10] the narrator foretells the end of enchantment by transforming Charles into that most Romantic of characters, the interesting hero:[11] "Il ne jouait pas la douleur, il souffrait véritablement, et le voile étendu sur ses traits par la peine lui donnait cet air intéressant qui plaît tant aux femmes" (1108; 573). Just as the narrator early in *Louis Lambert* anticipates the hero's future accomplishments on the basis of his intellectual superiority, so Eugénie sees in Charles's physical beauty the promise of moral virtue. The narrator tells us that Charles does not really deserve such sympathy: "Les germes de l'économie politique à l'usage du Parisien, latents en son cœur, ne devaient pas tarder à y fleurir, aussitôt que de spectateur oisif il deviendrait acteur dans le drame de la vie réelle" (1126; 579). Thus, the real drama lies not in the relationship between the two cousins, but rather in the relationship between father and daughter. Charles is a stock figure who only visits Saumur, but Eugénie will remain in her father's house, the earthly dwelling he, and Balzac, have prepared for her.

Accordingly, no sooner do Eugénie and Nanon bring Charles his breakfast than Grandet returns from his morning errands, summoning them back to his version of reality: "Un coup de marteau rappela les deux femmes à leurs places" (1107; 572). The miser orders preparations made for a dinner with the Cruchot family, the first act of his premeditated comedy. In a scene built on Grandet's long conversation with the servile Cruchot de Bonfons, Eugénie's future husband, and his uncle the notary, the narrator exploits the tension created by Grandet's affected stuttering to make the reader slow down his pace and follow quite closely the logic behind Grandet's calculations—a device similar to the clerk's long-winded sentence in *Le Colonel Chabert*. By liquidating his brother's estate, pacifying creditors with a small percentage of their due and waiting out Charles's return from the Indies—thus deferring and eventually escaping all other payments—Grandet will conveniently save the family honor without engaging his own money. As he instructs the agonizing Cruchots: "Je ne co, co, co, connais pas *lles malins* de Paris. Je . . . suis à Sau, au, aumur, moi, voyez-vous! Mes prooovins! mes fooossés, et, en, enfin, j'ai mes aaaffaires. . . . Voilllà tooout ce qu, qu, que je sais" (1112; 574). The financial drama, hidden under a verbal smokescreen, is all the more intriguing for its shamelessness; and Grandet's performance is so superb that in spite of ourselves we are eager to watch him carry off his plan.[12]

Grandet waits until the family falls asleep and then prepares with Nanon's help a financial *coup de théâtre*. In the middle of the night Eugénie, worried about Charles, suddenly wakes:

. . . une vive lumière qui passait par les fentes de sa porte lui donna peur du feu; puis elle se rassura bientôt en entendant les pas pesants de Nanon. . . .

"Mon père enlèverait-il mon cousin?" se dit-elle en entrouvrant sa porte avec assez de précaution pour l'empêcher de crier, mais de manière à voir ce qui se passait dans le corridor.

Tout à coup son œil rencontra celui de son père, dont le regard, quelque vague et inconscient[13] qu'il fût, la glaça de terreur. Le bonhomme et Nanon étaient accouplés par un gros gourdin dont chaque bout reposait sur leur épaule droite et soutenait un câble auquel était attaché un barillet semblable à ceux que le père Grandet s'amusait à faire dans son fournil à ses moments perdus. (1120; 577)

This scene, occurring almost exactly at the center of the novel, is truly its pivotal moment. Grandet and Nanon, master and servant, both struggle under the burden of Grandet's gold as if representing avarice and ignorance, polar opposites in capitalistic society. Eugénie, secretive and restless like her father, instinctively knows that something of value is being removed from the house. When her gaze meets his, Grandet apparently does not recognize her; but in that moment, when Eugénie becomes unwitting spectator, chance initiate to forbidden knowledge, it is as if Grandet communicates to her something of his corrupted intelligence. The blank gaze that fills her with terror may indeed reveal the space where genius meets amorality. It is the one time Eugénie, blinded by eros, sees clearly, the one time the narrator does not take us into Grandet's secret thoughts, the one time the miser is not completely self-possessed. This scene offers Eugénie and the reader a glimpse into that vast field of metaphysical speculation—the one reaped incessantly by impersonal death, lacking only the spectacle of Parisian vice and the complicity of daylight. It is this bleak Balzacian landscape that unifies city and province into a single country with its legions of characters and dozens of stories, its native language of despair. We are reminded of de Marsay and his sister locked in mutual contemplation, of Montriveau frozen by the stare of the Mother Superior, of the hapless Maulincour raked by the gaze of Ferragus, of the unforgiving madness of Chabert, of the unblinking eyes of Louis Lambert—moments in which the intelligence nails the world to its contradictions, flashing out of its social envelope and risking all in search of deeper meaning. In seeing her father as he is, Eugénie for a moment participates in the greater authorial vision that surpasses Grandet's own.

As if to ritualize her passage from innocence to experience, Eugénie turns to cross a thin band of light immediately after her father's departure: "Une bande lumineuse, fine autant que le tranchant d'un sabre, passait par la fente de la porte et coupait horizontalement les balustres du vieux escalier. 'Il souffre,' dit-elle en grimpant deux marches" (1121; 577). Finding Charles asleep in his chair, Eugénie caresses him and then gives in to the temptation of reading his correspondence:

... il se laissa faire comme un enfant qui, même en dormant, connaît encore sa mère et reçoit, sans s'éveiller, ses soins et ses baisers. Comme une mère, Eugénie releva la main pendante, et, comme une mère, elle baisa doucement les cheveux. Chère Annette! Un démon lui criait ces deux mots aux oreilles. "Je sais que je fais peut-être mal, mais je lirai la lettre," dit-elle.... Pour la première fois de sa vie, le bien et le mal étaient en présence dans son cœur. (1122; 577-78)

It is, of course, not his mother's presence, but Annette's to which Charles has grown accustomed; and in the rhetorical insistence of the simile "comme une mère" the narrator stresses the nature of Eugénie's attraction to Charles. The themes of evil, sexuality and reading converge, implicating Eugénie in her father's ethic—he who built his fortune on his wife's dowry, he who had plotted to dispose of Charles while reading his brother's suicide note. Eugénie's illicit knowledge of Charles's plight, gleaned from the unsealed letters on his desk, inspires her to commit the ultimate transgression in this, the Grandet household: she resolves to give her cousin the gold coins given her over the years by her father and other ancestors. This transgression reminds us, however, that there are boundaries to be respected; and, appropriately, the narrator, along with Eugénie, stops to take inventory of his fictional universe: "ce ne fut pas sans une vive émotion de plaisir qu'elle ouvrit le tiroir d'un vieux meuble en chêne, l'un des plus beaux ouvrages de l'époque nommée la *Renaissance,* et sur lequel se voyait encore, à demi effacée, la fameuse Salamandre royale" (1127; 579-80).

The wooden chest calls to mind the wooden doors inspected by the narrator in the first part of the novel and of which he said: "L'Histoire de France est là tout entière" (1028; 542). The barely visible figure of the royal salamander is reminiscent of the basilisk associated with Grandet, both mythological beasts resembling lizards and impervious to fire. When describing the coins Eugénie empties from the chest, the narrator lingers over such details as the provenance of each item and the sharply struck inscriptions. He sees what Eugénie cannot: the intrinsic esthetic beauty of these "véritables morceaux d'art" (1128; 580). The motif of portraiture, associated with the Grandet parlor and metaphorically with Eugénie's first sight of Charles, reappears when she exchanges her gold for miniatures of her aunt and uncle, "deux chefs-d'œuvre de Mme de Mirbel, richement entourés de perles" (1130; 581). Even when she deceives Grandet, Eugénie cannot escape his symbolic world; and when she defies her heavenly father, she demonstrates her ignorance of Grandet's actual power: "—Ma mère, je voudrais avoir pour un moment la puissance de Dieu, dit Eugénie au moment où elle ne vit plus le mouchoir de Charles" (1142; 585).

It is Grandet, of course, who could have easily redeemed his brother's name and fortune; and it is Grandet who, in the confines of his universe, possesses complete knowledge: "En ce qui concerne les affaires de la maison Guillaume Grandet, toutes les prévisions du tonnelier se réalisèrent" (1142; 585). A gaze that is "vague et inconscient" (1120; 577) has, however, for a moment symbolized that absolute authority ("*toutes* les prévisions"), and Eugénie's critical perception of that gaze serves much the same function as the narrator's distinction between "récit" and "histoire" in *Ferragus.* Grandet's vision has been reduced to the level of theme, and the narrator's perspective predominates. Appropriately, in the fifth chapter, "Chagrins de famille," the *process* of vision, rather than its range or authority, becomes a central theme, as if the narrator, having revealed the flaws in Eugénie's and Grandet's sight, would now begin to analyze its mechanisms in earnest. One can also see in the clash between father and daughter a dialectic between two similar ways of seeing, differing only as to object (gold and eros), ending in the reductive synthesis of Eugénie's joyless life—and in the rich synthesis of the narrative's own "principes de mélancolie."

What is perhaps most interesting about "Chagrins de famille," besides the marked turn of the plot to melodrama, is a phenomenon associated with Grandet and Eugénie: an intense preoccupation with symbolism on their part, a metonymic displacement of attention to an outward sign representing the original object of their desire. Eugénie creates a shrine of her cousin's former room, a temple of her beloved garden (1146-47; 587); she plots Charles's journey on a map emblematic of her world, flattened to the dimensions of a wishful illusion. When she would remember Charles, she does so through the medium of art, discerning his traits in the portrait of his mother. Grandet, similarly, must see and hold a tangible symbol of a fortune too vast to count, too dispersed to liquidate; accordingly, he becomes obsessed with the desire to see his daughter's gold. Unable to embrace their treasure, father and daughter develop the capacity to invest a symbol with its meaning; but for both of them the symbol becomes an object of devotion itself, inseparable in their minds from the entity it represents. The confrontation between Grandet and Eugénie therefore reveals their true selves, their true values, in keeping with Flannery O'Connor's dictum: "It is the extreme situation that reveals what we are essentially."[14] The impending dramatic distillation of character simply follows the lead of the characters' own concentration of attention upon a particular object: a miniature portrait encased in gold, a collection of gold coins.

On the New Year's Day after Charles's departure Grandet demands to see his daughter's gold:

> ... vous ne savez donc pas ce que c'est qu'un père. S'il n'est pas tout pour vous, il n'est rien. Où est votre or?
> —C'est un secret inviolable, dit-elle. N'avez-vous pas vos secrets?
> —Ne suis-je pas le chef de ma famille, ne puis-je avoir mes affaires?
> —C'est aussi mon affaire....
> —Mais l'on n'a jamais vu pareil entêtement, ni vol pareil, dit Grandet d'une voix qui alla *crescendo* et qui fit graduellement retentir la maison. (1154-55; 590)

The line between stubbornness and integrity is sometimes hard to draw. Significantly, Madame Grandet is stricken at this dramatic juncture, as if to confirm Eugénie's identity with her father; and Grandet chastizes his daughter for a sentimentality in matters of the heart uncharacteristic of a Grandet. His cruelty in the service of truth has her best interests at heart: "A quoi donc vous sert de manger le bon Dieu six fois tous les trois mois, si vous donnez l'or de votre père en cachette à un fainéant qui vous dévorera votre cœur quand vous n'aurez plus que ça à lui prêter?" (1158; 591). Deprived of the sight of gold, Grandet banishes Eugénie to her room; but this punitive gesture, though he loves his daughter, is not a form of self-sacrifice. Grandet has not designated Eugénie as one of his sacrificial lambs: "Quoi qu'elle ait pu faire, je ne la mangerai point" (1157; 591).

For Grandet Eugénie and his fortune are not mutually exclusive possessions, just as Eugénie's love for Charles does not preclude filial devotion:

> Le lendemain, suivant une habitude prise par Grandet depuis la réclusion d'Eugénie, il vint faire un certain nombre de tours dans son petit jardin. Il avait pris pour cette promenade le moment où Eugénie se peignait. Quand le bonhomme arrivait au gros

noyer, il se cachait derrière le tronc de l'arbre, restait pendant quelques instants à contempler les longs cheveux de sa fille, et flottait sans doute entre les pensées que lui suggérait la ténacité de son caractère et le désir d'embrasser son enfant. Souvent il demeurait assis sur le petit banc de bois pourri où Charles et Eugénie s'étaient juré un éternel amour, pendant qu'elle regardait aussi son père à la dérobée ou dans son miroir. S'il se levait et recommençait sa promenade, elle s'asseyait complaisamment à la fenêtre et se mettait à examiner le pan de mur où pendaient les plus jolies fleurs, d'où sortaient, d'entre les crevasses, des cheveux de Vénus, des liserons et une plante grasse, jaune ou blanche, un *sedum* très abondant dans les vignes à Saumur et à Tours.
(1163-64; 593)

Caught on the sharp contradictions of his own nature, Grandet strikes a tacit compromise with Eugénie, comically waiting out her acknowledgement of his authority. Although Eugénie believes herself pledged to Charles —"*Tout* c'était *lui*" (1161; 592)—she has given her entire allegiance to her father. Grandet has replaced Charles in the garden, and it is Grandet, not Charles or even herself, whom Eugénie sees in her mirror. Her long hair, secretively contemplated by her father, becomes figuratively entangled with the "cheveux de Vénus" she studies in their mutual charade, for Grandet and Eugénie have the same indivisible poetic setting:

... peut-être aussi serait-il également probable que, sorti de Saumur, le bonhomme n'aurait fait qu'une pauvre figure. Peut-être en est-il des esprits comme de certains animaux, qui n'engendrent plus transportés hors des climats où ils naissent. (1110; 573)

Mon père est maître chez lui. Tant que j'habiterai sa maison, je dois lui obéir. Sa conduite ne saurait être soumise à l'approbation ni à la désapprobation du monde, il n'en est comptable qu'à Dieu. (1163; 593)

Only Eugénie's renunciation of her right to succession to her mother induces Grandet to pardon her. It is as if her punishment is a rite of purification, rendering her completely Grandet: "elle est plus Grandet que je ne suis Grandet" (1155; 590). Appropriately, in the scene where the miser threatens to mutilate Charles's miniatures, Grandet symbolically equates Eugénie's blood with gold:

—Mon père, si votre couteau entame seulement une parcelle de cet or, je me perce de celui-ci. . . . Allez maintenant, blessure pour blessure?
Grandet tint son couteau sur le nécessaire, et regarda sa fille en hésitant. . . . Le tonnelier regarda l'or et sa fille alternativement pendant un instant. (1168-69; 595)

Both father and daughter are armed with weapons, like de Marsay and the Marquise in *La Fille aux yeux d'or,* Montriveau in *La Duchesse de Langeais* and Louis Lambert at equally crucial moments in these narratives. All these characters, when unable to dominate that which they most desire, threaten violence, the ineradicable inscription into flesh. Grandet solves the dilemma of separate identity by denying it, completely identifying himself with Eugénie: "Tiens, vois-tu, mémère, nous ne faisons qu'un maintenant" (1170; 595). The description of Grandet's death further confirms the efficacy of this solution:

> Eugénie lui étendait les louis sur une table, et il demeurait des heures entières les yeux attachés sur les louis, comme un enfant qui, au moment où il commence à voir, contemple stupidement le même objet; et, comme à un enfant, il lui échappait un sourire pénible.
> Ça me réchauffe! disait-il quelquefois en laissant paraître sur sa figure une expression de béatitude.
> Lorsque le curé de la paroisse vint l'administrer, ses yeux, morts en apparence depuis quelques heures, se ranimèrent à la vue de la croix, des chandeliers, du bénitier d'argent qu'il regarda fixement, et sa loupe remua pour la dernière fois. Lorsque le prêtre lui approcha des lèvres le crucifix en vermeil pour lui faire baiser le Christ, il fit un épouvantable geste pour le saisir et ce dernier effort lui coûta la vie, il appela Eugénie qu'il ne voyait pas quoiqu'elle fût agenouillée devant lui et qu'elle baignât de ses larmes une main déjà froide.
> Mon père, bénissez-moi? demanda-t-elle.
> —Aie bien soin de tout. Tu me rendras compte de ça là-bas, dit-il en prouvant par cette dernière parole que le christianisme doit être la religion des avares. (1175; 597)

Eugénie has not only become Grandet's steward: she symbolically becomes Grandet himself, even though she retains the illusion of Charles's love for her. The grotesque convergence of religion, avarice and vision into an image of "stupid" contemplation dramatizes the horror glimpsed earlier by Eugénie in the "regard... vague et inconscient" (1120; 577) of her father. Once again, as she looks on him, Grandet does not see her; this time, however, Eugénie does not draw back in horror, but remains kneeling by his side. Paying homage to his vision, Eugénie accepts as her blessing complete responsibility for her inheritance. In this way, the transference of perspective from Grandet to Eugénie is complete, awaiting only her disillusionment to be perfected.

Indeed, Eugénie's desire for independence has been turned against her metaphorically also; the image of the infant learning to see, conspicuously reappearing here, earlier described her meditations in the garden: "Quand les enfants commencent à voir, ils sourient; quand une fille entrevoit le sentiment dans la nature, elle sourit comme elle souriait enfait" (1073; 559). Infancy, now associated with its opposite, senescence, loses its usual connotations of freshness, curiosity, innocence. Experience, its harsh rigidity born of ingrained habit ("un épouvantable geste"), corrupts, by association, the religion of gold cultivated by Grandet and Eugénie's love for Charles; both gradually evolve into forms of mindlessness. The empty fixation of Grandet's gaze calls to mind the similar "expression de béatitude" of the cataleptic Louis Lambert. For Balzac the intelligence is sound only when it operates in its proper sphere: philosophical inquiry, at one point leading Lambert to reject Swedenborg; social organization, placating Chabert with the prospect of compromise; the manipulation of political power, giving the Treize temporary rule over Paris; the pursuit of pleasure and romance, inspiring Montriveau and de Marsay to feats of ingenuity and daring; the exploitation of economic structures, allowing Grandet to build his fortune. Thought contained within such systems, the mind functions freely, even admirably, in its inventiveness; but when one would find the infinite in a world subject to the laws of matter, one's vision, like Grandet's, fails, prompting intellectual and physical deterioration (*Louis Lambert, Le Colonel Chabert, Ferragus*) or desperate recourse to convention (*La Duchesse de Langeais, La Fille aux yeux d'or, Eugénie Grandet*).

In this instance of utter, open ambivalence of meaning—an image signifying a promise of new life for Eugénie and the imminence of death for her father—one finds concrete proof of the attitude of acceptance qualifying Balzac's realism.[15] The individual novel need not be edifying, only truthful, as a mirror of society: "Si je vous montre un avoué fripon, je vous l'accompagne d'un honorable avoué. Nucingen et Birotteau sont deux œuvres jumelles. C'est l'improbité, la probité, juxtaposées comme dans le monde."[16] It is because he repeatedly shows the hollowness of materialism that Balzac may speak of "le but de profonde moralité caché dans mon livre": each of the early, isolated works considered in this study leads inexorably to that insight. But how far, metaphysically speaking, does that hollowness extend? If an author proceeds to demonstrate the existence of the material and spiritual worlds by means of juxtaposition—by a collective work containing, for example, *Le Livre mystique* and the *Histoire des Treize*—he reduces ontology to a question of relativity, withholding judgments as to ultimate value. If, on the thematic level, the child image brings to light the author's necessary indifference towards the pleasure or displeasure his realistic portrait of society may provoke, it also reveals an oppressive ambiguity at the level of Balzac's metaphysics—the same exile of spirituality wistfully contemplated in *Louis Lambert*. For this reason Balzac's fiction, although, as he rightly insists, moral, cannot be called religious or mystical in the profoundest sense.[17] Eugénie Grandet may see through her father's blindness to the emptiness at its source, but that is all she sees, a Louis Lambert who dwells in despair and not insanity—in a world without angels.

Thus, in the dénouement, "Ainsi va le monde," we find the story enshrined in its original setting, as if fixed, petrified, immured within itself:

Enfin, hormis le nombre des personnages, en remplaçant le loto par le whist, et en supprimant les figures de M. et de Mme Grandet, la scène par laquelle commence cette histoire était à peu près la même que par le passé.... Si Charles fût arrivé du fond des Indes, il eût donc retrouvé les mêmes personnages et les mêmes intérêts.
(1180; 599)

Grandet and Madame Grandet are only figuratively absent; symbolically speaking, Eugénie has become her father—"vous avez toute la voix de défunt votre père, dit Mme des Grassins" (1192; 604)—and her mother—"Elle est toujours vêtue comme l'était sa mère" (1198; 606).

The virtually static tableau of provincial life serves to accentuate the nature of Eugénie's voyage, an interior one: "Epouvantable et complet désastre. Le vaisseau sombrait sans laisser ni un cordage, ni une planche sur le vaste océan des espérances" (1188; 602). Abandoned by Charles, Eugénie marries Cruchot de Bonfons, only to survive him, childless, the Grandet home and fortune intact: "La maison de Saumur, maison sans soleil, sans chaleur, sans cesse ombragée, mélancolique, est l'image de sa vie" (1198; 606). The novel ends laconically, as if, despite appearances, nothing has been resolved:

> Eugénie marche au ciel accompagnée d'un cortège de bienfaits. . . . Les gens de Saumur s'occupent d'elle et de M. le marquis de Froidfond dont la famille commence à cerner la riche veuve comme jadis avaient fait les Cruchot. Nanon et Cornoiller sont, dit-on, dans les intérêts du marquis, mais rien n'est plus faux. Ni la grande Nanon, ni Cornoiller n'ont assez d'esprit pour comprendre les corruptions du monde. (1198-99; 606)

Eugénie's way to heaven seems to mock the Biblical injunction to the rich young man: "Go, sell your possessions and give to the poor . . . and come, follow me" (Matthew 19:21). There is no sure way to heaven—"l'ironie est le fond du caractère de la providence" (1047; 550)—if indeed there is such a way; in the world of the novel there is only the somber, melancholy passage through the streets of Saumur. Knowledge precludes innocence and happiness in this world; the garden glimpsed through the grille has been the scene of an eternal primal drama; a banal one as well, profoundly unifying the currents of myth and mimesis flowing throughout the novel. Having gradually evolved detail by detail the inner life of a character whose stoicism is like a hieroglyph, the narrator ends his sustained exercise in discernment; he leaves us standing again as strangers before the heavy wooden doors of the houses of Saumur. The sad, disappointing dénouement of Eugénie's passion acknowledged, not denied, *Eugénie Grandet* has Balzac's paternal sanction. All we can conclude from the ending is the relation of intelligence to the problem of good and evil: "Ni la grande Nanon, ni Cornoiller n'ont assez d'esprit pour comprendre les corruptions du monde." The drama remains imprinted in the present tense. Like Eugénie, the narrator keeps an inheritance of irony, and of melancholy, shrewdly to himself.

CONCLUSION

On a peak high above the seas of Norway Balzac's angel figure, Séraphîtüs (*Séraphîta*),[1] glories in his exalted perspective, as he exclaims to his companion Minna:

> Mais ne sois pas injuste, Minna, vois le spectacle qui s'étale à tes pieds, n'est-il pas grand? A tes pieds, l'Océan se déroule comme un tapis, les montagnes sont comme les murs d'un cirque, l'éther est au-dessus comme le voile arrondi de ce théâtre, et d'ici l'on respire les pensées de Dieu comme un parfum. Vois? les tempêtes qui brisent des vaisseaux chargés d'hommes ne nous semblent ici que de faibles bouillonnements, et si tu lèves la tête au-dessus de nous, tout est bleu. . . . ici, disparaissent les nuances des expressions terrestres. (744; 332)

Even as he reaches the vanishing point of all human discourse, Séraphîtüs sees the world as his creator sees it: the theater for the *Comédie humaine*. The ocean resembles a carpet forming the stage; the mountains ring the shore like so many impassive spectators; and the sky acts as the ceiling, a veil between the infinite and man. The sea, routinely visited by death, recalls the landscape dominated by an absent reaper in *La Fille aux yeux d'or*; the vessel City of Paris, emblem of artistic and intellectual adventure, has its counterparts here in the ships lost in the Norwegian seas. But Séraphîtüs and Minna are too far removed to perceive the drama of individual destiny that might have led any one traveler to risk all in search of love, fortune or truth, like Montriveau, Charles Grandet or Colonel Chabert; the outlines of the scene are vague, the similes like helpless gesticulations; nature is inanimate. Séraphîtüs' exaltation is utterly prosaic. Soon after pronouncing these words, he leads Minna back down the mountain, as if to acknowledge that no narrative could possibly survive in such an inimical climate, one which absorbs and eliminates the distinctions made by language—and hence dispenses with language itself.

If, in defending *La Peau de chagrin*, Balzac insists upon the reciprocity of a novel's "sauvage enveloppe" and a hidden "but de profonde moralité," it is to remind readers that poetical discourse, because it constitutes vision in its own sphere, necessarily materializes thought in language—tends to the concrete and expressive detail: in Séraphîtüs' words, "l'on respire les pensées de Dieu comme un parfum." Séraphîtüs' retreat from a vertiginous silence, one implicitly made by the narrator of *Louis Lambert* as well, seems for Balzac to signify both religious skepticism and an affirmation of poetical discourse. Whether for Balzac the former is a condition of the latter would be the subject of another study, but much suggests that this is so. In the novels considered here Balzac demonstrates his faith in the hieroglyphs left by history and in the artistic and intellectual pursuits upon which he stakes his fictional mythology—and yet he denies his heroes success, happiness, equilibrium. The exemplary conduct of Eugénie Grandet and Derville's renunciation of Paris do not inspire admiration; they are as futile, unredeemed gestures. The perspective of Balzac's narrators accommodates an optimism with respect to language and intellectual inquiry, and a pessimism with respect to social structures and human effort. Surely this tension, qualified as it is by doubt of the possibility of an ultimate meaning for life, is at the heart of Balzac's vision and immense productivity.

It is impossible to isolate a persona or paradigm of the typical Balzacian narrator, to separate Balzac's narrative voice from the works themselves; but we can characterize the narrator in Balzac as a kind of guide or initiator, much like Virgil in the *Divine Comedy*. In Eliade's words:

> ... the need to find one's way into "foreign" Universes and to follow the complications of a "story" seems to be consubstantial with the human condition and hence irreducible. It is a difficult need to define, being at once desire to communicate with "others," with "strangers," and share in their dramas and hopes, and at the same time the need to know what *can have taken place*.[2]

This need no doubt impels the writer as well to adopt the various guises—possible, distinct, imagined perspectives—through which he can speak and build a number of fictional worlds. In these early, isolated works of *La Comédie humaine* we watch such worlds come into being: foreign by virtue of their origins in a receding, irretrievable era, and universal by virtue of their irreducible identities as dramas of human proportions and of possible destinies.

NOTES

Introduction

1. Maurice Bardèche, *Balzac: Romancier* (Paris: Plon, 1940), p. 183.
2. Paul Ricœur, *La Métaphore vive* (Paris: Seuil, 1975), p. 308.
3. Martin Kanes, *Balzac's Comedy of Words* (Princeton: Princeton Univ. Press, 1975), p. 224.
4. In the text of this study I have supplied page references to two of the most accessible editions of Balzac's work: first, *La Comédie humaine*, ed. Pierre-Georges Castex, 12 vols. (Paris: Gallimard, 1976-1980), the new Pléiade edition; and second, *La Comédie humaine*, ed. Pierre Citron, 7 vols. (Paris: Seuil, 1965-1966). The volume numbers for each work will be indicated in a note at the beginning of each chapter.

Chapter I

1. Page numbers in the text of this chapter refer first to Vol. XI of the new Pléiade edition of *La Comédie humaine*, and second to Vol. VII of the Seuil edition.
2. As Denise Levertov writes in *The Poet in the World* (New York: New Directions, 1973), p. 73: "the poet does not see and then begin to search for words to say what he sees; he begins to see and at once begins to say or sing, and *only in the action of verbalization does he see further.* His language is not more dependent on his vision than his vision is upon his language. This is surely one of the primary distinctions between poet and mystic."
3. Kanes, *Balzac's Comedy of Words*, p. 121.
4. Balzac, *Lettres à Madame Hanska*, ed. Roger Pierrot, Vol. I (Paris: Delta, 1967), p. 25.
5. I have made this distinction in light of Ricœur's remarks (*La Métaphore vive*, pp. 398-99): "D'une part, la poésie, en elle-même et par elle-même, donne à penser l'esquisse d'une conception 'tensionnelle' de la vérité; celle-ci récapitule toutes les formes de 'tensions' portées au jour par la sémantique: tension entre sujet et prédicat, entre interprétation littérale et interprétation métaphorique, entre identité et différence ... la poésie articule et préserve, en liaison avec d'autres modes de discours, l'expérience d'*appartenance* qui inclut l'homme dans le discours et le discours dans l'être. D'autre part, la pensée spéculative appuie son travail sur la dynamique de l'énonciation métaphorique et l'ordonne à son propre espace de sens. Sa réplique n'est possible que parce que la *distanciation*, constitutive de l'instance critique, est contemporaine de l'expérience d'appartenance, ouverte ou reconquise par le discours poétique, et parce que le discours poétique, en tant que texte et œuvre, préfigure la distanciation que la pensée spéculative porte à son plus haut degré de réflexion."
6. See Valéry's trenchant criticism of the novel quoted in Joyce A.E. Loubère, "Balzac: Le grand absent de chez Teste," *French Review*, 47, No. 6 (1974), 83.

7. Marthe Robert, *Roman des origines et origines du roman* (Paris: Gallimard, 1972), p. 287.

8. Otto Rank, *Art and Artist*, trans. Charles Francis Atkinson (New York: Agathon, 1968), p. 377.

9. The narrator's successive roles many also be described, first, as that of a teller-character—one who cannot withdraw from the action as such; and second, as that of a reflector-character—one who enjoys a privileged perspective while remaining outside the sphere of action (after the example, for instance, of the "omniscient" narrator of the *Histoire des Treize*). Thus, in *Louis Lambert* the narrator's account of his experience at the Collège de Vendôme reflects his capacity as teller-character and Lambert's disciple, and his reconstruction of Lambert's intellectual history after that period reflects his capacity as reflector-character and biographer. See Franz Stanzel, "Teller-Characters and Reflector-Characters in Narrative Theory," *Poetics Today*, 2, No. 2 (1981), 5-15. *Louis Lambert* is in some ways reminiscent of Rilke's *The Notebooks of Malte Laurids Brigge*; both Balzac and Rilke study at close range, through first-person narration, the problematic development of characters like themselves endowed with poetic consciousness. One might say that the narrator of *Louis Lambert* is like a poet attempting to write a novel, whereas the narrators of the other works considered in this study are clearly the instruments of a master storyteller.

10. Rank, p. 380.

11. Kanes, p. 70.

12. William Butler Yeats, "Louis Lambert," in his *Essays and Introductions* (New York: Macmillan, 1961), p. 441.

13. Ibid., pp. 441-44.

Chapter II

1. Page numbers in this chapter refer to Vol. III of the new Pléiade edition of *La Comédie humaine* and to Vol. II of the Seuil edition.

Chapter III

1. Page numbers in chs. 3, 4 and 5 refer to Vol. V of the new Pléiade edition and to Vol. IV of the Seuil edition.

2. José Ortega y Gasset, "Notes on the Novel," in his *The Dehumanization of Art*, trans. Helene Weyl (Princeton: Princeton Univ. Press, 1968), p. 79.

3. After referring to "la dépersonnalisation du créateur" in "Facio Cane," Jean Paris goes on to say that "le phénomène va si loin qu'il s'impose à soi seul pour thème évident ou secret de nombreux romans." Paris, "Notes sur Balzac," in his *Le Point aveugle* (Paris: Seuil, 1975).

4. Jonathan Culler, *Flaubert: The Uses of Uncertainty* (Ithaca: Cornell Univ. Press, 1974), p. 110.

5. John R. O'Connor, *Balzac's Soluble Fish* (Madrid: José Porrúa Turanzas, 1977), pp. 104-05.

6. Although the theme of this passage happens to be that of social convention, it is its esthetic function of creating certain expectations that is primarily important: "The Balzacian narrator, interestingly, adopts the *concept* of norms and draws it into

his own prose, quite apart from any connection to real forms drawn from the objective world . . . the Balzacian narrator is concerned to establish internal standards" (Kanes, p. 130).

7. "For [Balzac] the subjective-psychological demonism which is characteristic of his work is an ultimate reality, the principle of all essential action which objectivises itself in heroic deeds; its inadequate relation to the outside world is intensified to the utmost, but this intensification has a purely immanent counterweight: the outside world is a purely human one and is essentially peopled by human beings with similar mental structures, although with completely different orientations and contents." Georg Lukacs, *The Theory of the Novel*, trans. Anna Bostock (Cambridge, Mass.: M.I.T. Press, 1971), p. 108.

8. O'Connor, pp. 67-68.

9. See Moïse le Yaouanc, *Nosographie de l'humanité balzacienne* (Paris: Maloine, 1959), p. 110. The doctor tells Jules that to promote Clémence's recovery, "Il faudrait risquer le tout pour le tout par quelque réactif violent; mais je ne prendrai jamais sur moi de l'ordonner, je ne le conseillerais même pas; et en consultation, je m'opposerais à son emploi" (880-81; 45). One is reminded of the story "Adieu," in which similar therapy is actually carried out, with disastrous consequences. In her article "Women and Madness: The Critical Phallacy," *Diacritics*, 5 (1975), 2-10, Shoshana Felman discusses the relationship of the identity of the heroine in "Adieu" to the perspectives of the male characters and the narrator.

10. Paris, p. 113.

11. Marcel Proust, *Contre Sainte-Beuve* (Paris: Gallimard, 1954), pp. 262-63.

Chapter IV

1. Rainer Maria Rilke, "The Rodin Book: First Part," in *Where Silence Reigns*, trans. G. Craig Houston (New York: New Directions, 1978), p. 108.

2. Page numbers in the text of this chapter refer to Vol. V of the new Pléiade edition and Vol. IV of the Seuil edition.

3. Saint Teresa of Avila, *Le Chemin de la perfection*, trans. R.P. Cyprien de la Nativité de la Vierge (1650), quoted in the new Pléiade edition, p. 1473.

4. And Balzac writes elsewhere in *La Duchesse*: "Çà et là, dans le faubourg Saint-Germain, se rencontrent de beaux caractères, exceptions qui prouvent contre l'égoïsme général qui a causé la perte de *ce monde* à part" (927; 62; my emphasis).

5. See O'Connor, pp. 41-63.

6. See ibid., pp. 81-90.

7. Chateaubriand had been the target of Balzac's humor in the Preface to the *Histoire des Treize* (788; 10) and will be again in the image of Montriveau waiting outside the walls of the convent at the end of *La Duchesse de Langeais* (1034; 102), a very probable allusion to *René*.

8. O'Connor points out this transformation and interprets it in the context of Montriveau's renewed virility and power (pp. 158-63). He carefully draws the parallel between this scene and the earlier account, in the second chapter, of the character's adventures in Africa (944-46; 68-69), which correspond in effect to the Duchess' nightmare.

9. It is impossible to ignore the misogynistic overtones of the text and perhaps too convenient to reinsert them into the context of conventional morality Balzac so

lucidly portrayed. At the same time Madame de Langeais emerges as a full-fledged character, no mere stereotype, and here she passes judgment on a form of social oppression obviously recognized as such by Balzac. It is as if he transmits a cultural prejudice through his works and at the same time transcends it as artist and observer.

10. Or, as the Princess sardonically tells her niece, "Tu es deux siècles en arrière avec ta fausse grandeur" (1022; 97).

Chapter V

1. Page numbers in this chapter refer to Vol. V of the new Pléiade edition and to Vol. IV of the Seuil edition.
2. A detailed psychoanalytical reading of the novel can be found in Robert, pp. 261-70.
3. Christopher Prendergast, *Balzac: Fiction and Melodrama* (London: Edward Arnold, 1978), p. 64.
4. Victor Hugo, "Mors," in *Les Contemplations*, ed. Jean Gaudon (Paris: Le Livre de Poche, 1972), p. 280.
5. Edith Hamilton, *Mythology* (New York: New American Library, 1942), p. 35.
6. Leyla Perrone-Moïses analyzes de Manerville's words in terms of Balzac's use of euphemism in the story "Le Récit euphémique," *Poétique*, No. 17 (1974), pp. 28-31.
7. Fortassier has documented Balzac's literary sources in her introduction to *La Fille aux yeux d'or* in the new Pléiade edition (pp. 770-86).
8. In 1843 Balzac dedicated *La Fille aux yeux d'or* to Delacroix; at the time of its composition (1834-1835) he probably knew Ingres's "Grande Odalisque," then on exhibit at the Louvre.
9. The others are *"Quod erat demonstrandum"* (1054; 109) and *"les extrêmes se touchent"* (1094; 124).
10. See O'Connor, pp. 74-80.
11. Nicole Mozet likens the proletarians and lesbians in the novel as social outcasts, thus providing an ideological basis for this poetical association. See her "Les Prolétaires dans *La Fille aux yeux d'or*," *Année Balzacienne* (1974), pp. 91-119.
12. O'Connor compares the Marquise to Frenhofer in "Le Chef d'œuvre inconnu" (p. 180). This identification of the Marquise as artist is supported by biographical evidence because if Balzac drew the figure of Paquita in part from the actress Marie Dorval (Fortassier, p. 771), then there must have been a more than subliminal connection in his mind between George Sand and the Marquise de San-Réal.
13. See O'Connor, pp. 171-75.
14. See ibid., pp. 179-81.
15. The interpretation of Samsa as an image of the writer was suggested to me by my colleague Carl Singer at Bard College.
16. Virginia Woolf, "How Should One Read a Book?" in *The Second Common Reader* (New York: Harvest, 1960), p. 236.

Chapter VI

1. Page numbers in the text of this chapter will refer to Vol. III of the new Pléiade edition and to Vol. II of the Seuil edition.

2. Nicole Mozet, "Introduction" to *Eugénie Grandet* in the new Pléiade edition (p. 991).
3. Erich Auerbach, *Mimesis*, trans. Willard R. Trask (Princeton: Princeton Univ. Press, 1953), p. 472.
4. See Princeton University, "Thèmes religieux dans *Eugénie Grandet*," *Année Balzacienne* (1976), pp. 201-29.
5. Northrop Frye, *The Secular Scripture* (Cambridge, Mass.: Harvard Univ. Press, 1976), p. 164.
6. Mircea Eliade, *Myth and Reality*, trans. Willard R. Trask (New York: Harper and Row, 1963), pp. 192-93.
7. Ibid., p. 192.
8. See Mozet, "Introduction" to *Eugénie Grandet*, pp. 996-97.
9. Molière, *Oeuvres complètes* (Paris: Gallimard, 1971), II, 536.
10. See Janet Gurkin, "Romance Elements in *Eugénie Grandet*," *Esprit Créateur*, 7, No. 1 (1967), 20-21.
11. See Susan Sontag, *Illness as Metaphor* (New York: Farrar, Straus, Giroux, 1978), pp. 30-36.
12. In explaining the origins of Grandet's stuttering, Balzac resorts to an unfortunate literary stereotype of the Jew, using language that translates a vehement prejudice: ". . . Grandet, victime de son humanité, se crut obligé de suggérer à ce malin Juif les mots et les idées que paraissait chercher le Juif, d'achever lui-même les raisonnements dudit Juif, de parler comme devait parler le damné Juif, d'être enfin le Juif et non Grandet" (1110-11; 573). Having earned Grandet's grudging admiration, the figure is not entirely discreditable, much like Shakespeare's Shylock ("Hath not a Jew eyes? hath not a Jew hands, organs, dimensions, senses . . . ?" [*Merchant of Venice*, III, i, 52-65]). This expression of anti-Semitism and similar racist and misogynistic remarks tarnish the surface of Balzac's fiction, and yet they are contradicted on a deeper level by the poetic logic of his works, which reveals the emptiness at the heart of received ideas and of the social system that produces them.
13. In the new Pléiade edition the phrase reads: "vague et insouciant," with essentially the same meaning. According to Mozet, the word *insouciant* "signifie seulement que Grandet, se croyant seul, n'inspecte pas du regard les objets qui l'entourent" (p. 1701).
14. Flannery O'Connor, *Mystery and Manners* (New York: Farrar, Straus, Giroux, 1969), p. 113.
15. The same conciousness of the limitations of the intellect Balzac projects into the actions of his characters receives more introspective treatment in lyric poetry; the use of the child image in *Eugénie Grandet* anticipates the later association of childlikeness, disease and genius that Baudelaire will apply reflexively to poetical vision itself. See M.H. Abrams, *Natural Supernaturalism* (New York: Norton, 1971), pp. 414-15.
16. Balzac, "Lettre à M. Hippolyte Castille," in *Oeuvres complètes* (Paris: Calmann-Lévy, 1879), XII, 368. See Philippe Bertault's discussion of this letter in his *Balzac et la religion* (Paris: Boivin, 1942), pp. 504-06.
17. As Philippe Bertault writes (ibid., pp. 496-97): "L'angoisse pascalienne, il ne l'a jamais comprise, ni admirée; jamais la désespérance ne tenta le *chercheur d'absolu*. Quand il gémissait de se heurter au mystère, c'était de fatigue, de dépit, jamais d'effroi: un bon rire rabelaisien, une boutade sceptique le reposaient, et le lendemain il reprenait son effort.

Conclusion

1. The references are to Vol. XII of the new Pléiade edition of *La Comédie humaine* and to Vol. VII of the Seuil edition.
2. Eliade, *Myth and Reality*, p. 191

SELECTED BIBLIOGRAPHY

Works by Honoré de Balzac

Oeuvres complètes. 24 vols. Paris: Calmann-Lévy, 1870-1899.
Oeuvres complètes de M. de Balzac. Ed. Jean A. Ducourneau. 25 vols. Paris: Bibliophiles de l'Originale, 1965-1973.
Oeuvres complètes. 24 vols. Paris: Club de l'Honnête Homme, 1968-1971.
La Comédie humaine. Ed. Pierre Citron. 7 vols. Paris: Seuil, 1965-1966.
La Comédie humaine. Ed. Pierre-Georges Castex. 12 vols. Paris: Gallimard, 1976-1980.
Le Colonel Chabert suivi de Honorine et de L'Interdiction. Ed. Maurice Allem. Paris: Garnier, 1964.
La Duchesse de Langeais. La Fille aux yeux d'or. Ed. Rose Fortassier. Paris: Gallimard, 1976.
Eugénie Grandet. Ed. Pierre-Georges Castex. Paris: Garnier, 1965.
Histoire des Treize. Ed. Pierre-Georges Castex. Paris: Garnier, 1966.
Louis Lambert. Ed. Marcel Bouteron and Jean Pommier. Paris: José Corti, 1954.
Correspondance. Ed. Roger Pierrot. 5 vols. Paris: Garnier, 1960-1969.
Lettres à l'étrangère. 4 vols. Paris: Calmann-Lévy, 1906-1950.
Lettres à Madame Hanska. Ed. Roger Pierrot. 4 vols. Paris: Delta, 1967-1971.

Other Works Consulted

Abrams, M.H. *Natural Supernaturalism.* New York: Norton, 1971.
Affron, Charles. *Patterns of Failure in* La Comédie humaine. New Haven: Yale Univ. Press, 1966.
Auerbach, Eric. *Mimesis.* Trans. Willard R. Trask. Princeton: Princeton Univ. Press, 1953.
Baldensperger, Fernand. *Orientations étrangères chez Honoré de Balzac.* Paris: Champion, 1927.
Barbéris, Pierre. *Balzac et le mal du siècle.* 2 vols. Paris: Gallimard, 1970.
———. "La Pensée de Balzac: Histoire et structure." *Revue d'Histoire Littéraire de la France,* 67, No. 1 (1967), 19-54.

Bardèche, Maurice. *Balzac, romancier.* Paris: Plon, 1940.
Barthes, Roland. *S/Z.* Paris: Seuil, 1970.
Baudelaire, Charles. "Théophile Gautier." In his *Critical Studies.* Ed. D. Parmée. Cambridge: Cambridge Univ. Press, 1949, pp. 79-106.
Bayard, Pierre. *Balzac et le troc de l'imaginaire.* Paris: Minard, 1978.
Bérard, Suzanne. "Une Enigme balzacienne: La 'Spécialité.' " *Année Balzacienne* (1965), pp. 61-82.
Bershtel, Susan. "Fairy Tales and Success in Balzac's *Comédie humaine.*" *Comparative Literature,* 31 (1979), 47-62.
Bertault, Philippe. *Balzac et la religion.* Paris: Boivin, 1942.
Bilodeau, François. "Balzac et les frasques de l'imposture." In *L'Oeuvre littéraire et ses significations.* Ed. Renée Legris and Pierre Pagé. Quebec: Presses de l'Université de Québec, 1970, pp. 67-90.
Bodin, Thierry. "Balzac et George Sand." Mémoire pour l'obtention de la maîtrise de Lettres modernes, Université de Paris-Sorbonne, 1971.
Booth, Wayne C. *The Rhetoric of Fiction.* Chicago: Univ. of Chicago Press, 1961.
Brombert, Victor. "Natalie ou le lecteur caché de Balzac." In *Mouvements premiers: Etudes critiques offerts à Georges Poulet.* Paris: José Corti, 1972, pp. 172-90.
Brooks, Peter. "The Melodramatic Imagination." *Partisan Review,* 39, No. 2 (1972), 195-212.
———. "Romantic Antipastoral and Urban Allegories." *The Yale Review* (Autumn 1964), pp. 11-26.
Butor, Michel. "Balzac et la réalité." In his *Répertoire I.* Paris: Minuit, 1968, pp. 79-83.
Charreton, Pierre. "A propos du Paris de Balzac: Le principe de l'identité des contraires comme structure de l'imagination dans *La Fille aux yeux d'or.*" *Travaux de l'Université de Saint-Etienne,* 7 (1974), 1-67.
Chollet, Roland. "De *Dezesperance d'amour* à *La Duchesse de Langeais.*" *Année Balzacienne* (1965), pp. 93-120.
Citron, Pierre. *La Poésie de Paris dans la littérature française de Rousseau à Baudelaire.* 2 vols. Paris: Minuit, 1961.
———. "Le Rêve asiatique de Balzac." *Année Balzacienne* (1968), pp. 303-36.
———. "Sur deux zones obscures de la psychologie de Balzac." *Année Balzacienne* (1967), pp. 3-27.
Cohn, Dorrit. "The Encirclement of Narrative." *Poetics Today,* 2, No. 2 (1981), 157-82.
Culler, Jonathan. *Flaubert: The Uses of Uncertainty.* Ithaca: Cornell Univ. Press, 1974.

———. *Structuralist Poetics.* Ithaca: Cornell Univ. Press, 1975.

Curtius, Ernst Robert. *Balzac.* Trans. Henri Jourdan. Paris: Grasset, 1933.

Dargan, E. Preston, and Bernard Weinberg, eds. *The Evolution of Balzac's Comédie humaine.* Chicago: Univ. of Chicago Press, 1942.

———, et al. *Studies in Balzac's Realism.* Chicago: Univ. of Chicago Press, 1932.

Delattre, Geneviève. "De *Séraphîta* à *La Fille aux yeux d'or.*" *Année Balzacienne* (1970), pp. 183-226.

Dupuy, Aimé. "Balzac colonial." *Revue d'Histoire Littéraire de la France,* 50, No. 3 (1950), 257-79.

Eliade, Mircea. *Myth and Reality.* Trans. Willard R. Trask. New York: Harper and Row, 1963.

Eliot, George. *Middlemarch.* Ed. Bert G. Hornback. New York: Norton, 1977.

Eliot, T.S. "Beyle and Balzac." *Athenaeum* (30 May 1919), pp. 392-93.

Fargeaud, Madeleine. "Madame Balzac, son mysticisme et ses enfants." *Année Balzacienne* (1965), pp. 3-33.

Felman, Shoshana. "Women and Madness: The Critical Phallacy." *Diacritics,* 5 (1975), 2-10.

Fernandez, Ramon. *Balzac.* Paris: Stock, 1943.

Fortassier, Rose. *Les Mondains de* La Comédie humaine. Paris: Klincksieck, 1974.

Frangi, Françoise. "Sur *La Duchesse de Langeais*: Un essai de lecture stylistique." *Année Balzacienne* (1971), pp. 235-52.

Frappier-Mazur, Lucienne. *L'Expression métaphorique dans* La Comédie humaine. Paris: Klincksieck, 1976.

Friedman, Norman. "Point of View in Fiction: The Development of a Critical Concept." *PMLA,* 70, No. 5 (1955), 1160-84.

Frye, Northrop. *The Secular Scripture.* Cambridge, Mass.: Harvard Univ. Press, 1976.

Gauthier, Henri. "Un Projet d'étude de femme: *Les Amours* d'une laide." *Année Balzacienne* (1961), pp. 111-36.

Genette, Gérard. *Figures III.* Paris: Seuil, 1972.

Guise, René. "Balzac et le roman historique: Notes sur quelques projets." *Revue d'Histoire Littéraire de la France,* 75, Nos. 2-3 (1975), 356-72.

Gurkin, Janet. "Romance Elements in *Eugénie Grandet.*" *Esprit Créateur,* 7, No. 1 (1967), 17-24.

Hamilton, Edith. *Mythology.* New York: New American Library, 1942.

Hoffmann, Léon-François. "Balzac et les noirs." *Année Balzacienne* (1966), pp. 297-308.

———. "Eros en filigrane: *Le Curé de Tours.*" *Année Balzacienne* (1967), pp. 89-105.
———. "Mignonne et Paquita." *Année Balzacienne* (1964), pp. 181-86.
Hugo, Victor. *Les Contemplations.* Ed. Jean Gaudon. Paris: Le Livre de Poche, 1972.
James, Henry. *French Poets and Novelists.* London: Macmillan, 1893.
———. *Notes on Novelists.* New York: Charles Scribner's Sons, 1914.
Jameson, Fredric. "*La Cousine Bette* and Allegorical Realism." *PMLA,* 86 (1971), 241-54.
Kafka, Franz. *The Penal Colony.* Trans. Willa and Edwin Muir. New York: Schocken, 1948.
Kanes, Martin. *Balzac's Comedy of Words.* Princeton: Princeton Univ. Press, 1975.
Lamm, Martin. *Swedenborg.* Trans. E. Söderlindh. Paris: Stock, 1935.
Langer, Susanne K. *Feeling and Form.* New York: Charles Scribner's Sons, 1953.
Laugaa, Maurice. "L'Effet 'Fille aux yeux d'or.'" *Littérature,* No. 20 (1975), pp. 62-80.
Levertov, Denise. *The Poet in the World.* New York: New Directions, 1973.
Le Yaouanc, Moïse. *Nosographie de l'humanité balzacienne.* Paris: Maloine, 1959.
Loubère, Joyce A.E. "Balzac: Le grand absent de chez Teste." *French Review,* 47, No. 6 (1974), 82-91.
Lukács, Georg. *Balzac et le réalisme français.* Trans. Paul Laveau. Paris: Maspéro, 1967.
———. *The Theory of the Novel.* Trans. Anna Bostock. Cambridge, Mass.: M.I.T. Press, 1971.
McCarthy, Mary Susan. "Function and Participation of the Reader in Balzac's *Comédie humaine.*" Diss. University of Wisconsin-Madison, 1977.
Maurois, André. *Prométhée; ou, la vie de Balzac.* Paris: Hachette, 1965.
Miller, Henry. "Balzac and His Double." In his *The Wisdom of the Heart.* New York: New Directions, 1941, pp. 208-50.
Molière. *Oeuvres complètes.* 2 vols. Paris: Gallimard, 1971.
Mozet, Nicole. "Les Prolétaires dans *La Fille aux yeux d'or.*" *Année Balzacienne* (1974), pp. 91-119.
———. "Le Réalisme balzacien selon Pierre Barbéris." *Littérature,* No. 22 (1976), 98-117.
Nash, Suzanne. "Story-telling and the Loss of Innocence in Balzac's *Comédie humaine.*" *Romanic Review,* 70 (1979), 249-67.
Nathan, Michel. "Les Narrateurs du *Livre mystique.*" *Année Balzacienne* (1976), pp. 163-84.

Nykrog, Per. *La Pensée de Balzac dans* La Comédie humaine. Copenhagen: Munksgaard, 1965.
Oates, Joyce Carol. *New Heaven, New Earth.* New York: Vanguard, 1974.
O'Connor, Flannery. *Mystery and Manners.* New York: Farrar, Straus, Giroux, 1969.
O'Connor, John R. *Balzac's Soluble Fish.* Madrid: José Porrúa Turanzas, 1977.
Ortega y Gasset, José. *The Dehumanization of Art.* Trans. Helene Weyl. Princeton: Princeton Univ. Press, 1968.
Paris, Jean. *Le Point aveugle.* Paris: Seuil, 1975.
Perrone-Moïsés, Leyla. "Le Récit euphémique." *Poétique,* No. 17 (1974), 27-38.
Pichois, Claude. "Deux Hypothèses sur *Ferragus.*" *Revue d'Histoire Littéraire de la France,* 56 (1956), 569-72.
Poulet, Georges. *Les Métamorphoses du cercle.* Paris: Plon, 1961.
Prendergast, Christopher. "Antithesis and Moral Ambiguity in *La Cousine Bette.*" *Modern Language Review,* 68, No. 2 (1973), 315-32.
―――. "Balzac: Chance and Realism in *La Comédie humaine.*" *Forum for Modern Language Studies,* 10, No. 2 (1974), 109-20.
―――. *Balzac: Fiction and Melodrama.* London: Edward Arnold, 1978.
Princeton University. "Thèmes religieux dans *Eugénie Grandet.*" *Année Balzacienne* (1976), pp. 201-29.
Proust, Marcel. *Contre Sainte-Beuve.* Paris: Gallimard, 1954.
Rank, Otto. *Art and Artist.* Trans. Charles Francis Atkinson. New York: Agathon, 1968.
Rexroth, Kenneth. "Balzac." *Saturday Review* (7 September 1968), pp. 12-13.
Richard, Jean-Pierre. "Balzac, de la force à la forme." *Poétique,* No. 1 (1970), pp. 10-24.
Ricœur, Paul. *La Métaphore vive.* Paris: Seuil, 1975.
Rilke, Rainer Maria. *Where Silence Reigns.* Trans. C. Craig Houston. New York: New Directions, 1978.
Robert, Marthe. *Roman des origines et origines du roman.* Paris: Gallimard, 1972.
Senninger, Claude-Marie. *Honoré de Balzac par Théophile Gautier.* Paris: Nizet, 1980.
Shakespeare, William. *The Riverside Shakespeare.* Ed. G. Blakemore Evans. 2 vols. Boston: Houghton Mifflin, 1974.
Sontag, Susan. *Illness as Metaphor.* New York: Farrar, Straus, Giroux, 1978.
Stanzel, Franz E. "Teller-Characters and Reflector-Characters in Narrative Theory." *Poetics Today,* 2, No. 2 (1981), 5-15.

Suleiman, Susan, and Inge Crosman. *The Reader in the Text: Essays on Audience and Interpretation.* Princeton: Princeton Univ. Press, 1980.

Tremewan, P.J. "Balzac et Shakespeare." *Année Balzacienne* (1967), pp. 259-303.

Tritter, Jean-Louis. "Y a-t-il une linguistique balzacienne?" *Grammatica III*, 10 (1974), 27-33.

Van Laere, François. "Attitudes critiques à l'égard de *La Comédie humaine.*" *Revue des Sciences Humaines,* 33, No. 131 (1968), 435-64.

Vannier, Bernard. "Scriptural et pictural." *MLN,* 84, No. 4 (1969), 627-45.

Weber, Samuel. *Unwrapping Balzac.* Toronto: Univ. of Toronto Press, 1979.

Winkler-Boulenger, Jacqueline. "La Durée romanesque dans *Eugénie Grandet.*" *Année Balzacienne* (1973), pp. 75-87.

Woolf, Virginia. *The Second Common Reader.* New York: Harvest, 1960.

Yeats, William Butler. *Essays and Introductions.* New York: Macmillan, 1961.

Zéraffa, Michel. "Personnage et personne dans le roman français." *Revue d'Esthétique,* 12, Nos. 1-2 (1969), 3-23.

FRENCH FORUM MONOGRAPHS

1. Karolyn Waterson. *Molière et l'autorité: structures sociales, structures comiques.* 1976.
2. Donna Kuizenga. *Narrative Strategies in* La Princesse de Clèves. 1976.
3. Ian J. Winter. *Montaigne's Self-Portrait and Its Influence in France, 1580-1630.* 1976.
4. Judith G. Miller. *Theater and Revolution in France since 1968.* 1977.
5. Raymond C. La Charité, ed. *O un amy! Essays on Montaigne in Honor of Donald M. Frame.* 1977.
6. Rupert T. Pickens. *The Welsh Knight: Paradoxicality in Chrétien's* Conte del Graal. 1977.
7. Carol Clark. *The Web of Metaphor: Studies in the Imagery of Montaigne's* Essais. 1978.
8. Donald Maddox. *Structure and Sacring: The Systematic Kingdom in Chrétien's* Erec et Enide. 1978.
9. Betty J. Davis. *The Storytellers in Marguerite de Navarre's* Heptaméron. 1978.
10. Laurence M. Porter. *The Renaissance of the Lyric in French Romanticism: Elegy, "Poëme" and Ode.* 1978.
11. Bruce R. Leslie. *Ronsard's Successful Epic Venture: The Epyllion.* 1979.
12. Michelle A. Freeman. *The Poetics of* Translatio Studii *and* Conjointure: *Chrétien de Troyes's* Cligés. 1979.
13. Robert T. Corum, Jr. *Other Worlds and Other Seas: Art and Vision in Saint-Amant's Nature Poetry.* 1979.
14. Marcel Muller. *Préfiguration et structure romanesque dans* A la recherche du temps perdu *(avec un inédit de Marcel Proust).* 1979.
15. Ross Chambers. *Meaning and Meaningfulness: Studies in the Analysis and Interpretation of Texts.* 1979.
16. Lois Oppenheim. *Intentionality and Intersubjectivity: A Phenomenological Study of Butor's* La Modification. 1980.
17. Matilda T. Bruckner. *Narrative Invention in Twelfth-Century French Romance: The Convention of Hospitality (1160-1200).* 1980.
18. Gérard Defaux. *Molière, ou les métamorphoses du comique: de la comédie morale au triomphe de la folie.* 1980.
19. Raymond C. La Charité. *Recreation, Reflection and Re-Creation: Perspectives on Rabelais's* Pantagruel. 1980.
20. Jules Brody. *Du style à la pensée: trois études sur les* Caractères de La Bruyère. 1980.
21. Lawrence D. Kritzman. *Destruction/Découverte: le fonctionnement de la rhétorique dans les* Essais de Montaigne. 1980.
22. Minnette Grunmann-Gaudet and Robin F. Jones, eds. *The Nature of Medieval Narrative.* 1980.
23. J.A. Hiddleston. *Essai sur Laforgue et les* Derniers Vers *suivi de Laforgue et Baudelaire.* 1980.
24. Michael S. Koppisch. *The Dissolution of Character: Changing Perspectives in La Bruyère's* Caractères. 1981.
25. Hope H. Glidden. *The Storyteller as Humanist: The* Serées *of Guillaume Bouchet.* 1981.
26. Mary B. McKinley. *Words in a Corner: Studies in Montaigne's Latin Quotations.* 1981.

27. Donald M. Frame and Mary B. McKinley, eds. *Columbia Montaigne Conference Papers.* 1981.
28. Jean-Pierre Dens. *L'Honnête Homme et la critique du goût: Esthétique et société au XVIIe siècle.* 1981.
29. Vivian Kogan. *The Flowers of Fiction: Time and Space in Raymond Queneau's* Les Fleurs bleues. 1982.
30. Michael Issacharoff et Jean-Claude Vilquin, éds. *Sartre et la mise en signe.* 1982.
31. James W. Mileham. *The Conspiracy Novel: Structure and Metaphor in Balzac's* Comédie humaine. 1982.
32. Andrew G. Suozzo, Jr. *The Comic Novels of Charles Sorel: A Study of Structure, Characterization and Disguise.* 1982.
33. Margaret Whitford. *Merleau-Ponty's Critique of Sartre's Philosophy.* 1982.
34. Gérard Defaux. *Le Curieux, le glorieux et la sagesse du monde dans la première moitié du XVIe siècle: L'exemple de Panurge (Ulysse, Démosthène, Empédocle).* 1982.
35. Doranne Fenoaltea. *"Si haulte Architecture." The Design of Scève's* Délie. 1982.
36. Peter Bayley and Dorothy Gabe Coleman, eds. *The Equilibrium of Wit: Essays for Odette de Mourgues.* 1982.
37. Carol J. Murphy. *Alienation and Absence in the Novels of Marguerite Duras.* 1982.
38. Mary Ellen Birkett. *Lamartine and the Poetics of Landscape.* 1982.
39. Jules Brody. *Lectures de Montaigne.* 1982.
40. John D. Lyons. *The Listening Voice: An Essay on the Rhetoric of Saint-Amant.* 1982.
41. Edward C. Knox. *Patterns of Person: Studies in Style and Form from Corneille to Laclos.* 1983.
42. Marshall C. Olds. *Desire Seeking Expression: Mallarmé's "Prose pour des Esseintes."* 1983.
43. Ceri Crossley. *Edgar Quinet (1803-1875): A Study in Romantic Thought.* 1983.
44. Rupert T. Pickens, ed. *The Sower and His Seed: Essays on Chrétien de Troyes.* 1983.
45. Barbara C. Bowen. *Words and the Man in French Renaissance Literature.* 1983.
46. Clifton Cherpack. *Logos in Mythos. Ideas and Early French Narrative.* 1983.
47. Donald Stone, Jr. *Mellin de Saint-Gelais and Literary History.* 1983.
48. Louisa E. Jones. *Sad Clowns and Pale Pierrots: Literature and the Popular Comic Arts in 19th-Century France.* 1984.
49. JoAnn DellaNeva. *Song and Counter-Song: Scève's* Délie *and Petrarch's* Rime. 1983.
50. John D. Lyons and Nancy J. Vickers, eds. *The Dialectic of Discovery: Essays on the Teaching and Interpretation of Literature Presented to Lawrence E. Harvey.* 1984.
51. Warren F. Motte, Jr. *The Poetics of Experiment: A Study of the Work of Georges Perec.* 1984.
52. Jean R. Joseph. *Crébillon fils. Economie érotique et narrative.* 1984.
53. Carol A. Mossman. *The Narrative Matrix: Stendhal's* Le Rouge et le Noir. 1984.
54. Ora Avni. *Tics, tics et tics. Figures, syllogismes, récit dans* Les Chants de Maldoror. 1984.
55. Robert J. Morrissey. *La Rêverie jusqu'à Rousseau. Recherches sur un topos littéraire.* 1984.
56. Pauline M. Smith and I.D. McFarlane, eds. *Literature and the Arts in the Reign of Francis I. Essays Presented to C.A. Mayer.* 1984.
57. Jerry C. Nash, ed. *Pre-Pléiade Poetry.* 1984.

58. Jack Undank and Herbert Josephs, eds. *Diderot: Digression and Dispersion. A Bicentennial Tribute.* 1984.
59. Daniel S. Russell. *The Emblem and Device in France.* 1985.
60. Joan Dargan. *Balzac and the Drama of Perspective: The Narrator in Selected Works of* La Comédie humaine. 1985.

French Forum, Publishers, Inc.
P.O. Box 5108, Lexington, Kentucky 40505

Publishers of *French Forum*, a journal of literary criticism